THE LONDON

idea

Library Learning Information

To renew this item call:

020 7364 4332

or visit

www.ideastore.co.uk

TOWER HAMLETS

Created and managed by Tower Hamlets Council

THE
LONDON
FOOTBALL COMPANION

A Site-by-Site Celebration of the Capital's Favourite Sport

ED GLINERT

BLOOMSBURY
LONDON · BERLIN · NEW YORK

First published in Great Britain 2009

Copyright © by Ed Gilbert 2009

Bloomsbury publishing Plc
36 Soho Square
London W1D 3QY

www.bloomsbury.com

Bloomsbury Publishing, London, New York and Berlin
A CIP catalogue record for this book is available from the British Library

ISBN 978 0 7475 9516 8

10 9 8 7 6 5 4 3 2 1

Typeset by Hewer Text UK Ltd, Edinburgh
Printed and bound in Great Britain by Clays Limited, St Ives plc

Mixed Sources
Product group from well-managed
forests and other controlled sources
www.fsc.org Cert no. SGS-COC-2061
© 1996 Forest Stewardship Council
FSC

To the memory of Martin Rose

Contents

Acknowledgements

Like much in football *The London Football Companion* has been a team effort. Many have been the fellow fans, even those of other clubs, who have chipped in with a perfectly floated anecdote and expertly weighted suggestion, so many thanks to Richard Aron, Bela Cunha, Peter Golds, Mark Gorman, David Grant, Lakh Kaira, Gill King, Glenn Masters, Martin Morris, John Naughton, Tim Richard, Juliet, Martin and Simon Rose, David Stone, Katy Walsh Glinert, Alison Weardon and Ian Wilson.

Considerable thanks go to David Stone and Tim Richard for all those nights spent ruminating over a hot kebab in the Yildiz Okacbasi, to Peter Golds for similar in the North Sea fish 'n' chip emporium (but not the Yildiz), and to Katy Walsh Glinert for helping me unravel the difference between Thames and Thames Ironworks, Upton Park FC and West Ham United (who play in Upton Park but not West Ham), and for noticing that Clapton play not in Clapton, Chelsea in Walham Green not Chelsea, and Queen's Park Rangers not in Queen's Park.

Back in the stands, Bloomsbury publishers came up with the signing-on fee, but halfway through the match (okay, the writing) editor Mike Jones was substituted by Bill Swainson. Many thanks to both, along with my agent Faith Evans, for tackling, tactics and distribution.

Introduction

Football is *not* a funny game, well not particularly so, but those who play, run and watch it, especially those who do so in London, are a peculiar lot. Take, for instance, Midget Moffat, the legendary winger, who was offered a trial by Arsenal, but on arrival in London went to what he thought was the club's ground – in Woolwich – unaware that Arsenal had moved to Highbury.

Players have been acting in ever more amusing ways since, their arrival in the capital after a childhood in a sunless Gorbals tenement or dust-choked pit village the cue for reckless hedonism that will fill a thousand newspaper columns and give their performances on the pitch that extra edge. Frank McAvennie left St Mirren for West Ham in the 1980s and was soon the new George Best, scoring on and off the pitch even though, as he himself admitted: 'I had such a strong Scottish accent no one knew what I was talking about. When I was shouting in training the other players thought I was trying to pick a fight.' McAvennie bought himself a Capri 2.8 and a tasteful registration plate: UP U2. Sadly the car was stolen the day after he bought it, but McAvennie simply went out the next day and bought himself another.

One Friday night before a game Frank was drinking at a West End club into the late hours when Wimbledon's John Fashanu, who was suspended at the time, noticed it was 4.30 a.m. and that McAvennie was still lording it up. 'Haven't you got a game tomorrow?' asked the centre-forward. 'Aye,' smiled the Scot and strode off. The next day Fashanu woke late, put on the results and noticed that McAvennie had scored a hat-trick.

It's not just players who do strange things, managers are not immune to peculiarities and peccadilloes. Don Revie was a no-nonsense, bluff

Yorkshireman, straight as a die, or as straight as a man with a penchant for bribing opponents to throw matches and pick up backhanders – 'Don Readies' they called him – could be. His 1960s and 1970s Leeds teams were clinically and brutally successful, practically inventing the concept, since perfected by Manchester United, of criticising and challenging every adverse refereeing decision no matter how much they knew the ref was right and that one of their men had cheated. He took a team that had never challenged for honours to League titles, FA Cups, even European finals. He achieved that not just by trying to grease a few palms but with some astute tactics and selections as well. But all the good habits were ditched once Revie came to London permanently in 1974 to be England boss. He began handing out caps to practically anyone in the First Division who had been born in England, produced convoluted dossiers about the opposition that no one, least of all he himself, could understand, and tried odd methods to relax players before games, while tormenting himself with a host of strange superstitions.

At least modern-day managers are more level-headed (apart perhaps from Alan Curbishley, who a few years ago began the trend that by 2008 had become endemic of claiming that English managers are 'not allowed' to manage the really big clubs and are therefore unable to gain the experience of playing in the European Champions League that would make them viable contenders for the England manager's job) Arsene Wenger, for instance, is known as 'The Professor'. But this is not because he has passed the required examinations in an academic subject but came about from the confusion of an Arsenal fan who saw a picture of Wenger standing by a library of works on a bookshelf and assumed they were learned tomes when in fact they were simply bound volumes of old Arsenal programmes.

Are the fans any better? You might think that those who have flirted with success at the highest level, whose team had won Championships, cups galore and European trophies, would be so pleased at gaining some silverware after years of failure that their fans would be eternally grateful to the managerial mastermind who had guided them to the trophies. Instead Tottenham fans, 1999 brand, were nonplussed as their side won the League Cup; the same League Cup that was ecstatically greeted when it was won nine years later. The reason? The manager was an Arsenal man, George Graham, so it didn't really count.

At least there are the football writers to bring a touch of sanity and sobriety to proceedings ... Or rather, not. Here there is some very funny business going on. A large squad of supposedly neutral 'professionals', educated at university or college, dispensing a diet of non sequiturs and non-stories, an endless list of imminent transfers, almost none of which have any chance of coming off, paraded as 'exclusives'. These are the initiators of many of the great footballing myths. The myth that José Mourinho has been good for football. The myth that the Premier League/Premiership is somehow a higher division than the old Football League Division One. The myth that football has changed over the past few generations. (The rules have barely altered and the team that scores the most goals still wins the game.) The consequent absurdity that the tier of football that normal people still call the Second Division (the one that Crystal Palace often fall into and struggle to get out of – that one) is the Championship or that what is really the Fourth Division should be allowed to trade under the name League Two. The myth that Arsenal players under Arsene Wenger are more prone to being sent off than their rivals.

Above are some of the reasons why *The London Football Companion* has been written. Those football fellas keep doing infuriating, frustrating and fulsome things, they keep generating such great copy with their funny and furious antics. *The London Football Companion* gathers together some of the best stories the game has thrown up in the capital in the last 150 years, from the first attempt to codify and unify the rules to José Mourinho's tantrums. For London is central to the never-ending game that is football. It was in London, in Covent Garden – not somewhere associated with football – that in 1863 those rules were drawn up by a body that called itself the Football Association. The idea of everyone playing by the same rules – from Tottenham to Tashkent to Tasmania to Tucson Arizona and back round the world to Tottenham again – was and remains revolutionary. Other sports like rugby and cricket are inferior because they have allowed mavericks to invent inferior versions of the master game (one-day nonsense as opposed to Test cricket, rugby league rather than rugby union) but there is only one type of competitive football. It was also in London that the FA Cup, the world's oldest competition, was invented and where the final has mostly been played. It is to London that the great, the good and the gormless have long gravitated, not to improve their game but to practise their off-the-ball antics. Here, despite what Newcastle folk might argue, the fans are as mad and manic as those who wear but a black-and-white-striped shirt on the fiercest wintry day. If only the capital's clubs, well one of them, could match the string of trophies won by Liverpool.

How to use *The London Football Companion*

The tales included within have been presented geographically rather than chronologically, thematically or club by club. *The London Football Companion* begins with Central London – Bloomsbury, the City, Covent Garden and so on – followed by the suburbs in turn. Within those geographical chapters stories are told in the locations where they happened.

So if you want to read how officials from Arsenal plied their counterparts from Bolton Wanderers with strong alcoholic drink to diddle them out of a few bob when buying David Jack for a record fee in 1928 then look under the place where it happened – the Euston Hotel at Euston station. Naturally there are sizeable entries for the big clubs like Tottenham and smaller entries for smaller fry like Leyton Orient. There are even entries on defunct clubs (Thames) and long demolished places like Anderton's Hotel, Fleet Street, these inclusions denoted by an unusual typeface.

To direct the curious reader to similar stories and places I have inserted what I hope are helpful links at the end of entries pointing to a different location elsewhere in the book. Finally, in the interests of the kind of non-biased professional impartiality that the great football writers claim guides them I have tried my utmost to remove all bias towards my favourite club and hostility towards their sworn enemies. It's not my fault that my club is so successful and upright and that their rivals are so venal and risible.

1 Central London

No major football club is based in the centre of London, but it was here that the game was first codified and regulated in the mid-nineteenth century, that the first leagues were formed, and that the FA Cup was invented – despite Elizabeth I's sixteenth-century decree that 'no foteballe play to be used or suffered within the City of London'. It is here also that many of the capital's most exciting nightclubs can be found, their plush sofas, well-stocked bars and seductive sirens forever enticing London's finest players as night moves into dawn.

BLOOMSBURY, WC1

Imperial Hotel, Russell Square

The Imperial was the London hotel the touring Moscow Dynamo football team stayed in during their extraordinary visit to England in 1945, the first by a continental side. The stay wasn't prearranged, for although it was known the Russians were coming they hadn't confirmed the date of their arrival and landed at Croydon airport in November with little warning. At first, the FA couldn't find a single hotel in London willing to put them up, but after the Russians had spent a restless night at the Wellington Barracks in Westminster the Imperial came to their rescue, even if the hotel manager did fret over whether the Russians had 'sheets on their beds'.

There were thirty-nine people in the Soviet party: twenty footballers and nineteen trainers, minders and journalists, including one woman, an interpreter, Alex Elliseyeva, who said little and whom Fleet Street soon dubbed 'Alexandra the Silent'. The Russians ate no meals at the hotel and travelled to the Soviet embassy in Kensington for sustenance, for there was no rationing at the embassy and plenty of chocolate, steak and butter available.

Moscow Dynamo played four games in Britain. They beat Cardiff 10–1 and Arsenal, who included three ringers – Stanley Matthews, Stan Mortensen and Joe Bacuzzi – in fog so thick visibility was almost impossible, 4–3. They drew with Chelsea and Glasgow Rangers, and returned to the Soviet Union unbeaten. Not everyone was impressed by the visit. George Orwell in a famous essay wrote that it had confirmed for him that sport was 'an unfailing cause of ill-will, and that if such a visit as this had any effect at all on Anglo-Soviet relations, it could only be to make them slightly worse than before'.

→ **Arsenal** *v* **Moscow Dynamo at White Hart Lane, p. 127**

Russell Hotel, 1–9 Russell Square

Charles Fitzroy Doll's 1898 hotel, Victorian architecture at its most flamboyant, was where the Sunderland football team were dining on 3 September 1939 when prime minister Neville Chamberlain announced on the wireless that 'this country is at war with Germany'. Hearing the sound of the air-raid sirens, the players instinctively rushed out into the street, but were quickly chased back into the hotel by the police, who made them take refuge on the *third* floor, believing it would be the place safest from flying glass.

The victorious Manchester United side stayed at the Russell before and after the 1968 European Cup Final. Manager Matt Busby, remembering the many Manchester United players who had died ten years previously in the Munich air disaster, found it hard to celebrate and sat among the families of those who survived singing 'It's a Wonderful World'.

One who didn't join them was Bobby Charlton. He was too overcome with emotion and stayed in his room. 'Bobby couldn't take complete strangers coming up and slapping him on the back and telling him what a wonderful night it was,' Charlton's wife, Norma, later recalled.

In December 1973 Alan Hudson, the gifted but wayward 22-year-old Chelsea midfield star, was invited to meet Stoke City manager Tony

Waddington in Russell Square to discuss a transfer from Chelsea, who were short of cash, to Stoke, then enjoying the most successful spell in their history. When Hudson arrived in the square he couldn't see the Stoke manager, but after a few moments Waddington suddenly appeared from behind a phone box. 'I thought he was a crank,' Hudson later told the journalist Rob Steen.

The two men sat on a park bench, and Waddington somehow convinced the Chelsea man to join the Potteries side. At Hudson's first training session in the north Midlands he was given a green bib to wear over his shirt while the other players were told: 'Whenever you get the ball, pass to the man in the green bib.' Hudson's debut for Stoke at Anfield was so remarkable that Liverpool manager Bill Shankly invited Waddington into the Liverpool dressing room, usually out of bounds to all bar Liverpool stalwarts – no other opposition manager had ever previously been allowed there – and told him Hudson's performance was the finest he had ever witnessed in his career. Stoke finished fifth in the 1973–74 season – their second highest League placing ever.

CITY OF LONDON, EC1–4

Ansbacher, 1 Mitre Square

The Tottenham manager Terry Venables and the computer magnate Alan Sugar announced their decision to join forces and take charge of the club at this merchant bank on 21 June 1991. Tottenham Hotspur were at the time desperately short of cash. Needing a rich investor, they had been courting Robert Maxwell, the corrupt owner of Mirror Group newspapers, who in the late 1980s was desperate to become a major player in football. It looked as if Maxwell might take charge, but Alan Sugar phoned him and after an exciting conversation Maxwell for once backed down.

By the summer of 1991, with Tottenham having just won the FA Cup for a record eighth time, Sugar was poised to take over, and he teamed up with the manager who had just taken the club to that FA Cup success. Many feared the relationship between Sugar, the ruthless electronics magnate, and Venables, the so-called 'lovable' chirpy cockney, could never work.

It took as long as two years for it not to. Sugar ousted Venables as chief executive of Spurs a few days before the 1993 Cup Final between Arsenal and Sheffield Wednesday, a boardroom coup immediately captured in song by the Arsenal fans who filled the Wembley air with the ditty: 'Just a spoonful of sugar makes the Venables go down . . .'

Corinthians' birthplace, Paternoster Square

Corinthians, the English game's most famous amateur club, were founded here in 1883 by N. L. 'Pa' Jackson, assistant secretary of the Football Association. He was opposed to professionalism, which was rapidly gaining hold, albeit mostly in the North, and wanted the club to be the preserve of the best amateurs. Or as he put it, 'Football is a game for gentlemen that should be played by gentlemen.'

Jackson decided to call his new club Corinthians, hoping that a classical name would infuse them with the most desirable qualities of Ancient Greece. Initially they refused to play competitive matches, and would arrive for their friendly games wearing top hats and brandishing canes. On the field Corinthians played the short passing game in the Scottish style rather than the dribbling game of the English public schools. Most of their players turned out for other sides as well, and until the end of the nineteenth century Corinthians could match the best professional teams.

FA Cup birthplace, *Sportsman's offices*, 139–140 Fleet Street

It was at the *Sportsman*'s offices on 20 July 1871, in front of delegates from the leading clubs of the time, that the Football Association's secretary, Charles Alcock, unveiled what would become football's greatest competition: the FA Cup.

Alcock based the idea on matches at his old school, Harrow, in which teams would compete to be the 'Cock House'. He wanted the FA Cup to be a 'Challenge' Cup, which meant that the winners earned the automatic right to play in the following year's final in which they would be challenged by the best of the rest, a format that was soon dropped. Another odd rule stated that if a match was drawn *both* sides would progress. But at least there was to be no seeding, something which to this day ruins so many knock-out cups, such as the Wimbledon tennis tournament.

Alcock's creation met with universal approval from FA members, fifteen of whom registered to play in the first competition. They were Barnes, Civil Service, Clapham Rovers, Crystal Palace, Donington School, Hampstead Heathens, Harrow Chequers, Hitchin, Maidenhead, Marlow, Queen's Park, Reigate Priory, Royal Engineers, Upton Park and Wanderers. All the teams were from London or the Home Counties apart from Donington who came from Lincolnshire and Queen's Park (Glasgow).

The first Cup began late in 1871. Donington School withdrew without playing a game, Royal Engineers enjoyed a walkover against Reigate Priory, and by the quarter-finals there were only five teams left instead of the expected eight. An unfair anomaly saw Queen's Park allowed to reach the semi-finals automatically because of the cost of travelling to London. When their semi-final against the Wanderers ended in a draw the idea of allowing both teams to progress became ridiculous. The FA ordered a replay but the Scots ran out of money and withdrew from the competition.

In the other semi-final Royal Engineers beat Crystal Palace 3–0. In the first final the Wanderers beat the Royal Engineers 1–0 at the Kennington Oval (→ p. 165). The winning team was presented with the trophy a few days later at the Pall Mall Restaurant, and it was that cup which was eventually stolen from a shop window after Aston Villa won it in 1895 and reputedly melted down so that it could be converted into half-crowns – although there are those who believe it languishes on its own in Birmingham City's trophy cabinet.

Football League birthplace, Anderton's Hotel, 164 Fleet Street

The long-gone Anderton's Hotel was the 1888 birthplace of the Football League, the archetype for the weekly football competition played throughout the world to determine which team is the best. The League was the brainchild of William McGregor, a director of Aston Villa, and he wrote to Blackburn Rovers, Bolton Wanderers, Preston North End, West Bromwich Albion as well as Aston Villa:

Every year it is becoming more and more difficult for football clubs of any standing to meet their friendly engagements and even arrange friendly matches. The consequence is that at the last moment, through cup-tie interference, clubs are compelled to take on teams who will not attract the public.

I beg to tender the following suggestion as a means of getting over the difficulty: that ten or twelve of the most prominent clubs in England combine to arrange home-and-away fixtures each season, the said fixtures to be arranged at a friendly conference about the same time as the International Conference.

This combination might be known as the Association Football Union, and could be managed by a representative from each club. Of course, this is in no way to interfere with the National Association; even the suggested matches might be played under cup-tie rules. However, this is a detail.

My object in writing to you at present is merely to draw your attention to the subject, and to suggest a friendly conference to discuss the matter more fully . . .

I am, yours very truly, William McGregor (Aston Villa F.C.) P.S. How would Friday, 23rd March, 1888, suit for the friendly conference at Anderton's Hotel, London?

J. J. Bentley, secretary of Bolton, suggested the invitation be extended to Accrington, Burnley, Notts County, Stoke and Wolverhampton Wanderers, and those teams formed the first League – not the Association Football Union as McGregor suggested – with his original five as well as Derby County and Everton. Three further teams – Mitchell St George's (of Birmingham), Halliwell (Bolton) and Old Carthusians (Surrey) were interested but never made it into the League.

There was some heated debate about the status of the twelve clubs that formed the first League. The choice of the pedestrian Accrington perplexed many. *Athletic News* noted that the club 'are not particular whether they win or lose matches with clubs admittedly inferior to them', which may have accounted for their imminent collapse.

A month later a number of leading northern clubs which had been excluded – Crewe, Blackburn Olympic, Blackburn Rovers – decided to form a rival league, the Combination. And when Preston, who many believed to be the best club in the country, failed to respond to McGregor's original letter, it looked as if two rival and more or less equal leagues might soon be up and running. The problem was solved on 17 April, at a second meeting of the Football League, this time held in Manchester, when all twelve clubs who eventually formed the original League, including Preston, attended. The Football League soon became a reality while the Combination flopped.

The first Football League season began on 8 September 1888, yet it wasn't until 21 November that the points system was finalised. Six clubs were from the North – Accrington, Blackburn Rovers, Bolton Wanderers, Burnley, Everton and Preston North End (the first champions); six from the Midlands – Aston Villa, Derby County, Notts County, Stoke City, West Bromwich Albion and Wolverhampton Wanderers. They were all professional. Preston won the first championship without losing a game (of their twenty-two) and Stoke finished last. Complaints that Accrington were inferior to the rest and that some of those excluded, particularly the Wednesday, were too good not to be involved were soon eased by the formation of a second division in 1892.

On 2 February that year those southern clubs who wanted to play professional football like their northern and Midlands counterparts met here to consider once again the idea of forming their own league. Two years previously an attempt to start such a league with the blessing of the London FA had foundered after a meeting at the Salutation (→ p. 8).

Behind the latest venture were Woolwich Arsenal, who sent a circular to suitable clubs. They had already turned professional, for which they had been expelled by the London FA and refused entry to local cup competitions. This time it looked as if the Southern League might take off. At the meeting Arsenal's Fred Beardsley proposed that 'a league be formed for London and the South', a motion seconded by William Henderson of Millwall and carried. Twelve clubs were elected, the vote won by Chatham and Luton. Those also voted in included Ilford, Millwall, Swindon, Reading, Woolwich Arsenal and the now lesser known Chiswick Park, Marlow, Old St Marks, West Herts and Crouch End who pulled out despite being elected. Bottom of the list were Tottenham Hotspur with one vote – their own.

Once again the scheme went into abeyance and it needed another meeting at Billiter's on Fenchurch Street in 1894 for the Southern League to take off. Anderton's was demolished in 1939 and replaced by Hulton House, an office block which contained a number of publishing houses including, ironically, that which produced Charlie Buchan's *Football Monthly*.

→ **Formation of the Southern League, see below**

St Paul's School, St Paul's Churchyard

The famous school founded in the shadow of St Paul's Cathedral in 1509 played a part in the early development of football. Richard Mulcaster, headmaster of St Paul's in 1596–1608, introduced a game with small-sized teams controlled by a referee, and urged that there be no violence. 'The Footeball strengtheneth and brawneth the whole body . . . it is good for the bowels, and driveth downe the stone and gravel from both the bladder and kidneys,' he explained.

Southern League birthplace (1), Salutation Tavern, 17 Newgate Street

In the wake of rising interest in professionalism at the end of the 1880s the London Football Association, which was then still amateur, convened a meeting at the Salutation Tavern on 13 March 1890 to consider a proposal to form a Southern League. Behind the venture was former England international Charlie Bambridge. He hoped the new league would rival the Football League, which then consisted entirely of professional clubs from the Midlands and the North. However, the old boys' network of clubs whose players were drawn from the public schools of the South rejected the idea. The main opponent was N. L. 'Pa' Jackson, who went on to found the fanatically amateur Corinthians club, and he proposed a motion that stated 'it was not desirable to form a league', which was narrowly passed by 47 votes to 46. Consequently, no further developments in the South's still unfinished battle to wrest dominance in football from the North took place for two years.

Southern League birthplace (2), Billiter Coffee Rooms, 19 Billiter Street

After two unsuccessful meetings in the City the Southern League finally got underway after a meeting here on 12 January 1894 with representatives from Chatham, Clapton, Ilford, Luton, Millwall, Reading and the 2nd Scots Guards. A second meeting was called for a week later, invitations to which were also sent to Casuals, Crouch End, Crusaders, London Caledonians, Old Carthusians, Old Westminster, Royal Ordnance Factories, Swindon and Woolwich Arsenal, even though the latter were now in the Second Division of the rival, mostly northern, Football League. The ex-public school teams involved, such as Old Carthusians, refused to go along with the venture and they pressurised the Scots Guards to pull out as well.

The Southern League began in 1894 with nine clubs: Chatham, Clapton, Ilford, Luton Town, Millwall Athletic, Reading, Royal Ordnance Factories, Southampton St Mary's (who replaced Scots Guards) and Swindon Town. Of these, Clapton, Ilford, Reading and Royal Ordnance Factories were all amateur sides. Millwall Athletic won the first League title and repeated the feat the following season. Ironically the club (as Millwall) has never won anything comparable since.

There was also a Second Division but it had just seven teams: Bromley, Chesham, Maidenhead, New Brompton, Old St Stephens, Sheppey United and Uxbridge. Woolwich Arsenal wanted to enter their reserve team but were turned down. The Southern League teams played football of a high standard – many said it was equal to the Football League's Second division – until 1920 when its best teams hived off to form the new Third Division.

World Cup replica workshop, George Bird's silversmith's, Fenchurch Street
When the World Cup, the Jules Rimet trophy, was stolen from an exhibition at Westminster's Central Hall in March 1966, FA secretary Denis Follows visited silversmith George Bird at his workshop in Fenchurch Street, before news of the theft was made public, and hired him to make a replica from the same solid gold as the original. The work was to be hush-hush; not even FIFA chief Stanley Rous could be told.

Within a week the stolen cup was found, by a dog in Norwood (→ p. 182), but from then on Bird's replica trophy, not the real cup, which was safely ensconced at FA headquarters, was taken from exhibition to exhibition by Bird on his bike, concealed only by a cloth.

On the day of the final, Saturday 30 July 1966, the police took the real trophy from the FA's Lancaster Gate headquarters to Wembley, where it was given to the Queen who presented it to the victorious England captain, Bobby Moore. Minutes later on the pitch Bird's replica was given to the England players for their celebrations, and it was that cup, not the real Jules

Rimet trophy, which was taken to the Royal Garden Hotel in Kensington for the post-match celebrations. Not that anybody in the crowd would have been able to notice the difference.

When it came to the next finals, in Mexico in 1970, it was time for the FA to return the trophy to FIFA, who run the international game. But which trophy did the FA send back? After all, there were now two. The FA handed FIFA the replica. In Mexico, Brazil won the World Cup for the third time, and FIFA honoured the achievement by allowing Brazil to keep the Jules Rimet trophy outright. Thirteen years later it was stolen again, never to be found. This time it was in Brazil, which was ironic given that back in 1966 when it first went missing Brazilians said the theft was a sacrilege that would never have happened in their country, where even the thieves loved football.

By then the real World Cup was hidden under George Bird's bed. Twice his house was burgled, and twice the thieves failed to come across the trophy. After Bird died in 1995 his family auctioned the cup, which was described in Sotheby's catalogue as a replica. It should have had a scrap value of around £1,500, yet it sold for £254,500. The successful buyer? FIFA. Officials from football's world governing body then brought in experts to examine their expensive acquisition, only to discover that they had indeed bought a replica – made of bronze!

As Simon Kuper explained in the *Financial Times* in 2006, no one really knows what has happened to the original. Perhaps it has been melted into gold bars, or perhaps it is hidden away under a bed; maybe in Latin America, maybe somewhere in the Home Counties.

→ The World Cup is stolen, p. 43

CLERKENWELL, EC1

Charterhouse School (1611–1873), Charterhouse Square

The public school that moved to Surrey in the mid-nineteenth century was instrumental in the creation of the modern game when it was still based in Clerkenwell. Pupils played football – Gownboys *v* Rest of School – in the cloisters, a space that was seventy yards long, twelve feet wide and paved with smooth flagstones. Because there was little room for manoeuvre, or to kick the ball high or long, players had to learn to dribble, which was particularly difficult when there were often as many as fifty or so boys pushing and shoving for the opportunity to use the ball. Recalling those games, two old boys who wrote a history of the school, E. P. Eardley-Wilmot and E. C. Streatfield, noted that 'shins would be kicked black and blue; jackets and other articles of clothing almost torn into shreds; and Fags trampled underfoot'.

It was a former Charterhouse pupil, Charles Wreford-Brown, who coined the word 'soccer'. Leaving his Oxford digs one day dressed in playing gear, he was asked where he was going. 'I'm off to play football,' Wreford-Brown replied. 'Rugger or Association?' the man asked. 'Soccer,' Wreford-Brown replied. The word caught on but is now erroneously seen as an Americanism.

→ Harrow school, p. 142

COVENT GARDEN/HOLBORN/STRAND, WC2

Alhambra, 24–27 Leicester Square, east side

After winning the FA Cup for the first time in 1909 the victorious Manchester United team were taken to the Alhambra Theatre where they were entertained by the great comedian George Robey (who once played for Millwall). The clientele that night included a strange mixture of United fans from the North in tweed caps and jackets, and the usual Saturday-night crowd in the dress circle clad in their evening jackets and bow ties. The next morning the lid of the cup couldn't be found, much to United's chagrin. It eventually turned up in inside-left Sandy Turnbull's jacket where a practical joker had hidden it.

Football Association birthplace, New Connaught Rooms (former Freemasons' Tavern), 61–65 Great Queen Street

The Football Association was founded at the Freemasons' Tavern (since refurbished into the New Connaught Rooms) on 26 October 1863 by representatives of eleven clubs: Barnes, Blackheath, Blackheath Proprietary School, Crystal Palace, Crusaders, Forest, Kensington School, No Names Kilburn, Perceval House (Blackheath), Surbiton and War Office.

Football had been played in an anarchic and rule-free form since time immemorial, but in the nineteenth century several influential establishment sporting figures began moves to codify the game nationally with a set of rules and a regular programme of fixtures. The catalysts were the two major advances in communications recently pioneered: the railways and the telegraph. These inventions meant it was now possible for a team to journey easily from one town to another some distance away, and to discuss the idea within a few minutes as opposed to a few days.

By the 1840s almost every public school had its own rules. At some, players could pass a ball using their hands. At others, they could hack down an opponent legitimately. And the numbers in a team varied greatly. In 1846 H. de Winton and G. C. Tring from Cambridge University met representatives of the schools to standardise the regulations. Their eight-hour deliberations led to the so-called 'Cambridge Rules', of which no original copies exist. Tring himself published another set in 1862 for what he called 'The Simplest Game'.

Behind the parallel move to form a football association was Ebenezer Cobb Morley, a solicitor at the Temple, and it was he who invited representatives of eleven leading clubs to the October 1863 meeting here on Great Queen Street. Absent were the great public schools of Eton, Winchester, Harrow, Rugby and Westminster, which had done so much to promote the game. Harrow even sent a strongly worded letter that read: 'We cling to our present rules, and should be sorry to alter them in any respect whatsoever.'

The clubs who were interested in an 'association of football clubs' and did send representatives had mostly been formed by ex-public schoolboys. Forest, founded by a group of Old Harrovians, played at Snaresbrook by Epping Forest. They later became the Wanderers, who dominated the FA Cup in its early years. Crystal Palace were the works team from the palace itself, the huge glass and iron exhibition hall which had served as the centrepiece of the 1851 Great Exhibition in Hyde Park and had been shifted to south London. Although they are the only one of the eleven whose name survives as a club, the current League side have no connection with the FA founders. Indeed none of the original FA clubs survives in the same form.

Thus did the Football Association come into being. It was not the English Football Association, but simply *the* Football Association; there were no others.

The original eleven clubs continued to meet here a number of times over the next few months to agree on the rules. The main point of contention was over the issue of 'hacking' – kicking the shins. Many saw it as a sign of manliness. 'Hacking is the true football game,' F. W. Campbell of the Blackheath club explained. To Campbell, those who disagreed 'liked their pipes and grog or *schnaps* more than their manly game of football'. He went on to claim that 'if you do away with hacking you will do away with all the courage and pluck of the game, and I will be bound to bring over a lot of Frenchmen who would beat you with a week's practice'. Blackheath were also keen on having a rule approved that allowed a player 'to run with the ball towards his adversaries' goal if he makes a fair catch'. Nevertheless Campbell and Blackheath lost the crucial vote over hacking and handling at the December meeting, and football developed as a game that outlawed both.

Later that December the FA drew up its first set of rules. They were:

1. The maximum length of the ground shall be 200 yards, the maximum breadth shall be 100 yards, the length and breadth shall be marked off with flags; and the goal shall be defined by two upright posts, eight yards apart, without any tape or bar across them.
2. A toss for goals shall take place, and the game shall be commenced by a place kick from the centre of the ground by the side losing the toss for goals; the other side shall not approach within 10 yards of the ball until it is kicked off.
3. After a goal is won, the losing side shall be entitled to kick off, and the two sides shall change goals after each goal is won.
4. A goal shall be won when the ball passes between the goal-posts or over the space between the goal-posts (at whatever height), not being thrown, knocked on, or carried.
5. When the ball is in touch, the first player who touches it shall throw it from the point on the boundary line where it left the ground in a direction at right angles with the boundary line, and the ball shall not be in play until it has touched the ground.
6. When a player has kicked the ball, any one of the same side who is nearer to the opponents' goal line is out of play and may not touch

the ball himself, nor in any way whatever prevent any other player from doing so, until he is in play; but no player is out of play when the ball is kicked off from behind the goal line.

7. In case the ball goes behind the goal line, if a player on the side to whom the goal belongs first touches the ball, one of his side shall he entitled to a free kick from the goal line at the point opposite the place where the ball shall be touched. If a player of the opposite side first touches the ball, one of his side shall be entitled to a free kick at the goal only from a point 15 yards outside the goal line, opposite the place where the ball is touched, the opposing side standing within their goal line until he has had his kick.

8. If a player makes a fair catch, he shall be entitled to a free kick, providing he claims it by making a mark with his heel at once; and in order to take such a kick he may go back as far as he pleases, and no player on the opposite side shall advance beyond his mark until he has kicked.

9. No player shall run with the ball.

10. Neither tripping nor hacking shall be allowed, and no player shall use his hands to hold or push his adversary.

11. A player shall not be allowed to throw the ball or pass it to another with his hands.

12. No player shall be allowed to take the ball from the ground with his hands under any pretext whatever while it is in play.

13. No player shall be allowed to wear projecting nails, iron plates, or *gutta percha* on the soles or heels of his boots.

For a few years the FA held its annual meeting at the Freemasons' Tavern. In January 1885 the first debate on legalising professionalism in the game was held here.

In 1910 the venue was rebuilt as the luxurious Connaught Rooms, named after the first Duke of Connaught, Grand Master of the Freemasons whose Grand Lodge is situated alongside.

Football Association headquarters (1863–90), 51 Holborn Viaduct

After formulating the first official football rules at a series of meetings on Great Queen Street (→ p. 11) in 1863 the new Football Association set up offices here. At first members of the organisation were confined to London, where the body had been formed, and most local clubs refused to join the FA or simply ignored its directives. For instance, in 1866 No Names Kilburn, one of the founder members, complained that there were only two other teams, Barnes and Crystal Palace, who were willing to play them according to the new FA rules. That year a London side played Sheffield in Battersea Park using a bizarre hybrid set of laws which saw the home side win by two goals and four touchdowns to nil. Within a year there were only ten teams in the Football Association – one fewer than the number that had formed the body – but matters improved in 1868 when two public schools, Charterhouse and Westminster, joined. However, it was the Sheffield club, the only member outside the capital, that pushed to exclude touchdowns and the use of the hand.

By 1872, the year in which the FA Cup was first played, there were around 120 Association clubs, fewer than the number of those playing rugby. But football surpassed the oval-ball game in popularity that decade thanks to the enthusiasm of the northern working-class teams. In 1877 all references to rugby-like conventions were removed when it was agreed that only the goalkeeper could handle the ball. By 1881 the FA had 128 members, but it was not until 1914 that all professional and amateur clubs agreed to recognise it as the single football governing body in England.

Gamages, 116–128 Holborn

The huge, much-mourned Holborn store was the major seller of match balls in the early years of the professional game. A 1906 advertisement explained that Gamages provided 'everything for football – Beware of Foreign Rubbish!' Much touted was the Universal ball which sported 'cowhide cases and rubber bladders'.

→ Florin Raducioiu shops at Harvey Nichols, p. 197.

The High Court, Strand

Of the many legal battles involving football that have taken place at the country's leading civil court, none has had such an impact as the case of George Eastham and Freedom of Contract in the early 1960s.

Eastham was a skilful inside-forward with Newcastle who in 1959 declined the offer of a new contract. The club were no longer obliged to pay him and could now sell him to whoever they chose.

Eastham held out for seven months without playing, taking a job outside the game arranged by businessman Ernie Clay, who went on to become chairman of Fulham. He also trained with amateur Reigate and Redhill, and played for a showbiz XI alongside Tommy Steele and unfunny comedy duo Mike and Bernie Winters. He then moved to Arsenal for what was at the time a big fee (£47,500).

Meanwhile, the Professional Footballers' Association, with Jimmy Hill as chairman, decided to challenge football's 'Retain and Transfer System'. They were helped by Conservative MP Philip Goodhart who described it as 'documents a fifteenth-century apprentice might view with suspicion'. Eastham agreed to be a guinea pig and take his case to the High Court. Lawyers advised the PFA that they only had a 50 per cent chance of getting the transfer system declared a restraint of trade, but Mr Justice Wilberforce announced on 4 July 1963 that rules restricting a player out of contract from taking up employment elsewhere were indeed restrictive.

In December 1979 the High Court overturned on appeal a ten-year ban on Don Revie's involvement in domestic football imposed after the England manager had announced his resignation from the job in an exclusive interview with the *Daily Mail*, before telling even the FA. Soon after he took a post with the United Arab Emirates.

The High Court banned Terry Venables from being a company director for seven years in January 1998.

Karen Parlour, ex-wife of Arsenal's 1990s midfield player Ray, won the award of a third of his future earnings as part of their divorce settlement at the Court of Appeal here in 2004.

→ Terry Venables at Knightsbridge Crown Court, p. 197

Howard Hotel, Temple Place

Elton John met Bobby Moore at this hotel in May 1977 and nearly appointed him as manager of Watford. The singer-pianist had recently taken over at Watford Football Club, and needed a new manager. He approached Moore, who was coming to the end of his playing career, and promised to call him to finalise the details. A further meeting was scheduled for five days later at the Memories of China restaurant in the West End, but earlier that day

Elton phoned to postpone it. A few weeks later the job went to Graham Taylor who took Watford into the First Division for the first time in 1982 and to second position behind Liverpool in 1983.

→ **Wimbledon at Cannizaro's hotel, p. 230.**

Mills Music, 20 Denmark Street
In the 1960s Chelsea players would congregate here in the afternoon, where they would be served by the tea-boy, Reg Dwight, who later changed his name to Elton John.

Savoy Hotel, Savoy Court
Once London's most stylish hotel and currently being refurbished, the Savoy was where the victorious Tottenham team celebrated after winning the Second Division Championship in 1950, a rare feat given that it had been nearly thirty years since their previous trophy. Three hundred and fifty guests were joined by Jack Kirwan, the only surviving member of the 1901 FA Cup-winning team.

Remarkably, a year later, Tottenham were back, as First Division champions. It was the last time a team won the top two divisions in English football in successive seasons. That year Spurs also had the highest average attendance figures in the country. Ten years later they were back at the Savoy, having won the Double. There have been no further championship celebrations for Tottenham since, either at the Savoy or any other hotel.

When Johnny Haynes, then one of the leading players in England, drove up to the hotel in his MG sports car for a function in 1959 a flunkey rushed up and breathlessly purred: 'Good evening, Mr Haynes, if you'd like to give me the keys I'll park the car for you.' Right behind Haynes in his less grand Triumph Herald was Alan Mullery, then an unknown teenage hopeful at Haynes's club, Fulham. Mullery tossed his keys to the Savoy attendant, but instead of offering Mullery the same service the attendant asked him: 'What are these for?' 'I'm with him,' responded Mullery, hopefully. 'Bugger off and park your own car,' came the reply.

In 1961, Ipswich held a dinner at the Savoy to celebrate their unlikely championship, masterminded by Alf Ramsey as manager. During Ramsey's speech, club chairman John Cobbold kept interrupting the future England boss from behind the curtains, hissing at him, 'C'mon Ramsey, stop boring everyone.'

→ Alf Ramsey growing up in Dagenham, p. 82

Stringfellow's, 16–19 Upper St Martin's Lane

Stringfellow's was *the* footballers' nightspot in the 1980s. At first the club wanted little to do with them for players' earnings had not then risen beyond human computation. The management was also worried about footballers' 'lager lout' image; there was certainly no glamour attached to the era's finest London-based talents such as Liam Brady and Glenn Hoddle. But this changed within a few years with the arrival in the capital of two playboy Scots: Charlie Nicholas and Frank McAvennie. Indeed it was Stringfellow's that influenced Nicholas to sign for Arsenal, rather than Liverpool or Manchester United, in 1983, even though the London club was then way behind the two northern ones in terms of success.

McAvennie, the bleach-blond West Ham and Scotland striker who seemed to spend as much time at Stringfellow's as on the training pitch, adopted his playboy lifestyle practically as soon as he first arrived in London. At Heathrow airport he was met by West Ham manager John Lyall who whisked him off down the King's Road in his Jag to show him the sights of 'Swinging London'. But the Scot initially hated London. In an interview with the *Newcastle Chronicle* in 2004 he recalled: 'I had such a strong Scottish accent no one knew what I was talking about. When I was shouting in training the other players thought I was trying to pick a fight.' Once McAvennie began putting the goals away for West Ham he became a minor tabloid celebrity and bought himself a snazzy registration plate (UP U2) for his new Capri 2.8. Sadly, the car was stolen the day after he bought it, but McAvennie simply went out the next day and bought himself another.

One Friday night John Fashanu, the Wimbledon striker, was at the club, his excuse being that he was suspended, when he noticed it was 4.30 a.m. and that McAvennie was still lording it up. 'Haven't you got a game tomorrow?' asked the Wimbledon centre-forward. 'Aye,' smiled the Scot and strode off. The next day Fashanu woke late, turned on the results and found out that McAvennie had scored a hat-trick.

McAvennie told the *Chronicle* that he had been a great club man: 'West Ham, Celtic, St Mirren, oh and Stringfellow's and Brown's. I've always enjoyed life and enjoyed the nightclubs. I drank nothing but champagne at one time. I had a few model birds. It goes with the territory. If you have a couple of quid in your pocket you're everybody's friend.'

In 1995 he had £100,000 seized by Customs, who claimed it was going to be used to fund a major drugs deal and didn't believe McAvennie's explanation that the money was for investment in an expedition to raise a sunken treasure ship.

McAvennie told the *Observer* his lowest ebb came in autumn 2000 when he went on trial at Newcastle Crown Court charged with conspiracy to supply £110,000 worth of ecstasy tablets and amphetamines. He spent a month on remand in Durham jail and faced up to ten years in prison if convicted. The jury, however acquitted him, at which he broke down in tears.

→ **China White, p. 27**

Tavistock Hotel, Piazza at James Street, east side
The hotel was popular with provincial clubs in the late nineteenth century. For instance, Aston Villa made the Tavistock their headquarters when they won the Double in 1897. But when the well-known football journalist J. A. H. Catton told the team he was disappointed because their triumph meant that Preston were no longer unique in winning the League and Cup in the same season, things got rather heated and Villa players threatened to throw Catton out of the window.

Officials from Chelsea engaged in staunch canvassing of Football League officials at the hotel in May 1905 in order to get the club elected to the Football League before they had even kicked a ball. Chelsea boasted of having financial stability (£3,000 in the bank) and a high-quality stadium, and claimed that they were assembling a strong team. League officials were not swayed initially, but once the directors of the new club had bought them a few drinks they changed their minds. Chelsea duly became one of only two clubs ever to be elected to the League before they had played a match. (The other one was Bradford City.) Chelsea's remarkable elevation led opposing fans to mock them for decades by twisting the club's own 'carefree' song into an alternative version that went, 'Carefree, wherever you may be, Chelsea ain't got no history . . .'

→ **Chelsea at Stamford Bridge, p. 204**

FITZROVIA, W1

Oxford Music Hall, 14 Oxford Street
In 1912 George Robey, one of the great music-hall stars of the day, an avid football fan and occasional Millwall player, had a vision of the game of the future. He imagined the Oxford Music Hall demolished to make way for a vast stadium, home to London United, where the crowd would number 'a quarter of a million, each paying a sovereign for a game against St Petersburg Athletic'. The music hall has since gone but London United and indeed St Petersburg Athletic have yet to be formed.

→ **Arsenal at the** Windsor Castle Music Hall**, p. 181**

Soho Ramblers, Atlantic Machines Office, 28 Windmill Street
The Soho Ramblers were a 1960s charity football team that included some of London's most notorious late-twentieth-century gangsters, among them veteran jailbird 'Mad' Frankie Fraser and Eddie Richardson, one of the so-called Richardson 'torture' gang. The headquarters were Fraser and Richardson's West End offices, where the two villains ran their fruit-machine business. Their 1965 fixture list included an official invitation to play at Parkhurst prison where the governor and prison officers treated them like stars, rather than as prospective inmates. The team inevitably broke up when several of the participants returned to their old ways and got nicked.

MARYLEBONE, W1

Harley Street

Drugs scandals in football go back further than modern-day tales of top players knocking back the odd line of coke or missing drugs tests. In January 1925 a Harley Street doctor, and Arsenal fan, worried about his team's form, approached Leslie Knighton, the Arsenal manager, and offered him some 'courage pills' that would boost the side's chances in a forthcoming FA Cup game at West Ham. Perhaps not so reassuringly, he added, 'Don't worry. The pills have no after-effects.'

Knighton collected the pills and the Arsenal players downed them a few hours before kick-off – only to find the game postponed owing to thick fog. Things might have been fine had the players been given the chance to run around in a match, but forced to remain relatively immobile they became increasingly frustrated. They developed an unquenchable raging thirst and a bitter taste to boot. When the game finally went ahead the players again popped the pills, but succeeded only in obtaining a draw. There *were* unwelcome side-effects and the players told Knighton not to hand them out again – especially after they lost the replay.

Selfridges, 400 Oxford Street

Alex James, one of London's most celebrated between-the-wars footballers, had a day job as a sports demonstrator at the leading store after joining Arsenal from Preston in 1929. At that time wages for footballers were paltry so it made sense for James to take on extra work. But James wasn't that keen on the job. He had been expecting some kind of 'financial inducement' to move south, and when he found out the incentive was a job at Selfridges he assumed it would be a nominal position requiring him to do little other than show his face and knock a ball or two up for a few minutes. James was amazed to find he had to work as many as fifty hours a week (for £250 a year), although most of them were spent simply signing autographs. James won four League Championship and two FA Cup medals with Arsenal, sporting the baggiest shorts in existence to hide the long johns he wore to alleviate his rheumatism.

→ Alex James's sweetshop, p. 88

MAYFAIR, W1

Bond Street

A horde of Northern barbarians invaded London on Saturday, strolling
in their big boots up Bond Street, staring into the peaks of their cloth
caps, giving an unintelligent glance or two ... many with big fists and
brawny shoulders, slouched along in their ready-made suits ... hard
and dour in the mould of their faces, nor softness nor grace or elegance.
London was a strange unknown to them and like sheer savages, they
went stupidly about.

> Philip Gibbs, *Daily Graphic*, 29 April 1911,
> before the FA Cup Final between Bradford
> and Newcastle at the Crystal Palace

Clipper's Bar, 160 Piccadilly

This part of London has long been packed with expensive bars luring
footballers away from an early night. In the 1930s Arsenal's diminutive and
baggy-shorted inside-forward Alex James would go to Clipper's Bar, not
to celebrate winning or to drown his sorrows after a bad result, but before
games. When Arsenal fan George Frey dropped into the bar one Friday
night in 1930 he was astonished to see James drinking with a large group of
friends even though it was 1 a.m. and the Arsenal man was due to play in the
afternoon. Frey, as he told the writer Jon Spurling, approached the Scottish
inside-forward and chatted to him. When it got to 3 a.m. he asked James
when he planned to quit drinking. 'When the sun comes up,' came the reply.
James put in an inspirational performance on the field later that day.

Dorchester Hotel, 53 Park Lane

A world-renowned hotel built in 1931, with 600 bedrooms and walls of
reinforced concrete soundproofed with seaweed and cork, the Dorchester
has often played host to footballers visiting the capital for the Cup Final.
For instance, in 1961 the Leicester City team booked into the hotel before
playing Tottenham Hotspur in that year's final. Also staying there were
the actors Elizabeth Taylor and Richard Burton, then Hollywood's most
glamorous couple. They were soon spotted by the young Leicester centre-

half, Frank McLintock (later the Double-winning captain at Arsenal), who was amazed to find Ms Taylor making eyes at him. The craggy Scot became somewhat agitated when the actress sidled up to him, only to whisper in his ear: 'You've still got your bicycle clips attached to the bottom of your trousers.'

When the much lusted after 70s actress Raquel Welch visited Stamford Bridge for a Chelsea match in 1972, she invited the team to a post-match cocktail party at the Dorchester also attended by various Beatles and Rolling Stones.

It was at the Dorchester in 2003 that Ken Bates, owner of Chelsea, met Roman Abramovich to discuss selling the club to the Russian. The two men talked for twenty minutes. Bates had a bottle of wine, Abramovich, who is teetotal, water. The Russian billionaire then offered Bates £17 million – £16,999,999 more than Bates had paid for Chelsea in the early 1980s.

Embassy Club, 29 Old Burlington Street

One of the main late-night partying zones for Premiership footballers in the early twenty-first century, the Embassy was where Jermaine Pennant drank four glasses of red wine on the night of 23 January 2005 before driving away while serving a sixteen-month driving ban and being uninsured.

Pennant then crashed the Mercedes he was driving in Aylesbury into a lamp-post which he began to drag along. When the police caught up with the winger and asked for his name, he was so shaken he momentarily forgot his identity and told the officers he was Ashley Cole, then a team-mate at Arsenal. He was close; the car belonged to Cole. Pennant was jailed for three months for the offence (drink-driving, not impersonating Ashley Cole), suffered the humiliation of playing with a prison identity tag on his ankle after he was released early, and still endures the chant from opposing fans of 'You're supposed to be in jail'.

A year later in January 2006 Chelsea's Joe Cole enjoyed a few drinks at the Embassy with West Ham's Bobby Zamora and Anton Ferdinand before leaving for a party in Chiswick. There he claims he was attacked by a big, beefy, bruisy bloke. The England international fled the house at 5.30 a.m., climbing out of a window, bare-chested and shoeless.

Thoughts that high-profile players might now be more circumspect in their behaviour after a night out at the Embassy were dashed later that year when Cole's Chelsea team-mate Wayne Bridge was involved in a 'disturbance' in the street outside while celebrating the end of another gruelling season. He suffered a cut and bruising to his face.

It was around that time that Ashley Cole came to the Embassy to get what he so eloquently described in his autobiography as 'hammered' after Arsenal fans snubbed him during the post-match celebrations marking the club's departure from Highbury. 'Thierry Henry and I sat in the centre circle after the final whistle. His name was sung from the rooftops while my contribution was recognised by a deafening silence,' the hard-done-by Cole noted. Rather than trying to work out how to win the fans back, Cole mutinously celebrated with several Chelsea players who were at the Embassy after winning the Premiership. He joined Chelsea soon after.

Grosvenor House Hotel, 87–89 Park Lane

Football folk have long gathered in this luxury hotel, designed in the 1930s by Edwin Lutyens, but have not always behaved impeccably. At the testimonial dinner for long-serving Arsenal centre-half David O'Leary in 1984 the new powerbroker at the club, David Dein, joked about Tottenham's Keith Burkinshaw, who had just been dismissed. 'I hear Selfridges have already hired their Father Christmas for this year,' he told guests. 'It's Keith Burkinshaw who has just been given the sack by Spurs.' The joke didn't go down too well and Peter Shreeves, Burkinshaw's successor, walked out. Dein later apologised to Tottenham.

In October 2003 the Grosvenor House was the setting for a series of sordid events that gripped the newspaper readers of the nation, especially those acquainted with the racier tabloids. The story revolved around the practice of 'roasting' – mass sexual congress between a group of footballers and one girl – so named because the perpetrators liken it to stuffing a chicken with sausage before cooking it.

A friend of a number of Premiership stars had supposedly organised a roast in the hotel's Room 316. But who had roasted whom, the world of football wanted to know? There were five players involved, the early reports revealed, including one from Chelsea and one or two from Newcastle. The five-a-side team had met the girl at 1 a.m. Saturday morning at the Funky Buddha nightclub on Mayfair's Berkeley Street, moved on first to another nightclub, Brown's, and then to the hotel, where, according to the footballers, she willingly participated in group sex. Two players were later named in the papers, Carlton Cole of Chelsea and Titus Bramble, the Newcastle United defender, but both men were eventually cleared of any wrongdoing.

The hotel is also regularly used for football functions, such as get-togethers of the 1966 World Cup winners, and annual awards ceremonies. At the 2003 Professional Footballers' Association awards bash that took place here the comedian Dominic Holland opened his act in front of more than 1,000 footballers and 400 hangers-on with a nod to the recent roasting allegations: 'So here we are, lads – 800 football players at the Grosvenor House Hotel. Are you all staying the night, 'cos you'll need what, four or five rooms between you?'

Langan's, Stratton Street

The finer points of Teddy Sheringham's transfer from Nottingham Forest to Tottenham Hotspur in the summer of 1992 were hammered out at this upmarket brasserie. Sheringham was then one of England's most feared strikers, and both clubs were challenging for top honours. There was one major problem: the legendary Forest manager, Brian Clough, 'liked a bung' – an illicit payment in a brown envelope that went into his pocket, rather than the selling club's bank account through the official channels.

The announced fee was £2.15 million but Forest's accounts showed receipt of only £2.1 million. As for what happened to the other £50,000, Brian Clough took that secret to his grave.

Park Lane Hotel, 112 Piccadilly

The hotel has long associations with the Bracewell-Smith family, major shareholders at Arsenal, and ironically it was here that Arsenal manager George Graham met his nemesis, the Norwegian players' agent Rune Hauge, in the bar just before Christmas 1991. After a chat Hauge presented Graham with a little something contained in a holdall 'as an appreciation of all you [Graham] have done to help me to open doors here in England'. When Graham got home and opened the bag he found £140,000 in £50 notes inside. He also received a banker's draft for a further £285,000, and deposited some of the money in a Jersey bank, later claiming it was an unsolicited gift. In 1994 Graham decided to pay the money to Arsenal, and agreed with the club to leave quietly at the end of the season. However, when news of the 'gift' leaked out Arsenal sacked him and the FA banned him from football for a year.

→ George Graham at Arsenal, p. 98

Playboy Club (1960s–1970s), 45 Park Lane

After England won the World Cup the victorious team enjoyed their post-match dinner at the Royal Garden Hotel in Kensington, then turned up at the Playboy Club, epitome of swish, swinging sixties London, where there was a sizeable crowd to greet them. When the players' hopes of being escorted to a table and served champagne were dashed by a flunkey who told them they would have to stand behind a rope and wait for an official photographer, Nobby Stiles, with two brief words, one a cuss, led the party outside, off to Danny La Rue's club on Hanover Square. Some stayed at the Playboy, however, including Mr and Mrs Bobby Moore, who celebrated in the company of the renowned songwriter Burt Bacharach. Moore even ended up on stage to sing Len Barry's '1–2–3'.

21 Club, 8 Chesterfield Gardens

The 21 Club was many a footballer's favourite nightspot during the days before swinging London, and was where Fulham's masterly Johnny Haynes introduced Bobby Moore and wife to the highlife at the start of Moore's career. For the Moores it was a chance to dine like the glitterati. On their first night at the club Haynes ordered the starter for the three of them. A large silver bowl arrived, lined with ice and overflowing with prawns. Soon Mrs Moore had a mountain of discarded heads and shells on her plate. She asked Haynes if they were expensive and he told her they were so expensive that the restaurant charged by the prawn. Tina was horrified and asked how they knew how many had been eaten. 'They count the shells and heads you leave,' Haynes explained. Whereupon she promptly emptied the remains into her handbag, unaware that the Fulham forward was winding her up, with the full knowledge of the West Ham half-back, of course.

→ Johnny Haynes at Fulham, p. 219

SOHO, W1

Café Royal, 68 Regent Street

The Café Royal has long been London's most elegant restaurant-cum-nightspot, even if by the 1990s it had also become a hang-out for David Beckham, Jamie Redknapp, Teddy Sheringham and Stan Collymore.

The venue opened in 1865, and with its lavish decor, velvet seats, and ornate mirrors soon started to attract flamboyant members of the Aesthetic Movement such as Oscar Wilde. Later, directors of Arsenal began to come here. In the 1930s, board member Clive Carr was responsible for revamping Regent Street as well as the Café, and on Friday nights Arsenal would treat visiting team managers and directors to dinner.

The Arsenal players celebrated here after securing the Double in 1971. The club's less successful early twenty-first-century Dutch reserve, Quincy Owusu-Abeyie, was arrested outside in 2005 after five men were caught brawling in the street by the entrance at 3 a.m. on the night of the Professional Footballers' Association awards.

After the Chelsea *v* Moscow Dynamo match of 13 November 1945, a friendly that was one of the first ever matches between English and continental clubs, Chelsea held a dinner here for officials and players of both clubs. Gifts, including inscribed cigarette lighters, were exchanged.

When Hungary came to Wembley in November 1953 and beat England 6–3 the FA were so mortified they called a meeting of all top managers at the Café Royal to discuss how to save English football. Amazingly the England manager, Walter Winterbottom, merely took notes and spoke not once in a discussion dominated by the Scot Matt Busby, manager of Manchester United.

Prime minister Harold Wilson was speaking here at a testimonial dinner for Sir Alf Ramsey in 1974 when a mouse ran across the top table. The boxer Henry Cooper caught it and handed the rodent to a waiter who stamped on it. There were hoots of laughter and cries of 'aah' and 'ooh'. Wilson thought the audience were commenting on his speech.

China White, 6 Air Street

China White has become the West End late-night club of choice for the best-paid Premier League footballers. For instance, Rio Ferdinand was photographed here after Manchester United had given him compassionate leave to attend his grandmother's funeral in London. Another regular visitor is Mark Bosnich, the coke-snorting former United and Chelsea goalkeeper. After his nine-month ban for drug-taking ended in 2003 Bosnich told journalists: 'I really don't give a toss about football any more. F*** football. It would take me a year to eighteen months to get back into the form I was. And I really can't be bothered. I have had enough. I want to try and make it as a sports star in America. I don't know what type of sports I would do. But that is what I want to do.'

Stan Collymore is also often to be seen at China White. He stopped playing football at the age of thirty in 2001, prompting Geoff Hurst's wife to ask her husband: 'Retired? Retired from what?' When Collymore was sixteen he was at lowly Walsall. Tommy Coakley, who took him on as a trainee, recalled: 'Even at sixteen, Stan was very much his own man, with his own ideas about absolutely everything. Sadly, most of his ideas were usually wrong. I felt from day one that he'd either be one of the best players in the world, or that he'd have a very short career.'

In 1995 Collymore became Britain's most expensive player when Liverpool bought him for £8.5 million. Three years later during the 1998 World Cup he kicked and punched his then girlfriend, Ulrika Johnsson, in a Paris bar, and in May 2004 was bound over in the sum of £500, agreeing to keep the peace after facing four charges including threatening to kill his estranged wife, Estelle. Nevertheless he now broadcasts on Radio 5 Live where evidently standards have slipped.

Daft on a bus

Paul Gascoigne engaged in one of his craziest madcap escapades on Oxford Street in the heart of the West End in 1997. Gascoigne, then with Rangers, had come down to London to join up with the DJ Chris Evans and journalist Danny Baker for a jaunt to the bright lights. The group travelled into town in Evans's chauffeur-driven Bentley, parked near Marble Arch, and went walkabout.

The fun soon began. The England man decided to hijack a bus and, seeing a double-decker stopped at the lights, beckoned to the driver, climbed in beside the amazed man and somehow persuaded him to let him take the wheel, where he was soon leading the passengers in a chorus of 'Summer Holiday'.

A few minutes later Gascoigne decided to turn his hand to the state of the roads. Spotting some workmen digging up the street, he got out of the bus and persuaded them to let him have a go on their pneumatic drill. Before long the England midfield star was wielding the drill, wearing a hard hat and earphones.

For their next stunt the group stopped a taxi and persuaded the driver to let Gascoigne borrow the vehicle. The cabbie climbed in the back with Chris Evans while Gascoigne negotiated the road. A few yards later the footballer stopped, beckoned to a passer-by and announced: 'You'll never believe who I've got in the back of the cab – Chris Evans!' The pedestrian, who didn't recognise the England international, peered into the back, where he failed to recognise Evans either, and replied: 'No, it isn't, this is a wind-up'.

The FA Premier League, 30 Gloucester Place

The top division in English football, officially the Barclays Premier League, previously the Premiership, has its own offices in the heart of austere Georgian Marylebone. The League was formed in 1992 from the old First Division and triumphantly announced its arrival as if it were a distinct new football entity. Taking advantage of the nation's illiteracy, the new body convinced the football world that there was something more elevated about the word 'Premier' than the word 'First', that somehow 'premier' meant more 'first' than 'first', and succeeded in getting the Football League to rename the Second Division the First Division.

Football semantics became even more obtruse in 2004 when the First Division (in reality the Second Division) was renamed the Championship and the old Third Division became the First Division. In reality the Premier League/Premiership was simply football's First Division with a new name and greater sponsorship. The nature of the competition was the same, with all teams playing each other twice, home and away, in a season, gaining three points for a win, one for a draw and none for a defeat.

And the outcome at the end of the season remained the same: the team that had the most points became champions and those at the bottom were relegated to the next League down. What did change was that more money flooded into the game, from television companies, sponsorship and the fans' pockets, and the players got richer.

Some experts claim the standard of football is now higher. However, in the first fifteen seasons of the Premier League its sides won the European Cup only twice, whereas in the previous fifteen (relevant) seasons of the old First Division, they won it seven times.

→ The FA at Soho Square, p. 31

Premier League off the bench

✪ The first ever Premier League/Premiership goal was scored by Brian Deane for Sheffield United against Manchester United in August 1992.

✪ Soon after the League was set up Blackburn paid Southampton a British record fee of £3.3 million for Alan Shearer. By September 2006 the record was £30 million, paid by Chelsea to AC Milan for Andriy Shevchenko. Amazingly the highest fee was once (in 1995) paid for Stan Collymore.

✪ Two of the original signatories to the deal that set up the Premier League were Luton and Notts County neither of which has ever played in it.

✪ In the League's first seventeen years two teams – Swindon and Barnsley – have won promotion to the Premiership/Premier League and lasted only one season before being relegated.

✪ During the Premier League era (up to 2009) only four clubs have won the title. Surprisingly these are not the same four regarded as the Big Four – Arsenal, Chelsea, Liverpool and Manchester United – but include Blackburn at the expense of the once all-powerful Liverpool. During the same period the FA Cup was always (bar once) won by the 'Big Four', each of whom has also won at least one European competition.

Football Association (2001–), 25 Soho Square

The Football Association moved from the Victorian chaos of Lancaster Gate in Bayswater three miles east to stylish Soho Square in 2001 as part of the organisation's desperation to shed its fusty image.

In charge of Operation Streamline was 35-year-old chief executive Adam Crozier, formerly of the advertising agency Saatchi and Saatchi, whose lack of tie dismayed many FA officials used to a blazer and slacks culture. Crozier set about the task of improving the Association's image at a time when Glenn Hoddle had only recently been sacked as England manager in 1998 for bizarre quasi-religious pronunciations, and the FA had shamefully allowed the 1999 FA Cup winners, Manchester United, to withdraw from the following season's competition so they could play a series of meaningless friendlies in Brazil to boost England's chances of hosting the 2006 World Cup.

Crozier made a sterling effort to restore the stature of the FA Cup. He also insisted the FA took a moral stance over the selection for England of two Leeds players, Lee Bowyer and Jonathan Woodgate, who were being investigated for a racist attack on a student, of which they were subsequently cleared. As part of his streamlining Crozier replaced the FA's cumbersome ninety-one-strong board with a body of just twelve and showed a number of antiquated time-servers the door, even if he did replace them with sharp-suited advertising types spouting New Labour nonsense in tortuous Blairspeak. Crozier also implemented an instant and long overdue cost-cutting exercise, cancelling the FA's £25,000 account for blazers at Aquascutum.

Two huge stories dominated the Crozier era that ushered in the FA's tenure at Soho Square: the much delayed and costly rebuilding of Wembley stadium (→ p. 152) and the controversial appointment of a foreigner, the Swede Sven-Goran Eriksson, as England manager. The Wembley project achieved little worthwhile, banished the FA Cup Final to Wales for six seasons of misery for fans attempting the impossible – namely, to get from England to Cardiff on time and back home the same day – and cost nearly £1 billion in doing so. The appointment of a non-English manager to the England job likewise.

After Kevin Keegan resigned in October 2000 Crozier and Arsenal vice-chairman David Dein travelled to Rome to persuade Eriksson to leave

Lazio and take the England job. If the idea of a team representing a non-independent country such as England was absurd, how much more absurd the hiring of a non-English manager?

Sven-Goran Eriksson secured a five-year contract that made him the highest-paid coach in the world (even though he'd never won the World Cup or European Championship), and though he had few problems qualifying for the three major tournaments of his tenure – surely the base line for any England manager – Eriksson's teams flopped when it came to the crunch.

In friendlies between qualifying games Eriksson was wont to use every player in the squad as a substitute, so much so that the line-up at the end of the game bore no relation to the starting eleven. In some games he played potentially important players out of position, presumably to justify dropping them in a subsequent competitive match for performing so badly in the friendly. Such was the case with the player who more than any other would have enhanced England's 2006 World Cup, Andy Johnson, who in a friendly against Holland was played not in his rightful attacking role but on the right wing.

Eriksson's teams, stuffed with players from the so-called 'Golden Generation' (Frank Lampard Jnr and Ashley Cole), reached three successive quarter-finals but froze each time at the big occasion and crashed out of the tournaments in the most frustrating manner when a little oomph from the soporific Swede in charge might have propelled England into the success zone.

At the 2002 World Cup the team's general performances were ineffectual, the manager's tactics questionable, and his selections ridiculous given the lack of full fitness of Beckham, and the plethora of English right-backs better than Danny Mills and reserve goalkeepers more deserving than David James. England went out of the tournament with a 2–1 defeat to Brazil, despite taking the lead. When Sven lost his nerve tactically, the country's well-rehearsed excuse-mongers called a forty-yard free-kick by Ronaldinho a fluke – as if that would somehow make it count less.

Euro 2004 was even more frustrating. At least England qualified, unlike four years later under Eriksson's successor, Steve McClaren. But Eriksson inexplicably promoted David James to first-choice goalie, and James justified his critics' fears when he not only conceded a goal scored directly from a free-kick by France's Zinedine Zidane to let France equalise, but then moaned that the video of France's games which FA officials had provided him with hadn't included any Zidane free-kicks. During that France game Eriksson took off Wayne Rooney for Emile Heskey, something akin to Pope Julius II removing Michelangelo from the Sistine Chapel and replacing him with a painter-decorator. England eventually went out of the tournament on penalties (again).

By the time it came to the 2006 World Cup in Germany everyone knew the script. Neither Eriksson nor England disappointed. With disregard for basic professionalism, Sven allowed the players' wives, partners and girlfriends to travel to Germany and distract their concentration. Eriksson decided to include only four attackers in the squad. Out of the four, only one of them (Peter Crouch) was both fit and able to play at this level. One (Wayne Rooney) was not fully fit. He returned to the side, well into the tournament but, uncontrollable under Eriksson's management, got himself sent off in the Portugal match. Another (Michael Owen) had been injured for most of the season and was soon injured again. The fourth (Theo Walcott), barely out of school, was presumably selected as part of a jokey *Jim'll Fix It* stunt, for he had played only twenty-one games of first-team football (scoring four goals) and Eriksson had never seen him perform.

In the quarter-final Portugal were insurmountable for the third time in four tournaments, and England went out on penalties with only one player of the four able to find the net from the spot-kick.

And just to liven things up between games there were plenty of juicy scandals and dramas in Svenworld. There were the affairs with Ulrika Johnsson and FA employee Faria Alam. There were the close encounters with a potential new employer while under contract with England. (When Eriksson met Roman Abramovich to discuss taking over the Chelsea job just a month before the 2006 World Cup, the FA responded by increasing his annual pay to £4 million.) There was the way Sven was duped by a reporter posing as a sheikh looking to buy an English club. He identified Aston Villa as a likely target, and indicated that he would happily become manager and prise David Beckham away from Real Madrid. More embarrassingly, Eriksson told the fake sheikh that Wayne Rooney's temperament was down to 'coming from a poor family'. He also called Rio Ferdinand 'lazy'.

McClaren Formula 0

Adam Crozier resigned as chief executive in November 2002. He was replaced by the hulking, brooding ex-professional footballer Mark Palios, who had become a chartered accountant. Like Crozier, Palios considered the FA to be a 'shambles'. Like Crozier he didn't last long. But Palios did make one significant contribution to the history of football. When Manchester United and England centre-half Rio Ferdinand forgot to attend a drugs test in September 2003, leaving himself open to a ban, Palios insisted Sven-Goran Eriksson drop him from the England team for a vital Euro 2004 qualifier to make an example of him, warning others who might also forget in the future.

The Professional Footballers' Association and the England players, with breathtaking arrogance and totally out of touch with the normal rules of decency and fairness, flew into an incandescent rage. Led by self-styled 'shop steward' Gary Neville, they threatened to go on strike. Palios stayed firm. He told the *News of the World*: 'After this case, I don't think any club will allow a player to miss a drugs test again.' Ferdinand contacted team-mates and urged them to play, and so the so-called 'Golden Generation' forwent the picket line for the touchline and achieved a creditable 0–0 draw that led them to qualification.

But Palios himself was playing away. His game was an affair with FA secretary Faria Alam, who had also featured in Sven-Goran Eriksson's bedroom. Palios quit in August 2004. Another scandal, another chief executive. The new man, Brian Barwick, had edited *Match of the Day* and *Sportsnight*, and sported a fine Adolf Hitler moustache. His appointment came with an excellent PR campaign presenting him as the saviour of English football, his 'passion' for the game honed inevitably during the '66 World Cup. The English football public, reared on generations of disappointment courtesy of the FA – failure to enter the early World Cups; failure to appoint Brian Clough as England manager, followed by the appointments of Graham Taylor, Glenn Hoddle et al., the withdrawal of innocent English clubs from European football in 1985 after the Heysel incident; the needless destruction of Wembley's twin towers – steeled itself for fresh disaster.

Soon enough Barwick was presiding over a fiasco. It surrounded the appointment of the next England manager after Eriksson. Barwick wanted

Luiz Felipe Scolari, manager of Portugal, regular humiliators of England, but the FA's courting of Scolari, who had won the World Cup with Brazil in 2002, was a little too public. On 24 April 2006 the journalist Harry Harris revealed in the *Daily Express* that Scolari had got the job. Brian Barwick travelled from Soho Square to Lisbon on 27 April to begin negotiations, while the FA, livid that the news had been leaked, began an investigation into how Harris had got his scoop. Anyway, one day Scolari found twenty journalists camped outside his door and asked not to be considered.

Barwick now turned to a shortlist of four. One of the names on that list was a man of quiet, studious intelligence, obvious integrity and a record of reasonable success as a manager with a club that doesn't usually win things.. As a player he had won the League and the European Cup. Martin O'Neill was not just the superior candidate, he was the only acceptable candidate – and was without a club at the time. The FA insulted O'Neill, first by lining him up on a catwalk with uglier models, and then by criticising aspects of the interview he gave. They feared O'Neill wanted too much control – not that that ever stopped them promoting and rearing Howard Wilkinson.

Eventually Eriksson's successor was chosen. The football world was aghast to find that it was Steve McClaren. It was not as if the FA had even sat down and worked out after painstaking reflection that McClaren was the best candidate. No. He was no one's preferred candidate. He was the compromise choice. After appointing McClaren to the top managerial job in English football, Barwick then insulted the public by claiming that McClaren had been the FA's first choice all along. Many did not believe him.

· At Middlesbrough McClaren had won the League Cup (well, at least here was an English manager who had won *something*, unlike Sam Allardyce, Alan Curbishley, Paul Jewell, Steve Bruce and others) and reached the UEFA Cup Final (where they were thrashed by Seville). These were extraordinary heights for a club with a history of success as non-existent as Boro. But a glance at the playing style of McClaren's sides should have been sufficient warning of impending doom, let alone a glance at the man's demeanour: the ruddy complexion of an overgrown schoolboy who has been out in the open air too long, the elaborately contrived balding hairdo (fussily protected by a multi-coloured umbrella during England's Euro 2008 exit); the fulsomely shiny shoes and shinier teeth; the appalling suits. As Boro's Italian striker Massimo Maccarone once put it, 'Only in England could someone with such evident limits become the head of the national team.'

McClaren had his priorities askew from the beginning. One of his first tasks was to hire a PR man. He took lessons in media presentation, which must have included practising a stick-on smile, and armed himself with an inexhaustible supply of meaningless, New Labour-style soundbites. He appointed Terry Venables as his assistant merely to win over Venables's dwindling media fan club, even though the man was now a busted flush ten years after failing to emulate Alf Ramsey in winning a major tournament on home soil, his stock considerably diminished after unsuccessful stints with Crystal Palace (second time around), Leeds, Portsmouth and Australia. McClaren rightly dropped David Beckham but then brought him back when he began playing for a cartoon club in LA.

The football public knew that McClaren would fail the one thing he needed to pass in – getting England to the 2008 European Championships. By the summer of 2007 it looked as if England weren't going to make it to Switzerland/Austria after dropping vital points against Macedonia and Croatia. Barwick came out with more senseless spin: 'Steve has seen the highs and lows of the job, some of the frustrations. I am here to support him. He is very diligent, works very hard. He is a contemporary thinker in coaching, in sports psychology. He has worked very hard at his man-management. He has tried very hard with the media. He hasn't ducked much.' Even Barwick couldn't have believed that someone as uninspiring as McClaren was a 'contemporary' thinker.

By the end of November 2007 England needed only a draw at home to Croatia to qualify, but McClaren underwhelmed the nation. Having proved to himself at previous games that Steven Gerrard cannot play alongside Frank Lampard Jnr he again picked both. Knowing that Paul Robinson had become error-prone in goal McClaren had friendly after friendly to try out an understudy but rarely used the option. He stuck with Robinson through thin and thinner right up till the last, the Croatia match, when he dropped the Tottenham man and went for Scott Carson, who had no previous caps in competitive matches. Carson, inevitably, screwed up. Although he must have known that hoofing a long ball Watford/Wimbledon 1980s style to a big bloke (Peter

Crouch) who occasionally might head it down for a nippy, on-rushing striking partner was so passé it would be laughed out of Wembley by the skilful Croatian defence, he carried on regardless, but didn't even bother handing Crouch anyone alongside to pick up the knock-downs. At least Watford and Wimbledon played anti-football properly. And all the time McClaren, instead of sending Owen Hargreaves to tighten the back of the midfield, instead of telling his players to cut out the long-ball lumping, dithered and doodled under his umbrella in the Wembley rain. 'The Wally With The Brolly' ran the tabloid headline the next day after England lost 3–2.

The game showed that the FA had learned little since the last time they had let in three at home in a competitive match – against West Germany in 1972. At least that had been to a team overflowing with major players, playing for Europe's top clubs with a comparable population. But this was to Croatia, a country barely fifteen years old, a team filled with nobodies and Premiership reserves, but who at least were trying to play football the way it is meant to be played.

Steve McClaren became England's shortest-lived manager. He refused to resign after the Croatia fiasco. That would have been the honourable thing to do, but he preferred the extra hand-out that came with the sack. At the press conference announcing his departure the even less inspiring FA chairman, Geoff Thompson, began discussing the future of Steve *McQueen*, to mass laughter, and then compounded the felony by referring to McQueen's 'Great Escape', as in the popular film of the same name, even though the screen-bound McQueen failed to escape and like McClaren never made it to Switzerland.

'The Golden Generation'
How could England have failed to win at least one of the first five international tournaments of the twenty-first century with the array of talent at their disposal: David Beckham, Michael Owen, Frank Lampard Jnr, Steven Gerrard, Gary Neville, Rio Ferdinand, Ashley Cole, Joe Cole, Sol Campbell, John Terry, Keiron Dyer and Wayne Rooney?

There were endless inquests in the tabloids, the radio phone-in shows, on Sky Sports panels and in pub discussions across the land about the so-called 'Golden Generation', a term originally applied to the higher-achieving Portuguese squad but deflected on to England by Adam Crozier when he was chief executive of the FA.

At the start of Euro 2000 many were convinced England would win in Belgium and Holland, especially after swamping Germany in a group game. When defeat to Romania in the next match put paid to that dream, the World Cup in 2002 came to the rescue. 1–0 up against Brazil in the quarter-final. Can't fail. But fail England did. Euro 2004 beckoned in Portugal. Wayne Rooney demolished Switzerland and Croatia and the stage seemed set, but again England flopped in the quarter-final, where once again they couldn't beat Portugal. Surely World Cup 2006 would see everything put right? Forty years on . . . England to get the ultimate revenge on Germany in Berlin . . . But once again the quarter-final was the limit. Elimination on penalties after a 0–0 against Portugal. Ronaldo's fault.

That left Euro 2008 as the swansong for a fine group of players. They didn't even qualify. So where did it all go wrong? Was it bad luck, bad management or was it years of avoidable personal mistakes which psychologically drained their resources and led them to perform at a lower level than expected? Comparison with highly successful Italy bears fruit. Whereas the Italians devote every waking moment to the task at hand, not just training impeccably but refraining from alcoholic indulgence *all the time*, eating only healthy food, concentrating intensely, even when their own domestic football is racked by corruption and violence, the England players always have an excuse, a bit of history, multiple distractions, youthful indiscretions.

Beckham and his naff wedding, obsession with hair and clothes – time that could be spent practising penalties. Michael Owen with his gambling binges. Lampard's appearance in a sex video (along with Rio Ferdinand and Keiron Dyer) made in Ayia Napa in 2000, in which they romped with two girls — events later dismissed in his autobiography as an 'error of judgement'. Lampard with his drunken abuse of American tourists in the wake of 9/11. Lampard thinking 'This is England's year. This is our time,' as he took the first penalty for England against Portugal in the 2006 World Cup quarter-final, rather than concentrating on justifying his grossly inflated salary by kicking the ball into the net. Gary Neville the shop steward and his embarrassing 'I hate Scousers' line.

Rio Ferdinand missing *that* drugs test, which resulted in his ban from Euro 2004; being questioned by police after Jody Morris's stag night when guests at the Hertfordshire hotel were sprayed with fire extinguishers; losing his licence for drink-driving; being cautioned by police after his arrest over a fracas with a photographer. Ashley Cole getting 'hammered' at the end of a gruelling season rather than learning a sense of moderation that might have seen him stay at Arsenal where he was already earning a fortune and would have improved as a human being and a footballer. Joe Cole clubbing. Sol Campbell walking out on Tottenham, walking out on Arsenal at half-time. John Terry and his fights. Wayne Rooney snarling and sniping his way to another sending-off that weakened the team.

Of the Golden Generation only Steven Gerrard is a scandal-free zone; a truly inspirational figure whose stature transcends club loyalties, but even he was unable to carry the England team single-handedly as he did for Liverpool in the 2005 European Cup Final and 2006 FA Cup Final.

England and Italy. Two football-mad countries with comparable populations. Two English teams have won the European Cup in the sixteen years since they were allowed back in Europe (with two defeats in finals). Italian teams have four wins and another seven final appearances. At international level twenty-first-century England have three quarter-finals; Italy the Euro 2000 Final

(England have never got that far) and capturing the World Cup in 2006 in a foreign country (England have never managed the final outside England).

Will anything change in the future? Will a new generation of skilled players emerge who don't drink, who turn their mobiles off when they undress a female, who can win a penalty-kick competition, who can at least behave like human beings in public? An incident from the 2002 Under-21 tournament in Switzerland suggests there is still a long way to go. At breakfast the AC Milan and Italy midfielder Andrea Pirlo could be seen behaving like a normal educated young man, chatting with 'civilian' guests. A few hours later the young England players were spotted in the street walking primary-school style in a group crocodile, the only way they could be let loose on society.

The Italian job

Post the Croatia defeat England set in motion the unenviable task of finding a successor to McClaren. They needed an intelligent, no-bullshit winner as Croatia had found in Slaven Bilic. Roy Keane, of all people, pointed out that it needed to be someone who could rein in the oversized egos (presumably he meant Frank Lampard Jnr and Ashley Cole but he didn't elaborate). Also needed was someone to address the bigger problem – exacerbated in the past by the over-promotion of Charles Hughes, Howard Wilkinson and Les Reed to technical director, not to mention McClaren to England boss – to change the basic philosophy. At present it begins at schoolboy level and winds all the way to the England team and dictates that a kid with skill on the ball and the confidence to wait and think before making a positive pass fears he needs to 'get rid of it' as soon as possible, preferably to a bigger lad standing nearer the goal, or risk not getting picked again.

There was no real rush to find a replacement for McClaren, given that there would be no competitive matches for nearly a year. Many, despite all the evidence, wanted José Mourinho (the *Guardian* acted as if he had already been appointed), others, astonishingly, Alan Shearer, citing the case of Germany that had appointed a recently retired leading international with no managerial experience (Jürgen Klinsmann) and nearly won the World Cup. They forgot that Klinsmann was a multilinguist who had won the very same trophy as well as the European Championships and the UEFA Cup twice as a player, whilst the barely monoglot Shearer had only a League Championship medal and seemingly little more to offer than the ability, as Harry Pearson put it, to run backwards while aggressively hectoring a linesman.

Remarkably the man picked as the new England manager *was* a man with the right qualities. Fabio Capello had won league titles in Spain and Italy, as well as the Champions League. Little known in England, he at least immediately looked capable. England began to win matches. What a pity he was still picking David James in goal.

The Football Association off the bench

✪ The Football Association's previous headquarters were: 51 Holborn Viaduct (1863–90); 61 Chancery Lane (1890–1902); 104 High Holborn (1902–10); 42 Russell Square (1910–29); 22 Lancaster Gate (1929–71) and 16 Lancaster Gate (1971–2001).

✪ The Football Association is the governing body in charge of the game – from schools football to the Premiership. It runs the sport in England only. Other parts of the United Kingdom have their own associations, which is why Great Britain alone of Europe's developed countries fails to enter a team for the World Cup and the European Championships.

✪ There is little signage outside No. 25 to proclaim that this is the headquarters of the game's governing body. Nor is entry to the great domain easy, as a reporter from the *Sun* discovered when he arrived at Soho Square to present England manager Sven-Goran Eriksson with an imitation P45 after England lost shamefully to lowly Northern Ireland in 2005.

✪ One thing the FA doesn't lack is money. When England played Northern Ireland in Belfast in 2005 the FA sent forty-two officials to keep the twenty-two players in the squad company, and they all stayed at the expensive Culloden Hotel at a combined cost of £50,000. It is to finance such extravaganzas that the price of Cup Final and internationals tickets is so high.

Palm's Café, 4 Brewer Street

It was at this takeaway half an hour before midnight on 17 May 1998 that Paul Gascoigne met his nemesis – a chicken kebab – following an extended drinking session with showbiz pals Danny Baker and Chris Evans. Unluckily for the England midfield star a student with a camera spotted the group and took a shot of Gascoigne holding the kebab and two bags of chips.

One of the party grabbed the camera, which went flying, ending up under a car, but the damage was done. The press was contacted and Gascoigne had some explaining to do to England manager Glenn Hoddle. Although Gazza couldn't deny having been there, he insisted he was in bed by midnight. Hoddle wasn't impressed and a few weeks later omitted Gascoigne from his World Cup squad.

For months afterwards Palm's Café sold a £3 Gazza kebab. 'It's just a chicken kebab, but we're doing a roaring trade,' explained one member of staff. The takeaway has since closed.

WESTMINSTER, SW1

Buckingham Palace, The Mall

To save an English side being humiliated by visiting Russians, George VI put pressure on Arsenal to field Stanley Matthews, then England's leading player, as a 'guest' in their celebrated match against Moscow Dynamo in 1945, when many of the Arsenal team were still overseas with the army clearing up after the Second World War. Matthews duly played for the Gunners for the only time but Arsenal still lost: 4–3.

George Best was arrested for drink-driving outside Buckingham Palace in November 1984.

→ Arsenal *v* Moscow Dynamo, p. 127

Central Hall, Storey's Gate

The World Cup itself – the Jules Rimet trophy – was stolen from an exhibition held at Central Hall on 20 March 1966, four months before it was due to be presented to the winning team.

The trophy was on display as part of the Stanley Gibbons stamp company's Stampex exhibition and was supposed to be guarded at all times. On the day of the theft the guards began their security circuit at noon but ten minutes later noticed that someone had forced open the display case and the rear doors of the building. The Jules Rimet trophy was missing!

Blame and recrimination were swiftly bandied about. The head of the security firm guarding the trophy told newsmen that security had been 'perfectly adequate', even if he did add disingenuously, 'I don't think it would have made any difference if we'd had barbed wire and machine guns.'

Two days later FA chairman Joe Mears, a Chelsea director, received an anonymous phone call from a man who said a parcel would be sent to Stamford Bridge the next day. A parcel was indeed delivered, but to Mears's home. Inside was the lining from the top of the trophy, a demand for £15,000 in £1 and £5 notes, and an illiterate ransom note from the thief – 'Jackson' – that read: 'Dear Joe Kno [sic] no doubt you view with very much concern the loss of the world cup. To me it is only so much scrap gold. If I don't hear from you by Thursday or Friday at the latest I assume it's one for the POT.'

Worried that the thieves would melt the trophy down should their demands not be met, Mears contacted the police, and Scotland Yard swung into action to retrieve the Jules Rimet trophy – unmelted. 'Jackson' would be met at the gate of Battersea Park, not by Mears, who was too ill, but by an 'assistant' (in reality a police officer). At the meeting 'Jackson' never noticed that the ransom money was mostly scrap paper, nor did he spot the coppers waiting at various points nearby. After a chase the police apprehended the ransomer, who turned out to be Edward Betchley, a well-known petty thief and used car dealer. He was later convicted of demanding money with menaces and intent to steal and was jailed.

But where was the trophy? On 27 March, eight days after it was stolen, the World Cup was sniffed out of bushes in Norwood, south-east London, by a dog called Pickles. The Football Association made a replica of the trophy for the public celebrations (→ p. 258) and both cups featured in the 1966 Final at Wembley (→ p. 148). Later the trophy was caught up in even more dramatic developments (→ p. 9).

East India, Devonshire, Sports and Public Schools Club, 16 St James's Square

The well-known amateur club Pegasus were formed on 2 May 1948 after a meeting of representatives from Oxford and Cambridge universities at this St James's club. One of those involved was Harold Thompson, a scientist who later became chairman of the Football Association and enjoyed a tempestuous relationship with 1970s England manager Don Revie (→ p. 241). The team's aim was to revive the classical ideal of amateurism previously embodied by the Corinthians team (→ p. 4) and they chose as their symbol aspects of the logos of Oxford (a centaur) and Cambridge (falcon).

Pegasus enjoyed a successful 1950s, winning the Amateur Cup in 1951 and 1953 in front of Wembley crowds of 100,000. The FA's abolition of the distinction between professional and amateur clubs in the early 1960s destabilised the club, which folded in 1963.

Foreign Office, King Charles Street

Whenever the England football team or England fans run into trouble overseas (it is rarely followers of Scotland, Wales or Northern Ireland) the Foreign Office is obliged to intervene. And never more dramatically than during the 1970 World Cup when the England captain, Bobby Moore, was accused of stealing a bracelet from a shop in Bogotá, Colombia. British embassy officials, realising straight away that Moore had been set up, spared no efforts to secure his release, and immediately cabled the foreign secretary who was at a NATO meeting. One diplomat noted at the time that 'we ensured that the magistrate concerned was privately made aware of the awkward implications of the case for Colombia because of the strong interest of British and world opinion.'

The Colombians agreed to 'stretch' the law so that Moore could stay at the home of a local football official rather than in jail while investigations continued. He was later cleared of any wrongdoing but the incident had the desired effect of destabilising the England party and their World Cup preparations.

Houses of Parliament, St Margaret Street

Football is a world with its own arcane and bizarre laws but sometimes a powerful outside agency – the government – intervenes. After thirty-nine Juventus fans died following a charge by Liverpool supporters at the 1985 European Cup Final in Brussels, prime minister Margaret Thatcher advocated the introduction of an identity scheme for all fans wishing to watch league football. Inevitably the scheme was abandoned due to its lack of coherence and clarity.

Quaglino's, 16 Bury Street

'If Dean Holdsworth scores twenty goals this season, I will kiss his backside,' promised Wimbledon owner Sam Hamman at the beginning of the 1993–94 season, 'and take him for dinner at Quaglino's. If he doesn't, he can kiss my backside.' Holdsworth scored twenty-four goals, and Hamman was true to his word, planting a smacker on the naked Holdsworth bum – but not during dinner at this smart restaurant.

10 Downing Street

Since the days of Harold Wilson, prime ministers have often sought to display their love of football in a desperate effort to win support from 'ordinary voters'. Wilson claimed to be a Huddersfield Town fan, but showed little understanding of the mechanics of the 1966 World Cup, held in England, when speaking to FA officials as the tournament approached. His contemporary Conservative rival, Ted Heath, showed no interest in the game, nor did his Labour successor, James Callaghan. In one of life's weird coincidences, he, like Wilson, shared a surname with a member of the victorious 1966 England squad.

In 1985, during the premiership of Margaret Thatcher, thirty-nine football fans died at the 1985 European Cup Final in Brussels after a charge by Liverpool fans on their Juventus rivals. Two days later officials from the Football Association stood outside No. 10 and announced that they had banned all English clubs – including even those who had committed no crime – from playing in Europe, thereby subverting 750 years of post-Magna Carta notions of justice for the innocent and punishment for the guilty.

Margaret Thatcher supported the ban, adding: 'We have to get the game cleaned up from this hooliganism at home and then perhaps we shall be able to go overseas again.' She invited seven leading football journalists to No. 10 to discuss the implications of the violence, among them the doyen of English football writers, Brian Glanville, who cycled there from Notting Hill.

'I want to know what you think. I want to know your opinions. I think we want to get decent fans to voice their disapproval,' the prime minister told them. An unworkable suggestion came out of the meeting, that of a nationwide identity card system for anyone wanting to attend a match. Only thirteen of the ninety-two league clubs implemented the scheme by the deadline date, and ID cards were eventually shelved when it turned out that the police were against them and Lord Justice Taylor condemned them in his report following the next football tragedy, the Hillsborough disaster of 1989.

Thatcher's successor, John Major, was a real football fan, having started watching Chelsea as a schoolboy in Brixton in the 1950s. Tony Blair was less football savvy but on becoming prime minister in 1997 set up a 'task force' to help combat racism, improve disabled access and encourage more affordable ticket pricing and merchandising. Blair and his advisers rightly criticised the 'obscene' wealth at the top and the poverty at the bottom of the game. But in a capitalist democracy in which the government *doesn't* run football (unlike Romania under Ceauşescu, for instance) politicians can only try to influence, not interfere. After more than a decade of Labour in No. 10 football remained corrupt, rampantly avaricious and uncontrollable, and the slightest expression of disquiet by MPs about players' salaries (Labour's Gerry Sutcliffe in November 2007 condemned John Terry's wages as 'obscene') swiftly led to denunciations from the game's apparatchiks.

Tramp, 40 Jermyn Street

An exclusive basement disco, Tramp's was a favourite haunt of George Best, who described in his autobiography, *The Good, The Bad and the Bubbly*, how in the 1960s the restaurant sold expensive sausage and mash in the shape of the male genitalia. Best was banned from Tramp after punching Michael Caine and Tim Jeffries (Mr Koo Stark) – in separate incidents.

Victoria station

There was much excitement when the Italy team arrived at Victoria on the boat train to play England in 1934, a time before such games became regular occurrences. There was a huge crowd of Soho-based Italians and a smattering of non-Italians amazed at how glamorous the players looked, this being the days when the typical Italian footballer was more Marcello Mastroianni than Massimo Maccarone. Even England centre-forward Ted Drake was impressed: 'They seemed to be from a different planet. They were a good-looking bunch of lads. Then there was the England team with broken teeth and cauliflower ears.' The two sides soon clashed in a violent match at Highbury (→ p. 94).

Thousands turned up at Victoria in November 1953 to cheer the Hungarian team on to the boat train taking them back to the continent after the 'Mighty Magyars' thrashed England 6–3.

Vincent Square

Westminster School *v* Charterhouse, first played in 1863, is the oldest continuous fixture played in England, and was originally played in this square near Victoria station.

Wellington Barracks, Buckingham Gate

The touring Moscow Dynamo team had to stay at these army barracks near Buckingham Palace when they came to London for their ground-breaking 1945 tour as initially no hotel was willing to accommodate them. On arrival at the barracks the Dynamos' party saw a drill sergeant putting a squad of defaulters through their paces. Believing they had been sent to a British gulag, the Russians refused to leave the coach. Eventually they disembarked, but were horrified at the austerity of the rooms, which were even more spartan than their own Soviet flats.

The beds were hard and unaccommodating, and there were no sheets or pillows because Stanley Rous, the FA secretary, had briefed the quartermaster that the Russians wouldn't need them. The touring party threatened to go home, but were placated by being sent the following night to the luxurious Park Lane Hotel (→ p. 25) owned by Sir Guy Bracewell Smith, the Arsenal chairman. What the Soviets didn't realise was that they wouldn't be staying in rooms at the hotel but in makeshift beds set out in the ballroom, which led to more complaints. Eventually the Moscow team were found adequate accommodation at the Imperial in Bloomsbury (→ p. 1).

Westminster Abbey, Broad Sanctuary

The memorial service for Denis Compton at the Abbey on 1 July 1997 gave rise to more applications for tickets than any previously held here, with more than 2,000 people left outside. Whether those who turned up had come to pay their respects for Compton's prowess as a Test cricketer or as an Arsenal winger – or both – is not known.

Westminster School, Great College Street

This famous public school was instrumental in the evolution of the game in the nineteenth century. The game was played in the school cloisters until it was banned in 1820 for being too rough. 'When running the enemy tripped, shinned, charged with the shoulder, got down and sat upon you . . . in fact did anything short of murder to get the ball from you,' one old boy later recalled.

2   East London

London's darklands – impoverished, industrialised, brutalised by years of deprivation and violence – gave birth to two major football clubs: Millwall (now based in south-east London) and West Ham United. Millwall were formed by the Thames docks, close to where ships were built in the mid-nineteenth century, but their founders actually worked in a jam factory. Further east were the Thames Ironworks where many of the great ocean-going vessels of the era were spliced together. The workers there, led by a teetotal fan of cycling, formed a football team that became West Ham. East London is also the home of Leyton Orient, the least successful League team in London history, though they have at least survived, unlike Thames FC.

ALDGATE/THE EAST END, E1

Arsenal on Brick Lane?

The long narrow street that connects Bethnal Green and Whitechapel has become one of the most fashionable in London in recent years thanks to its Victorian atmosphere, curry houses and urban edginess. Surprisingly it also nearly became the home of Arsenal in the late 1990s. After the club decided to leave Highbury stadium, they identified a number of potential locations for their new ground, including Wembley, Alexandra Park, a site in King's Cross and the large plot of land west of Brick Lane that was occupied by the Bishopsgate Goodsyard. Eventually Arsenal chose to stay in north London, and the now demolished Bishopsgate plot remains undeveloped.

Mile End Road

The stylish 1970s midfielder Alan Hudson, who starred for Chelsea, Stoke and Arsenal, was nearly killed crossing busy Mile End Road in December 1997. The accident happened just after 9 p.m., 'the earliest I'd ever gone home', Hudson joked to journalists, adding, 'which just shows, you should never go home early'. Hudson spent eighty-nine days in hospital, slipping in and out of consciousness, and nearly had to have both legs amputated. His determination saw him through, and that year his engaging and excellently titled autobiography, *The Working Man's Ballet*, was published.

→ Kings of the King's Road, p. 209

BETHNAL GREEN, E2

York Hall, Old Ford Road

It was at a meeting held in this well-known boxing venue that the Professional Footballers' Association voted in favour of a strike at Football League games. Their anger was over the maximum wage, which they wanted abolished. Around 250 members of the players' union packed out York Hall and agreed unanimously to give the League a month's notice of strike action if they continued to enforce the maximum wage rule.

At two subsequent meetings held outside London the players maintained their hard-line stance, with nearly 700 of them supporting a strike and only eighteen against. The worried clubs considered using amateurs if the strike went ahead, but most doubted that it ever would. At the end of 1960, after a compromise between the League and the ministry of labour collapsed, a strike starting on Saturday 21 January 1961 looked certain. To keep fit, some of the biggest stars planned to play exhibition matches in Dublin's rugby stadium or turn out in full-strength teams in parks. However, on 18 January the strike was called off. The maximum wage was abolished soon after.

→ Football at the High Court, p. 15

CLAPTON, E5

Clapton (Leyton) Orient origins (1881), Glyn Road

Leyton Orient began in 1881 as the Glyn Cricket and Football Club, founded by members of the Homerton Theological College who played in Glyn Road, Clapton. In 1886 the club became the Eagle Cricket Club. The following year one of the cricketers suggested they start a football side and call it Clapton Orient, the name chosen in honour of his employers, the Orient Steam Navigation Company. But other members didn't like using the name of the area, Clapton, and it was decided to call the club simply 'Orient'. Friendlies were arranged on the Glyn Road pitch and the players changed in a shed. They wore red shirts (as Leyton Orient still do) on which was sown a large 'O' in white, hence the club's nickname, 'The Os'. In 1893 the club joined the Clapton & District League, which they won two years later, and moved to the Ponds Lane Bridge ground at the north-eastern end of nearby Millfields Road, a site now covered by an electricity substation.

There are several other versions of the club's early history. The writer Dave Twydell in *Grounds for a Change* talks about the Star, Trafalgar and Saracens football clubs that merged to form Orient.

Clapton Orient on Millfields Road (1896–1930), north-east junction of Millfields Road and Glyn Road

In 1896 Orient joined the London League and moved to land which belonged to the Bailey Fireworks Company, thus upsetting the *North London Guardian* which accused Orient of getting 'big ideas'. The first game at the new ground was an innovative Gentlemen *v* Ladies exhibition match. Spectators bored with the football on display could look over the fence and watch the whippet racing instead.

Soon came a name change from Orient to Clapton Orient following a suggestion by Jack Dearing, who told the meeting: 'With Clapton now being considered a good district socially, the name would give the club more respectability.' Facilities were poor at first, and so the club bought two railway carriages for the players to change in.

In 1902 the site became known as the Millfields Road ground. A year later the club turned professional, celebrating by beating Shepherds Bush

11–0. In October 1904 Clapton Orient joined the Second Division of the Southern League, then the highest standard outside the Football League itself. When the following March they applied for the First Division of the same League, Tottenham Hotspur objected. 'We're not going to have them on our doorstep,' thundered the north London side.

Clapton Orient were unperturbed. They ambitiously applied to the Football League itself and were accepted into the Second Division in 1905, promptly losing 1–0 to Hull. The East Yorkshire newspapers savaged the Clapton facilities. 'On Saturday it presented a thoroughly washed out appearance in the pelting rain.' Soon there were more pressing problems. A creditor sued for the club to be wound up and Orient were only able to keep going thanks to the generosity of a supporter who donated £50.

Clapton Orient finished bottom of the Football League in their first season. Re-election would not be a formality, and so club chairman Captain Henry Wells-Holland told the League management committee: 'Our ground at Millfields is nearly seven acres, one of the largest in the South of England, and can be easily made capable of holding upwards of 60,000. Therefore, I conclude, let us continue in the League so that all of East London can be proud of Clapton Orient FC.' It was a stirring speech and worked, but money was short and the club had to stage other sports to fund the football. For instance, in 1908 more than 3,500 saw Clapton Orient beat Fulham in the British Baseball Cup Final.

As the decade wore on, the ground was refurbished and a grandstand built on top of slag taken from a power company to hold 12,000 spectators. In 1914 the League fined Clapton Orient £25 for fixing the kick-off time against Leeds City so late, at 4.30 p.m., that encroaching nightfall and lack of artificial lighting meant there was time for only a two-minute break at half-time and the end of the game was played in near darkness. The Leeds keeper complained that he hadn't been able to see the ball as two late goals sailed past him, and interestingly Leeds missed out on promotion by only two points.

The following season, 1914–15, took place during the First World War, and forty-one players and officials from the club joined the footballers' battalion of the 17th Middlesex Regiment, the highest number recruited from a single football club during the conflict. The army took over the Millfields Road site for the rest of the war, hoisting an anti-aircraft gun on top of the Spion Kop to ward German planes off from the locale.

In 1923 a new state-of-the-art stand was built, but four years later the owners successfully added greyhound racing to the facilities. As football was no longer the main attraction Clapton Orient decided to move, which they did, to Lea Bridge Road (→ p. 65). The stadium continued to host greyhound racing until the 1970s, when it was demolished and replaced with the Millfield Estate.

EAST HAM, E6

Boleyn Tavern, 1 Barking Road

Not for the faint-hearted on match days, the Boleyn Tavern is the kind of no-nonsense old-fashioned east London boozer now disappearing from the capital. Ted Fenton, West Ham manager in the 1950s, recalled in his autobiography, *At Home with the Hammers*, how the club's early twentieth-century boss, Syd King, 'an outsize, larger-than-life character with close-cropped grey hair and a flowing moustache', would shout at him in his younger days, ' "Boy. Get me two bottles of Bass." Down to the Boleyn pub on the corner I would go on my errand and when I got back to the office Syd King would flip me a two-shilling piece for my trouble.'

→ The Lord Palmerston pub on King's Road, p. 200

Cassettari's, 35 Barking Road

When Ted Fenton, West Ham manager in the 1950s, arranged for the players to be given luncheon vouchers they could spend in this family-run caff near the ground it became an unofficial headquarters for the club's tactically astute players. Over steaming cups of tea and bacon sandwiches Malcolm Allison, John Bond, Frank O'Farrell and Noel Cantwell met after training to discuss how the game should be played, shaping the ideas that propelled many of them into management. Cantwell later recalled that they would be at Cassettari's 'for two to three hours talking football then sometimes we'd go back to Upton Park in the afternoon. We were a nightmare for the groundsman.'

Allison led the Cassettari discussions. He was West Ham's captain in 1953, the year that Hungary thrashed England 6–3 at Wembley. Believing that what West Ham were doing in training at the time was inconsequential, he became the driving force behind a wholesale change of attitude to preparation. The Cassettari crew's first foray on the field saw the club's two full-backs, John Bond and Noel Cantwell, play in a new style. They stroked the ball to each other unhurriedly, setting up a steady give-and-go style instead of hoofing the ball vaguely in the direction of Barking Abbey. To the watching crowd this was patience-sapping. From all around came cries of 'get rid of it' in the time-honoured English manner. When Fenton asked the players why they were playing in so strange a fashion the answer came back: 'What's wrong, boss? We weren't worried. There was no danger.'

The new thinking propelled West Ham to what was for them unparalleled heights. In 1957 they made it to the FA Youth Cup Final with a team that included future manager John Lyall at left-back. The following year the club won the Second Division Championship.

One of the younger players also learning how to analyse the game at the caff was Bobby Moore. Allison told the future England captain when he first broke into the team in the early 1960s, 'Take control of everything around you. Look big. Think big. Keep forever asking yourself, if I get the ball now, who will I give it to?' In 1964, with Bobby Moore now an integral part of the team, West Ham won the FA Cup for the first time, and the following year the European Cup Winners' Cup.

Allison put the ideas honed at Cassettari's in practice successfully at other clubs, particularly at Manchester City, who under his coaching surprisingly won the Championship in 1968, followed by the FA Cup, League Cup and European Cup Winners' Cup within the next two years. But some of Allison's innovations were more cosmetic than academic. He wore his socks pulled up with no shinguards, in the Italian style, and was the first player in the country to wear really short shorts.

Not all the experiences at Cassettari's were so inspired. In the late 1950s Harry Cripps, who later became a Millwall legend, was on West Ham's books as a youth player. He was once told to lose weight, and so he headed to the caff where he ordered a huge plate of cabbage. Feeling pleased after scoffing the lot Cripps immediately rewarded himself with a portion of jam pie and custard.

→ The Cliff Bastin Café, p. 141

Green Street

The street that is home to West Ham United was also the name of an unconvincing 2005 film about football violence. It stars Elijah Wood, playing an American college student who falls in with a hooligan outfit, the Green Street Elite, run by his brother-in-law. The Green Street Elite was based on West Ham's notorious InterCity Firm of troublemakers.

West Ham United (1904–), Boleyn ground/Upton Park, Green Street

Perennial underachievers, West Ham United moved to the Boleyn ground, popularly known as Upton Park, in 1904 after manager-secretary Syd King was given the task of finding a new home. He identified Boleyn Castle Field on Green Street, land adjacent to a large brick property, Green Street House, where Ann Boleyn had lived and where according to local legend she awaited her execution in 1536.

The land was owned by the Catholic Ecclesiastical Authorities and used by a Catholic school. West Ham needed permission from the Home Office and the department initially indicated that it did not approve of the land being used by West Ham. King, however, went to see the local MP, Sir Ernest Gray, and through his good offices, subject to 'certain conditions', as King explained, the club were allowed to move in.

Then came another difficult task: turning what had been a potato field into a playing surface. Club officials launched an appeal for a million pennies, but when they asked the local breweries to make a donation they further alienated their teetotal founder, Arnold Hills. At least the new ground had excellent public transport links and was closer to the large areas of population such as Stratford and Ilford than their previous Memorial Ground home (→ p. 77).

King wasn't paid much, so a bonus from the Oxo food company must have come in handy, and explains why on the eve of the 1904–05 season a small postcard of the team photograph was issued with the following text on its reverse:

> When training, Oxo is the only beverage used by our team and all speak of the supreme strength and power of endurance which they have derived from its use – E. S. King, Secretary, West Ham United F.C.

West Ham's first game at Upton Park was on 1 September 1904 against Millwall, the team that would become their fiercest rivals, and a crowd of 10,000 saw West Ham win 3–0. The *Daily Mirror* wrote that 'favoured by the weather turning fine after heavy rains of the morning, West Ham United began their season most auspiciously yesterday evening when they beat Millwall 3 goals to 0 on their new enclosure at Upton Park'. The result so upset the Millwall keeper, Tiny Joyce, he forced his fist through the dressing-room door. In September 1906 came another ill-tempered game against Millwall. Jarvis of West Ham smashed Millwall's Deans on to a metal advertising hoarding, and the FA banned him for fourteen days.

In the years leading up to the First World War West Ham excelled at non-League level. They also had a number of FA Cup runs, preparing for home ties with a day trip to Epping Forest or a visit to the brine baths at Southend. In spring 1919 West Ham won election to the newly expanded Football League along with Coventry, Rotherham and South Shields, and finished a creditable seventh in their first season in the Second Division. For West Ham 1923 was an *annus mirabilis*: they finished second in the Second Division, winning promotion to the top flight for the first time. More dramatically, the club also reached the first Wembley FA Cup Final (→ p. 144). For this momentous occasion they once again prepared with a trip to the brine baths of Southend. However, they lost 2–0 to Bolton Wanderers. It would be over forty years before they lifted the trophy.

Syd King managed to keep West Ham in the top division for nine years, but in 1932 they finished bottom and were relegated. At a board meeting that November King insulted one of the West Ham directors. They decreed King had been drunk and insubordinate, and suspended him for three months without salary. The following January King was sacked. He did not take the news well and committed suicide a few weeks later by drinking a corrosive liquid.

The academy of football
The middle years of the century were an uneventful time for the Hammers under Charlie Paynter, but during the 1950s manager Ted Fenton reared

a highly intelligent group of players – Malcolm Allison, Noel Cantwell, Frank O'Farrell – who helped take West Ham back to the top division, and whose interest in the way football was played secured for the club a reputation as an academy of the game. The hard work behind the scenes paid off. In 1964 with Ron Greenwood now in charge West Ham won their first trophy – the FA Cup – with a team, captained by Bobby Moore, that also included Geoff Hurst. The following year came West Ham's greatest triumph: winning the European Cup Winners' Cup at Wembley. In 1966 West Ham narrowly missed out on more cup success but could at least revel in having three players – Moore, Hurst and Martin Peters – in the England team that won the World Cup.

Yet West Ham were unable to turn these virtues into League success, and under Greenwood they rarely finished in the top half of the table. In late 1974 Greenwood moved upstairs to become general manager and appointed his assistant, John Lyall, as manager. The change was instantly successful, for West Ham won the Cup in 1975 and again reached the Cup Winners' Cup Final, although this time they lost. Surprisingly West Ham were relegated in 1978 but the board stuck with Lyall who rewarded them by securing another Cup triumph – from the Second Division – in 1980. They soon went up and now came their greatest League achievement. A team overflowing with talent – Alan Devonshire, Frank McAvennie, Tony Cottee – should have won the title in 1986 but faded at the last and came third. Yet again West Ham couldn't maintain the momentum and relegation followed three years later.

Harry's games

With Harry Redknapp in charge from 1994 to 2001, West Ham became headline news for the wrong reasons. An expert wheeler-dealer, Redknapp was the living embodiment of Del Boy from the hit TV series *Only Fools and Horses*, but without the bonhomie and lovableness. He bought and sold an astonishing 134 players in seven years of taking West Ham nowhere, his penchant being for hiring overrated foreign 'stars' whom he could secure cheaply (thanks to the Bosman ruling) but whom he paid for dearly in other ways.

There was Dani who came on loan in 1996 from Sporting Lisbon. He had a playboy image and there were rumours he'd made records, been in films and strolled along the catwalks of Europe. At a press conference Redknapp joked: 'He's so good looking I don't know whether to play him or screw him.' The same year saw the arrival of Paulo Futre. He had been one of the best players in Europe when at Porto and Atletico Madrid. Being a world-class superstar, Futre would wear only the superstars' number – 10 – as worn by Pele, Michel Platini and Dennis Bergkamp. When Redknapp gave him the No. 16 shirt the Portuguese announced: 'Me Futre. Me wear No. 10.' Redknapp explained that the club had a squad numbering system and he was No. 16. Futre turned to the manager and simply repeated: 'Me Futre. Me wear No. 10.' Me Futre then got into a cab and went home.

No. 10 at the club was John Moncur (not a world-class superstar) and he wouldn't relinquish the shirt. But Futre got his way. He gave Moncur a free holiday in his luxurious villa on the Algarve and offered to stump up £100,000 of his own money to reimburse fans who'd bought 'Moncur 10' shirts – somewhat excessive given that West Ham had sold only six of them. Futre sparkled in his first game, but there weren't many more; nine in all and no goals.

Worse still was Marco Boogers, signed in 1995. He never got as far as starting a game but he did come on as a sub against Manchester United, and after a few seconds made what the *Sun* called a 'sickening horror tackle'. It was only against Gary Neville but it was a shocker, leading to a swift red card as the United players queued up to make their feelings known. After the red card a depressed Boogers left for Holland. Club representatives went out to try to bring him back and found him living in a caravan.

Florin Raducioiu seemed a better prospect. He had starred for Romania in the 1994 World Cup and cost £2.4 million. But West Ham fans were unimpressed with his performances. Wags claimed he was called Florin because he was worth only about two bob. Raducioiu didn't turn up for one match. A furious Harry Redknapp rang him on his mobile phone, interrupting the forward on a shopping spree in Harvey Nichols. After six games Raducioiu was sold for £1.6 million; another £800,000 fleeced off the fans.

Javier Margas had played for Chile in the 1998 World Cup, so surely he would be a great signing, was the thinking. Fortunately, he didn't like shopping or nightclubbing. Unfortunately, he didn't like anything about

London. One day he went home, not to his luxury Essex pad, but to Chile ... without telling anyone. West Ham had no idea where he was, and when they tracked him down in South America he was unaware of the controversy his departure had caused.

Titi Camara had been top goalscorer for Liverpool in the 1999–2000 season. 'I've got a £10 million striker for £1.5 million,' Redknapp proclaimed. In three years at West Ham Camara failed to score a single League goal, while earning £30,000 a week. Gary Charles had played for England and cost West Ham £1.2 million. When Redknapp wanted to drop him after four games the chairman, Terry Brown, was amazed. 'Is he no good?' he asked Redknapp. 'What do you expect for £1.2 million?' Redknapp retorted. 'Well,' asked Brown, 'why did you buy him, then? We're paying him £1 million in wages.' 'They're all getting it,' was Harry's disingenuous response. (All this was forgotten in autumn 2007 when those with short memories were touting Redknapp as a suitable successor to Steve McClaren as England boss, perhaps to be the first England boss to get the national team relegated.)

On 9 May 2001 Harry Redknapp was sitting in chairman Terry Brown's office at Upton Park ready to sign a new contract, when Brown shockingly announced he was letting the manager go. Redknapp's tears made no difference.

The wit and wisdom of Harry Redknapp

✪ On tactics: 'I sorted out the team formation last night lying in bed with the wife. When your husband's as ugly as me, you'd only want to talk football in bed.'

✪ On Samassi Abou: 'He don't speak the English too good.'

✪ On his former West Ham striker: 'John Hartson's got more previous than Jack the Ripper.'

✪ On his own playing career: 'Even when we had Moore, Hurst and Peters, West Ham's average finish was about seventeenth. Which just shows how crap the other eight of us were.'

✪ On 'simulation': 'Abou retaliated but the fellow went down as if he was dead, and then started rolling around.'

⊛ On his relationship as Portsmouth's director of football with the club's then manager, Graham Rix, who had served a jail term for engaging in underage sex: 'I shall not be interfering with Graham Rix.'

⊛ On Samassi Abou's mystery ailment: 'The lad went home to the Ivory Coast and got a bit of food poisoning. He must have eaten a dodgy missionary or something.'

⊛ During a pre-season friendly against Oxford City in 1994 Redknapp, then assistant manager, brought on as sub a fan who had spent the first half giving Lee Chapman inordinate amounts of abuse. The fan was a true Hammer (he had 'West Ham' etched on his neck) and Redknapp asked him: 'Can you play as good as you talk?' Obviously the heckler felt he could. He changed into the proper kit and ran on for the second half. 'Who's that, Harry?' asked a journalist from the local Oxford paper. 'What? Haven't you been watching the World Cup? That's the great Bulgarian, Tittyshev!' came back the ever-jocular assistant manager. It wasn't. It was a 27-year-old park player called Steve Davies and he even managed to score. The incident may seem surprising, but according to some commentators West Ham now regularly field such individuals in the first team.

End of the Roeder

Redknapp's replacement was not a famous name but Glenn Roeder, who had achieved little in management. Before being taken ill in April 2003 Roeder presided over a team doomed to go down, which they did while he was recovering. His replacement in October 2003 was a controversial choice. Alan Pardew left promotion rivals Reading, who at that time looked more likely to go up, but it proved a wise move. Pardew's team finished sixth, went up the following season, and a year later finished a commendable ninth in the Premiership as well as reaching the FA Cup Final, which they looked likely to win until the intervention of Steven Gerrard for Liverpool.

Of course this being West Ham such steady progress was never going to last. A boardroom tussle in summer 2006 resulted in the signing of two world-class Argentinians: Carlos Tevez and Javier Mascherano. They were so superior to the other players that they destabilised the team. Also arriving at Upton Park were new owners, an Icelandic consortium led by the gaunt figure of Eggert Magnusson. Astonishingly the new owners sacked Pardew, whose tenure had witnessed genuine improvement in the face of hostility, replacing him with Alan Curbishley. The former West Ham winger had achieved some success at Charlton – not by winning trophies but simply by staying in charge for more than fifteen years – but now he embarrassed himself with a disingenuous claim that English managers were not being given the chance to take charge of a team playing in the Champions League because the so-called Big Four clubs would only appoint foreigners. As if the make-up of the Big Four were set in stone; as if there were rules barring English-managed clubs from winning trophies or finishing higher than fifth.

As relegation loomed, news broke that West Ham might have infringed registration rules over the Tevez and Mascherano transfers. The FA Premier League fined the club £5.5 million for acting improperly and withholding vital documentation on the duo's ownership. Many, however, thought the football authorities should have docked West Ham points, which would have led to their relegation in 2007.

The Hammers are no longer known for stylish players in the Bobby Moore or Martin Peters tradition. The club's reputation has been sullied in recent years by the antics of Julian Dicks and Tomas Repka. Nor do they stick with a manager decade after decade, as with Syd King or Charlie Paynter. Lou Macari lasted less than a season, Glenn Roeder and Alan Pardew barely longer. Recent years have seen West Ham yo-yo between the top two divisions: never good enough to sustain a challenge for the title, often struggling, occasionally relegated from the top flight, but always too good for the second tier. A possible explanation is that though West Ham have the fan base – both real and potential – a regular presence of top-quality players, and supporters every bit as virulent as those who follow, say, Newcastle, the board have no ambition and many of those in charge are either too laid back (Trevor Brooking) or too lacking in vision (Alan Curbishley) to turn the club into a genuine power as Bill Nicholson did with Tottenham or David Dein with Arsenal.

The West Ham way is to introduce a high-quality youngster, as they did with Joe Cole in February 1999, who is soon targeted by a more ambitious club. West Ham deny they will sell but the bigger club always get their man. Worse still for Hammers fans, little of the money West Ham receive goes into strengthening the squad. Typical was the case of Rio Ferdinand, the best home-grown defender at the club since Bobby Moore. On 28 April 2000 Redknapp told the *Evening Standard*: 'Leeds did enquire about Rio, but we're not interested in selling any of our young stars. We want to go forward as a club and selling Rio now would be a backward step. The day we sell Rio and our other young players is the day when this club starts to die. I do not want to sell him because we have to build a football club around players like Rio, Joe Cole, Michael Carrick and even Freddie Kanoute.' On 25 November Redknapp reiterated this line, this time telling the *Standard*: 'We don't want to be seen as a selling club. Rio is going nowhere.' The following day Ferdinand joined Leeds for £17 million. None of the other players lasted long at E6 either.

West Ham off the bench

⚽ When West Ham took over the Boleyn ground in 1904 they found another team, Boleyn Castle FC, already playing there, but soon absorbed them into the West Ham set-up.

⚽ The song 'I'm Forever Blowing Bubbles', West Ham's signature tune, was written by Jaan Kenbrovin and John William Kellette just after the First World War, and West Ham took it up as their club song following the 1923 Cup Final. The connection was a West Ham schoolboy, Billy Murray, who resembled the curly haired boy in the Millais painting *Bubbles* that was then being used to advertise Pears Soap, and who knew club official Charlie Paynter.

⚽ West Ham were playing Tottenham Hotspur on 7 September 1940 – 'unofficial' wartime football – when the first German bombs of the Blitz fell on east London. At half-time West Ham were leading 4–1 and the crowd looked up as the sky blackened with German planes. A stick of bombs fell about a hundred yards from the stadium, and thousands fled through a rain of debris as shrapnel danced off the cobbles.

⊛ The club's most famous fan, the Rabelaisian TV character Alf Garnett, is fictitious. Garnett once clarified the minutiae of the club's history: 'We've got history, West Ham has, which none of yer other clubs have got. Anne Boleyn had a house right next door to West Ham's ground – Boleyn Castle – an' it was Henry the Eighth who founded West Ham so he'd have somewhere to go on Saturday afternoons when he was down at the Boleyn with Anne. That is why West Ham United play in the colours of Henry the Eighth, even till this day, claret an' blue; claret which was his favourite drink and the blue of your Royal blood. The directors' box at West Ham is actually built on the spot where Henry used to sit while he watched the lads play. I think it was at West Ham where he might have met Anne, because she was a local girl.'

⊛ When John Lyall, who went on to become one of the club's greatest managers, joined the playing staff in the 1950s, he helped the secretary, Frank Cearns, do the wages on a Friday. Being the son of a policeman, Lyall advised Cearns to vary the route he used from the bank to the club carrying the cash. Cearns explained that someone had indeed tried to rob him and then clenched his fist: 'I stuck this right up between his legs. No one came after that.'

⊛ Following crowd trouble in Madrid in October 1980 West Ham were made to play their Cup Winners' Cup home match against the Spanish team Castilla in an empty Upton Park stadium. This resulted in the world's smallest ever crowd for a first-class fixture, officially zero. Unofficially there were 262 spectators – members of staff from each side, a number of journalists, and sixteen ball-boys to retrieve the ball from the empty terraces. Outside the ground some 500 police patrolled the surrounding streets to deter anyone else from entering. West Ham, who had lost the away leg 3–1, won 5–1, thereby going through to the next round. The receipts for the game were exactly £0.

⊛ In 1991 West Ham launched a bond scheme to raise the £15 million that would help convert the ground into an all-seater stadium. Each of the 15,000 bonds would be sold at £500, £750 or

£975 and guarantee the buyer priority for a season ticket for fifty years. Supporters were outraged and staged a goalmouth sit-in at the 1992 Arsenal home match. Only 300 bonds were sold and the club withdrew the scheme.

⚽ Anton Ferdinand was meant to be at home resting in March 2007 when he decided to fly off to South Carolina in America to celebrate his twenty-second birthday. Just to complicate matters, Ferdinand told the club he was going to the Isle of Wight to visit his sick grandmother. Some commentators believe that Ferdinand assumed the Isle of Wight *was* part of the USA. When he was caught out, Ferdinand was 'severely' punished by being fined two weeks' wages, although it is doubtful he would have noticed losing £45,000 given that he once spent £64,000 on a watch.

FOREST GATE, E7

Clapton (1890–), Old Spotted Dog Ground, Upton Lane at Margery Park Road
Not to be confused with Clapton Orient (now Leyton Orient), Clapton severed connections with their nominal home over 100 years ago to play in Forest Gate. The club have the longest tenure at the same ground of any London football team but have continually endured a lowly existence. They were formed in 1887 as Downs FC in Downs Road at the Dalston end of Clapton. They changed their name to Clapton Football Club the same year and in 1888 moved to the Old Spotted Dog Ground, then a mostly rural location at the fringe of the fast disappearing West Ham part of Epping Forest.

In 1892 Clapton became the first English club to play on the continent, beating a Belgium XI 7–0 in Antwerp. Two years later Clapton helped form the new Southern League along with clubs who have since gone on to greater things, such as Luton, Millwall and Reading. Whereas Clapton's original rivals have prospered or folded Clapton have steadfastly remained at non-League level, despite winning the Amateur Cup five times. In recent years they they have been playing in the Essex Senior League, effectively the ninth division.

HOMERTON, E9

Hackney Marsh

The biggest collection of football pitches in the world can be found on land at the edge of Homerton by the River Lea. The marsh was used for storing bomb-damaged materials and debris in the Second World War, and flattened in 1947 to create 120 pitches. In recent years the number of pitches has shrunk by a third, and with the staging of the Olympic Games nearby in 2012 they may be scrapped altogether to be used for parking, despite the authorities' claim that the Games will benefit sport in the capital. Of the various professional footballers first spotted playing here the most famous current one is Lomana Lua Lua.

→ Welsh Harp training ground, p. 135

LEYTON, E10

Clapton Orient (1930–37), Lea Bridge, Rigg Approach

The team that became Leyton Orient moved to this eerily empty corner of east London in summer 1930, when they were still known as Clapton Orient, to share the ground with the Lea Bridge speedway team. It was not a suitable venue, despite the adjacent Lea Bridge station, for the speedway track ran around the football pitch and the perimeter fence was too near the touchlines. To improve things, the League insisted that Orient extend the pitch by a yard on both sides but unfairly gave them a seven-day deadline by which to do the work. The speedway owners were hardly likely to comply immediately and so Orient were forced to find a new ground only months after moving in.

Refused help by neighbours Leyton FC and Walthamstow Avenue, Orient found unlikely aid from the owners of Wembley Stadium. There some 10,000 watched Orient play Brentford on 22 November 1930 in the Third Division (South), mostly in support for the opposition. The *Daily Herald*'s correspondent, 'Syrian', was unimpressed and noted, almost accurately, 'I question if Brentford will ever play at Wembley again.'

Orient's next temporary home was Highbury, but they were soon back at Wembley, this time against Southend, for which only 2,500 turned up, the receipts failing to cover Wembley Ltd's guarantee. In the meantime the work at Lea Bridge went ahead and Clapton Orient returned. Unfortunately the awkward shape of the ground meant that new terracing took the form of odd constructions dotted haphazardly around the pitch.

By the mid-1930s there was talk of Orient merging with struggling Thames FC. Instead they moved to Brisbane Road, the home of amateur side Leyton FC, and that became their long-term home. The speedway stadium has since been demolished and the site has been taken over for industrial use.

Clapton Orient (1938–45, Leyton Orient (1946–), Matchroom Stadium, Brisbane Road

The least successful current League team in London football history – just one season in the top division, in which they finished bottom – are mainstays of east London, the spirit of which is embedded in the Orient part of their name.

Leyton Orient began in 1881 as the Glyn Cricket and Football Club, and in 1898 became Clapton Orient. When they arrived here, then the Osborne Road ground, in 1937 to take over the place from Leyton Amateurs, who could no longer afford the rent, the club were in the Third Division (South) and regularly finishing in the bottom half of the table. There was just one stand, which accommodated 475 people and was known as 'the orange box'. But things improved in the 1950s. Under the inspired management of Alec Stock Leyton Orient were runners-up in 1954–55 and the following season won the Third Division. The shock of losing Stock to Arsenal in February 1956 was relieved by his return fifty-three days later. 'Hard as I tried,' explained Stock, 'I could never stop thinking Orient. My mind said Arsenal, my heart Os. I realised that friendship to me is more important, much more valuable than all the progress and prestige I might have had at Highbury.'

A new East Stand was opened against Nottingham Forest in October 1956 but nearly burned down the same day, which led the chairman, Harry

Zussman, to quip: 'For years we hoped the old stand would catch fire to collect the insurance, and now the new one nearly goes up on its first day of use.'

Orient prospered at the elevated heights of the Second Division but nothing indicated the likelihood of the extraordinary success of 1961–62 when they finished runners-up to Liverpool. Life in Division One lasted one season. They finished bottom and have never returned. Like many clubs who overachieve (Northampton, Swindon, Barnsley), relegation from the First Division was soon followed by relegation from the Second. However, Jimmy Bloomfield turned out to be an enterprising manager, and the club returned to the second tier for the 1970s. That decade there were occasional flirtations with success. Promotion back to the top was just missed in 1974 and in 1978 Orient even reached the FA Cup semi-final, where they were thrashed by Arsenal.

Dog's dinner

When his Orient side came in at half-time losing to Blackpool in February 1995 manager John Sitton went into industrial mode. 'You, you f***ing little ****,' he ranted to one player, and turning to another added, 'and you, you f***ing big ****, when I tell you to do something, you f***ing do it. And if you want to come back at me we'll have a right sort out. Pair up if you like and pick someone to help you,' before adding the instant classic put-down, 'and you can bring your dinner, because by the time I'm finished with you, you're going to need it.'

Sitton kept it up for some time. 'You've all gotta go. You've all gotta go. Any of yer on thirty-five grand and all that, you've all gotta go. He [the chairman] wants to bring players in on 250 quid a week. He might be right! I think he is right! You're a disgrace!' The rant was captured by film student Jo Trehearne in her documentary about the club, which was shown on television the following October. Sitton was sacked at the end of the season and after finding it difficult to get employment in football became a black-cab driver. 'I made in excess of sixty applications for different jobs, all unsuccessful,' he explained, 'and by the end I was very bitter, twisted and disillusioned. I got caught out using the kind of language that is now accepted everywhere and which has earned Gordon Ramsay an eight-figure sum.'

The 1980s was the Frank Clark era at Brisbane Road. He took over as manager in 1981, fresh from helping Nottingham Forest win the European Cup, and later became managing director as well. But Clark had little to show for his involvement with practically everything taking place at the club other than relegation to the Third Division in 1985, although this was at least followed by promotion via the play-offs four years later. Financial problems in the 1990s resulted in the PFA having to pay the players' wages. In 1994–95 came the humiliation of failing to win away from home all season, as well as going eight games running without scoring at all. Orient finished bottom of the Third Division that year but nonetheless were still higher than Fulham and Wigan who have since reached the top. Off the pitch, chairman Tony Wood saw his coffee business collapse due to the war in Rwanda and the club unable to pay its milk bill.

Rescue came from wealthy sports promoter Barry Hearn who explained that the fans 'have had nothing to cheer for 100 years', to which one memorable riposte was 'In sixty years, I've cheered five or six times.' But Orient have prospered little since. In 1999–2000 they even nearly went out of the League, and remain a club that looks permanently marooned in the lower half of the League structure.

Orient off the bench
✪ Surprisingly Orient are London's second oldest League team, their entry (as Clapton Orient) predating those of Chelsea, Tottenham and West Ham. In their first season (in the Second Division) in 1905–06 they finished last, behind the now defunct Leeds City, and the long departed Gainsborough Trinity and Burton United, and haven't made much progress since.

✪ In the early years of the League the club were Clapton Orient, not to be confused with Clapton FC who have long played at some distance from Clapton in Forest Gate. In 1946 Clapton Orient, by now playing in Leyton, became Leyton Orient, which infuriated their non-League rivals Leyton FC. When the borough of Leyton was subsumed into Waltham Forest in 1965 Leyton Orient dropped the Leyton to become plain Orient. They reverted back to Leyton Orient in 1987.

✪ Terry Howard, Orient's longest-serving player, was sacked at half-time during John Sitton's infamous rant in February 1995. It was Howard's 397th appearance and he was told that not only was he being substituted, he was getting a free transfer and two weeks' wages. According to Sitton, 'he was one of a number of players whose performance against Blackpool lacked urgency and passion and could not be tolerated. But the decision was taken for several reasons, including economics.'

✪ Peter Shilton played his 1,000th league game, an unequalled record, on 22 December 1996 in Orient's 2–0 home win over Brighton. Only nine of these were for the east London club.

✪ The Leyton Orient ground, popularly known as Brisbane Road, is officially the Matchroom Stadium after Leyton Orient chairman Barry Hearn's promotion company, Matchroom Sport. It has shrunk over the years in the name of modernisation and now seats barely 10,000. Incongruously it also features blocks of flats at its corners. The club are considering moving to the stadium due to be built nearby for the 2012 Olympic Games.

Leyton, Leyton Stadium, 282 Lea Bridge Road

Not to be confused with Leyton Orient, Leyton predate the more famous east London club, having been formed as far back as 1868, but have been less successful even than their near namesakes, eternally plying their trade in non-League circles, although they did at least win the Amateur Cup in 1927 and 1928. The club have led a nomadic existence, playing at a host of venues including Brisbane Road, Leyton Orient's home. Twice Leyton have disbanded. In 1975 they merged with Wingate (→ p. 000) to become

Leyton-Wingate, but in 1992 reverted back to Leyton. Three years later came another merger, this time with Walthamstow Pennant to create Leyton Pennant (now Waltham Forest).

In 1997 a new Leyton Football Club formed, but it took a High Court case for them to be allowed to continue. As the lawyers explained:

> Please note that by Order of the High Court Chancery Division dated 26 July 2002, in an action brought against Leyton Pennant Football Club and the Football Association, Leyton Football Club (now incorporated as a Limited Company) of Wingate Stadium Lea Bridge Road Leyton has effectively been restored as Leyton Football Club, the unincorporated club formed in 1868; has had its membership to the FA restored; has had its history dating back to 1868 restored and the order also requires Leyton Pennant to refrain in any way from holding itself out to being Leyton Football Club.

As this made the current Leyton Football Club the legal continuation of the original team, Leyton can claim to be the second oldest existing club in the capital (after Cray Wanderers).

MANOR PARK, E12

Manor Park training ground, Grantham Street

In 1959 when Rodney Marsh was taken on by West Ham as a fourteen-year-old schoolboy on ten shillings a week, he would be the first to arrive at the Manor Park training ground on Tuesday and Thursday evenings to play in the same team as Harry Redknapp and Johnny Sissons. After nearly a year of this the club's chief scout, Wally St Pier, called him into his office. Marsh, somewhat optimistically, thought he was about to be promoted to the first team and follow in the footsteps of Bobby Moore, who had just stepped up from the reserves. Instead St Pier told Marsh that West Ham were releasing him. 'We believe there's a boy in our youth side who will become a better player than you. So we've decided to sign him instead and there's no room for you.' They were partly right. The 'boy in the youth side' was Geoff Hurst.

→ Bank of England training ground, p. 228

Victoria Street

Jimmy Greaves was born in Victoria Street in February 1940, early in the Second World War. Six weeks later the street was bombed and the family forced out. When he told the story years later, Greaves added a tale of how his dad had bumped into a pal coming out of the nearby station soon after the raid. His friend asked, 'Fancy a pint in the Black Lion on Victoria Street?' to which Greaves Snr replied, 'But the Black Lion ain't on Victoria Street.' To which his friend quickly retorted, 'It bloody well is now.'

→ Jimmy Greaves in Dagenham, p. 82

West Ham United as Thames Ironworks (1897), Browning Road

After being evicted from their Hermit Road ground (→ p. 81) for violating their tenancy agreement, Thames Ironworks (now West Ham) leased land here. It was evidently not a suitable venue. Long-time manager Syd King recalled in his 1906 *Book of Football*: 'For some reason, not altogether explained, the local public at this place did not take kindly to them and the records show that Browning Road was a wilderness both in the manner of luck and support.' The club soon found better land near Canning Town at the Memorial Ground (→ p. 77).

PLAISTOW, E13

World Cup winners' statue, junction Barking Road and Green Street

The West Ham trio of Bobby Moore, Geoff Hurst and Martin Peters, who played in the England team that won the 1966 World Cup, are commemorated by a statue in this prominent corner of east London, which also inexplicably features the non-West Ham left-back of that successful team, Ray Wilson. Moore was the captain, Hurst scored a hat-trick and Peters the other goal, which led terrace songsmiths to compose the ditty:

> I remember Wembley,
> When we beat West Germany.
> Peters one and Geoffrey three,
> Bobby Moore and his OBE.

POPLAR/ISLE OF DOGS, E14

Arsenal's first game (1886), Glengall Grove

Arsenal, as Dial Square, played their first ever game in Glengall Grove on 11 December 1886 against Eastern Wanderers. The team was made up of workers from the Dial Square workshop at Woolwich's Royal Arsenal armaments factory and changed in the local pub (the George) where they made so much mess the landlord charged them extra to cover the cost of cleaning. The pitch was simply a patch of grass lined with an open sewer from which the players had to retrieve the ball. There were no goalposts, cross bars, pitch markings or team colours, and, according to club secretary Elijah Watkins, the Dial Square players 'looked as though they had been clearing out a mud chute when they had done playing'. Dial Square won 6–0. Two weeks later players and officials met at the Royal Oak in Woolwich (→ p. 179) to decide how to continue the club. They never played a home game on the Isle of Dogs again.

Marriott Hotel, West India Quay

A few hours before their last match of the season against West Ham in May 2006, needing a win to get into the European Champions League, probably at the expense of Arsenal, Tottenham tried to get the game postponed because a number of players appeared to be suffering from food poisoning. The lasagne they had eaten at their hotel the previous night was suspected of being the cause. The authorities refused the request so Tottenham had to field players who had spent much of the night vomiting. Spurs lost the match, Arsenal won theirs, and it was they, not Tottenham, who qualified for Europe's major club competition.

Tests later showed the players were suffering from Norovirus, a viral form of gastroenteritis commonly known as Winter Vomiting Disease, which also induces diarrhoea. A cynical football world remained sceptical about the affair. Many believed that Tottenham had fabricated the problem to try to delay their game until after Arsenal had finished their season, so that Tottenham would know what result they needed.

Later that year Carlos Tevez and Javier Mascherano, West Ham's two new Argentinian internationals, stayed at the hotel. West Ham had found Tevez a two-bedroom flat but it proved too small when he decided to move nine members of his family in with him.

→ Why Tottenham Don't Do Very Well, p. 121

Millwall's beginnings (1885), J T Morton and Co., 2–4 and 19–21, West Ferry Road

Millwall began as Millwall Rovers in summer 1885, founded by workers from the Morton jam factory which stood where the Cascades block of flats can now be found. They took their name from the locale of the factory on the Isle of Dogs even though that of the waterside area by the factory, Sufferance Wharf, would have been more appropriate given the club's subsequent history.

Many of Morton's workers were of Scottish origin, having come south to take jobs in the mid-nineteenth century, and the club at first played in the Scots' national colours of navy and white. Asked about their origins, their first goalkeeper, Obed Caygill, explained that 'a few tinsmiths, engaged on the island, were the founders. First called the "Iona" it grew in importance till it reached its current position. It still continues practically as a working man's team, only one or two of its members being engaged in other occupations, such as clerkships.'

Rovers first captain was one Duncan Hean, a Dundee-born tinsmith, and their inaugural fixture was, somewhat incongruously, a cricket match at Clinker Valley between the Gentlemen and Tradesmen of Millwall. The new club set up their headquarters at the Islanders pub, 5 Tooke Street, from where they left in a three-horse brake for one of their first away fixtures, against Buckhurst Hill, which ended in a 1–1 draw, returning to a fireworks display staged by those who had not attended the match.

Millwall's first ground (1885–86), Tiller Road, south side

Millwall, then Millwall Rovers (see above), had their first ground by a rubbish tip at the western end of what was Glengall Road (now Tiller Road), a site covered by new houses. The first football game played here was against Old St Luke's in October 1885. After a year Millwall moved to a more suitable pitch behind the Lord Nelson pub at the southern end of the isle.

Millwall (1886–90), East Ferry Road, north-west junction with Manchester Grove

Millwall Rovers' second ground was situated on land behind the Lord Nelson pub, where the players changed, a site now covered by housing. They moved here in 1886, a year after forming, and now began charging admission money for the first time. The club joined the London Football Association, entered the London Senior Cup, and a year later won the East End Cup. After they won the competition three years in succession – heady success Millwall have never emulated in the 120 or so years since – the organisers let them keep the trophy.

Some matches here were played in apparent controversy. For instance, in a game against Crouch End the visitors scored two disputed goals. The north Londoners claimed they had won 2–0, but the local papers printed the score as 0–0, an impasse still unresolved to this day. In 1889 the owners of the land where Millwall played decided to replace football with a switchback railway, and the pub landlady gave the club twelve months notice to quit. Officials and players called a meeting in the pub to decide on Millwall's fate, the vote going to those who wished to carry on. A new ground was duly found on East Ferry Road.

Millwall (1890–1901), Crossharbour, east side East Ferry Road

After being forced off their pitch behind the Lord Nelson pub, Millwall Rovers took up residence near Millwall Dock station on East Ferry Road and moved their headquarters from the Lord Nelson pub to the George Hotel. The club planned to convert their new ground to a major sports complex with running track, cricket nets and tennis courts, and with this ambitious project in mind changed their name from Millwall Rovers to Millwall Athletic at a club dinner on 18 April 1889.

On the pitch things were improving too slowly. After Millwall lost at the first hurdle in the FA Cup to Schorne College, football was relegated to a back seat and club officials shifted their attention to cycling. However, the fad for other sports didn't outlive the summer and by September 1890 football was the main business once again. London Caledonians were the opponents for the first match at the upgraded stadium and were welcomed on to the pitch to the sound of bagpipes.

The new stadium was one of the best in southern England, everyone agreed, but the smell that emanated from the ground, little more than mud reclaimed from the nearby Thames, was nauseous. England international Fred Pelly, after playing here for Corinthians, remarked: 'I don't mind taking a tumble or two there, but when I fell to the ground I couldn't get rid of the smell for weeks.'

In 1894 Millwall Athletic became founder members of the Southern League (effectively the third tier of football at that time) and won the inaugural championship. In 1900 a run to the semi-finals of the FA Cup saw the press describe the club for the first time as the Lions, which Millwall later adopted as their nickname. A year later the Millwall Dock company gave the club notice to quit so that they could turn the site into a timber yard. It looked like the end for Millwall, but those who turned up to a meeting at Poplar Town Hall vowed to continue and found a new site at the tip of the isle in what was then optimistically called North Greenwich.

Millwall (1901–10), Isle of Dogs ground, east side East Ferry Road, immediately east of Mudchute station

Millwall's last home on the north side of the river, where they only had a seven-year lease, was a ground of mud and sand close to grazing cows and potato fields. The first game at the new venue, against Portsmouth, was marred by crowd trouble: Pompey's Smith was felled by a stone as he placed the ball by the corner flag, and at the end of the match the Portsmouth players had to run for their lives.

Despite scouring local sites for likely accommodation (much as some Arsenal fans did when they realised they would have to leave Highbury in the late 1990s), Millwall could find no suitable spot, and reluctantly announced they intended crossing the Thames. The news wasn't greeted positively at first. 'Keep it on the island' was the cry, a shout which could well have been directed at the Millwall players when they hoofed the ball. Millwall's final game on the Isle of Dogs was against Woolwich Arsenal in the London Professional Challenge Cup in October 1910. From then on supporters had to bid farewell to such pre-match institutions as Uncle Tom's Cabin sweet shop on British Street and forgo having their hair cut after the game at Elijah Moor's Toilet Club on East Ferry Road.

→ The Den, p. 168

Senrab, Barnes Street

Billy Payne who lived in Poplar's Barnes Street in 1962 decided to form a football club and called it after the name of the street spelt backwards – Senrab. It has since become the most successful boys' team English football has ever seen, blooding locals like Ray Wilkins, Ashley Cole, John Terry, Lee Bowyer, Jermaine Defoe, Ledley King, J'lloyd Samuel, Paul Konchesky and Bobby Zamora at its Wanstead Flats ground.

→ Len Shackleton at Arsenal, p. 102

STRATFORD, E15

Upton Park (1866–1911), West Ham Park, Portway

Entrants to the first ever FA Cup (in 1871–72) and four times quarter-finalists, Upton Park had no connection with the Upton Park location of West Ham United's traditional home. They played at West Ham Park and their attendances were large enough to convince near neighbours Thames Ironworks (who did later become West Ham United) to move to Canning Town.

In 1884 Upton Park complained that the Preston North End team they were playing in the FA Cup were being paid; that they were professionals. This was against the Cup rules, for football was then supposed to be amateur, and the northern club was disqualified from the competition. Upton Park's complaint brought the thorny issue of professionalism into the open, and it wasn't long before northern teams such as Preston went full-time and clubs openly paid their players. Eventually, the FA had no choice but to accept professionalism.

Upton Park ceased playing in 1887 but reformed four years later and briefly joined the Southern Alliance. The club even represented Great Britain at the 1900 Summer Olympics, held in Paris as part of that year's World Fair, and won the gold medal. Yet eleven years later they folded. Their most famous player was the unfortunately named Segar Bastard, who played for England in 1880, and was the last Bastard to play for England. Or maybe not.

West Ham station
Clyde Best, one of the first black players to succeed in League football, had a miserable start to his career in England in 1968. Invited over from Bermuda to have a trial at West Ham, he found to his surprise that there was no one to meet him at Heathrow, and that West Ham station, where he got off the tube, was nowhere near West Ham's ground, not realising that the right stop was Upton Park. Best asked various passers-by for directions and was eventually sent to the council house where John Charles, another black player who had appeared for West Ham, lived. Three years later Best was living in that council house, despite being a West Ham regular.

→ Gillespie Road station is renamed Arsenal, p. 104

West Ham United at the Memorial Ground (1897–1904), East end of Memorial Avenue
In their first guise as Thames Ironworks West Ham United moved to the Memorial Ground on Jubilee Day in 1897 to coincide with the sixtieth anniversary of Queen Victoria's accession. At that time the club were still non-League and known popularly not as the Hammers but the Teetotallers, so strongly was the owner, Arnold Hills, opposed to drink.

The Memorial was Ironworks' first proper ground and it offered superb facilities that included room for other sports such as swimming (in the longest pool in England) and cycling, which Hills saw as being as important as football. The ground could hold 100,000 spectators, a number so vast it must have affected Hills's thinking, for he told the FA it could accommodate as many as 133,000 and would therefore be ideal for the FA Cup Final. However, when representatives from the FA visited, they found there would be so little room for each spectator that they rejected the idea.

Despite the vast space only 200 turned up for Ironworks's first game in 1897 against Northfleet, and attendances remained low, probably because of the ground's inaccessibility. For this was no man's land – not really London (being east of the River Lea) and barely Essex. It stood on the wrong side of a delta of waterways abutting the East London Cemetery and was far from the main centres of population. Even when the London, Southern and Tilbury Railway Company built their line and opened a station near by – West Ham – few turned up.

Nevertheless the club continued to move towards professionalism, signing new players and choosing a new kit: Cambridge blue shirts, white shorts and a red cap. As it was becoming increasingly difficult to persuade the Ironworks employees to play for the team in case injury meant they were unable to work, the club committee decided to insure the players against loss of wages. This benefit came with the warning that anyone who had been injured in a match had to be home by eight p.m. every day – just to make sure they didn't try to ease the pain by going to the pub.

Hills continued to oppose professionalism but couldn't hold out for long. In summer 1898 the club ended its amateur status and joined the Southern League Second Division, which was of a higher standard than the London League that they were used to. Although Hills released funds for new players so that the club could secure their new status he insisted the football team break from the parent company. In July 1900 Thames Ironworks were relaunched as West Ham United. Hills allowed them to use the Memorial Ground rent free for the next three years until arguments about sponsorship by a brewery led to West Ham's move to Upton Park. At the final game at the Memorial Ground in 1904 both teams – West Ham and Swindon – played in the same kit until half-time.

→ **West Ham United at Upton Park, p. 55**

Station to station

The 1970s and 1980s were the time of the self-styled hooligan 'firms', each League club represented on the terraces, in the back streets and at the pubs by an army of psychopaths trained in quasi-military fashion, answerable only to a 'top boy' or 'face', intent on causing maximum damage to other clubs' hooligans, and occasionally to the police and property.

Chelsea's were the Headhunters, mostly fitters and fork-lift drivers from Carshalton Beeches or Kingston, and Millwall's the Bushwackers, who at their peak were possibly the most anti-social grouping London has ever seen, more outré than the Kray gang if slightly less insane than Al Qaeda. West Ham's were the InterCity firm or ICF, named after their use of the InterCity train network on which they travelled to away games. The living embodiment of the ICF was Cass Pennant, who wrote a number of books on football hooliganism in the late 1990s, including *Congratulations, You Have Just Met the ICF*, in which he helpfully explained that the ICF was not racist or right-wing as he himself was black. Another ICF 'face' was Bill Gardner, whose arrival at troublespots came with the deliberately understated announcement: 'Afternoon, gentlemen, the name's Bill Gardner,' the introduction alone often enough to provoke sheer terror in opponents.

The film-maker Alan Clarke based his anti-social mix of hardnuts on the ICF for his eminently watchable 1988 film *The Firm*, starring Gary Oldman in one of his best roles as the Top Boy, Bex Bissell. The less well-crafted 2005 film *Green Street* was also based on the ICF, who were renamed the Green Street Elite.

VICTORIA DOCKS/CANNING TOWN, E16

Ronan Point, Butcher Road
After a West Ham match in 1968 John Charles, the club's full-back and one of the first black players to make his mark in top-flight football,

met *the* John Charles, the revered ex-Leeds, Juventus and Wales striker who had been one of the world's greatest players in the 1950s. The two men went to the Black Lion pub near the ground and then to a party in Ronan Point, a new block of flats in Canning Town. As they were not enjoying themselves, the West Ham Charles suggested to the Welshman that they left. A few hours later Ronan Point collapsed, killing five people.

Thames, east side, Nottingham Avenue

The short-lived and intriguingly named club was founded as Thames Association FC in 1928 as a speculative venture by the owners of the West Ham speedway and greyhound stadium. Thames Association joined the Southern League where they soon prospered and even won election to the Football League Third Division (South) in 1930 when Merthyr failed to win re-election. Shortening their names to Thames, they struggled at this higher level and after finishing bottom in their second season, 1931–32, promptly resigned, to be replaced by Aldershot. The directors, realising that things had not worked out as planned, disbanded the club. Thames had set an unenviable record during their spell in the League: the lowest ever attendance, just 469 (in a 120,000 capacity stadium), who saw them beat Luton on 6 December 1930. The stadium was demolished in the 1970s.

→ Wimbledon, p. 230

West Ham United's origins (1895), Victoria Dock Road

The engineering and shipbuilding company Thames Ironworks formed a works football team of the same name (now West Ham United) in 1895. The venture was announced in the company newspaper, the *Thames Ironworks Gazette*, on 29 June by the firm's owner, Arnold Hills, who explained: 'Mr Taylor, who is working in the shipbuilding department, has undertaken to get up a football club for next winter and I learn that quoits and bowls will also be added to the attractions.' Hills said that he wanted to 'wipe away the bitterness left by the recent strike. Thank God this midsummer madness is passed and gone; inequities and anomalies have been done away with and now, under the Good Fellowship system and Profit Sharing Scheme, every worker knows that his individual and social rights are absolutely secured.'

The local newspaper praised Hills for forming the team: 'If this example were only followed by other large employers, it would lead to much good feeling.' Hills was himself a talented sportsman who had played for Oxford University in the 1877 FA Cup Final, won an England cap in 1879, and was also a top-class mile runner. He was teetotal and a non-smoker, and so were the players – officially. Indeed one of the club's first nicknames was the Teetotallers.

Training took place on Tuesday and Thursday nights in a gas-lit room at Trinity Church School in Barking Road and consisted mostly of army PE exercises. The club's first ground was on Hermit Road, Canning Town (see below). By that time the number of workers at Thames Ironworks had halved from the 6,000 employed a few decades earlier, due to competition from the Clyde yards.

West Ham United (1895–97), Hermit Road, north-east junction with Bethell Avenue

The club that became West Ham United had their first ground in 1895 on Hermit Road, a site previously used by Old Castle Swifts who were also a works team. 'A cinder heap', 'a barren waste', was how some described the ground which was surrounded by a moat and had canvas sheeting for fencing.

Ironworks played their first match here against Royal Ordnance on 7 September 1895, drawing 1–1. Soon they were pioneering floodlit football so that dock-workers could attend games at the end of the working day. On 16 December 1895 the Irons played Old St Stephen's at Hermit Road under twelve lights, each the equivalent of 2,000 candles. It didn't fully work. The lightbulbs, which were mounted on poles, kept going out and officials had to dip the ball in whitewash every ten minutes or so to make it easier to see.

At the end of 1896 Thames Ironworks were evicted for violating their tenancy agreement by erecting a pavilion, setting out a perimeter fence and charging admission. The club's owner, Arnold Hills, then leased a piece of land in Browning Road, Manor Park.

WOODFORD, E18

Forest, Hermon Hill

Forest, unconnected with Nottingham Forest, were one of the first football clubs and were based on Hermon Hill near Epping Forest. They were founded in 1859 by a group of Old Harrovians and became original members of the Football Association four years later. The team insisted on forcing opponents to abide by the new, and not always accepted, FA rules. These included such strictures as 'that in the event of the bursting of the ball a new one is to be placed in the centre of the ground' and 'that following any infringement of the rules of the game, a fine of two shillings and sixpence be inflicted'. Forest disbanded in 1864 and reformed as Wanderers who went on to win the FA Cup five times in its early years despite wearing a gruesome kit of orange, violet and black.

Further east

DAGENHAM

Jimmy Greaves, Terry Venables and Alf Ramsey are amongst the major football names to have emerged from Dagenham, the East End overspill area best known for the Ford car works.

Greaves grew up on Ivyhouse Road in the late 1940s. It was a time of rationing, and the family survived on powdered egg and milk, and tinned corned beef. Nearby was an Italian prisoner-of-war camp where the inmates grew potatoes they gave to the locals who converted them into the popular and ingenious feast of Italian Prisoner of War Camp mixed grill: chips, boiled potatoes and mash.

The young Venables lived on Bonham Road, as did at various times Les Allen (Tottenham 1961 Double winner), Ken Brown (manager of Norwich in the 1980s) and Dean Coney (1980s Fulham striker). At school Venables was warned by his teacher that it was very unlikely that he would make the grade. One boy in a million might become a professional footballer, the teacher explained. 'That's OK,' replied Venables. 'I'm that one boy.' It was no idle boast. Venables became the first and only player to represent England at every level – schoolboy, youth, under-23, amateur and full international.

Ramsey was born on 22 January 1920 in a cottage at Five Elms Farm; his father owned a smallholding which supplied hay for the cabbies' horses. He left school at fourteen and applied for a job at the local Ford plant but was rejected. Ramsey was a swarthy child, and was taunted by schoolmates who called him a gipsy. This slur followed him into professional football, and even one of his closest colleagues, Eddie Baily, assistant manager of Tottenham in the 1960s, once admitted that the England boss 'did look a bit Middle Eastern'. Driving through the Czech countryside on the way to an England game in 1973, the team coach passed some gipsy caravans, at which point Bobby Moore piped up: 'Hey, Alf, some of your relatives over there,' leaving the manager crimson with fury.

Ramsey went to great pains to disguise his humble origins. When asked once on the radio where his parents lived, he paused for a few pregnant seconds before venturing out with a 'Dagenham [further delay], I believe', as if it were a vague rumour about a couple of strangers. Ramsey's biggest fear was not being able to speak confidently in public and he took elocution lessons which rendered him mildly incomprehensible. According to Jimmy Greaves, the England manager ordering breakfast on the train sounded something like 'Hile half the baycorn hand scrambold heg. No thank you, I don't want no orange duce.'

Bonham Road

When a group of Chelsea players including Terry Venables broke their curfew in Blackpool before a big game in 1965 to sup the local ale, to the fury of their manager Tommy Docherty, the press converged on Venables's Dagenham home believing that it was their best chance of emerging with more juicy revelations. And Venables didn't disappoint. The Chelsea midfielder told reporters that the players had not done what had been suggested, which only excited the pressmen more as they had no idea what the players were supposed to have done in the first place. They didn't know at that stage that the players had secretly escaped from the hotel but had returned at half past three in the morning, at which point the hotel porter had informed the Chelsea manager. Nor did the press know that Docherty had burst into the room shared by Barry Bridges and the squeaky clean

John Hollins only to find them fast asleep. The manager woke them, and was told by the bleary-eyed players that they had no knowledge of any drinking session and had been fast asleep. But Docherty brazenly tore off the sheets and blankets on both beds revealing two players fully dressed in their best suits, ties and boots.

Docherty's punishment – dropping eight of the miscreants and playing reserves in their place – backfired when Chelsea lost two key games in the run-in to the title and narrowly finished third.

→ Tony Adams after a drink, p. 276

Dagenham and Redbridge (1992–), Victoria Road

Promoted to the Football League in 2007, Dagenham and Redbridge are a hybrid of a host of low-level London teams, formed following a merger of Redbridge Forest and Dagenham football clubs in 1992. Redbridge Forest had themselves come together only three years previously after Leytonstone/Ilford (themselves the obvious result of a marriage between Leytonstone and Ilford) joined with long-running non-League outfit Walthamstow Avenue, Amateur Cup winners in 1952 and 1961.

Dagenham and Redbridge's forerunners
- ⚽ Ilford 1881–1979
- ⚽ Leytonstone 1886–1979
- ⚽ Leytonstone/Ilford 1979–88
- ⚽ Walthamstow Avenue 1900–88
- ⚽ Redbridge Forest 1989–92
- ⚽ Dagenham 1949–92
- . . . *becoming* Dagenham and Redbridge 1992–

Pizza Hut, Hornchurch

After Arsenal's Tony Adams and Ray Parlour sprayed some Spurs fans with a fire extinguisher in Hornchurch's branch of Pizza Hut in 1993, manager George Graham savaged Parlour but simply shook his head at

Adams. When Parlour complained that he was being treated unfairly, Graham explained that 'He, Adams, does the business for me week in week out. You don't.'

→ **Gazza's kebab, p. 42**

3   North London

North London in football terms means only one thing: the rivalry between Arsenal and Tottenham Hotspur that has raged since the former left Woolwich for Highbury in 1913 against the latter's wishes. Just to compound the felony, Arsenal soon usurped their new neighbour's claims to a First Division place, despite having finished lower than them, where they have remained since for nearly a hundred years, winning thirteen titles to Tottenham's two.

ANGEL/ISLINGTON, N1

The Jolly Farmers, 113 Southgate Road

'From the first time I kicked a ball as a pro, I began to learn what the game was all about. It's about the drunken parties that go on for days, the orgies, the birds and the fabulous money,' explained Peter Storey, Arsenal and England's fiercely uncompromising tough-tackling early 1970s midfield hard man. 'Football is just a distraction, but you're so fit you can carry on with all the high living in secret and still play the game at the highest level.'

Fittingly, one of Storey's first post-football interests was running this pub in the non-bohemian end of Islington. He was also in charge of a massage parlour in Leyton, and in 1979, two years after leaving Arsenal, was fined £700 and given a six-month suspended jail sentence when the law decided the massage parlour was actually a brothel. Life then seriously deteriorated for the ex-player. In 1980 Storey was jailed for three years for financing a plot to counterfeit gold coins. Ten years later came a twenty-eight-day spell inside for attempting to import twenty pornographic videos from Europe hidden in a spare tyre.

→ **George Best at the Phene Arms, p. 201**

King's Cross station

After scoring an excellent goal to help England beat World Champions West Germany at Wembley in 1954 Sunderland forward Len Shackleton was handed a third-class rail ticket for the overnight sleeper back to Wearside by the FA. When he asked: 'Couldn't you raise enough money for a first-class ticket?' the official told him they had all been sold.

It was of course a lie. Shackleton was able to upgrade easily at the station, and he calculated that by the time he'd paid for the new ticket, and taken off tax and expenses for playing in the game he was left with less than £20 of his £50 fee, even though the receipts for the match totalled more than £50,000. Despite being one of the great stylists of the era, Shackleton, like Matt Le Tissier, was mostly overlooked by England selectors who seemed to be frightened of talent. This attitude was summed up by one committee member who, when asked why Shackleton had won only five caps, explained: 'because we play at Wembley Stadium, not the London Palladium'.

→ **Bolton Wanderers duped at Euston Station, p. 131**

Noel Road

This elegant side street in the fashionable part of Islington was caught up in two media frenzies in the 1960s and 1970s. In 1967 it was where the playwright Joe Orton was killed by his gay lover, who then poisoned himself.

Four years later George Best, then in decline as a footballer if not as a playboy, arrived with actress Sinead Cusack for a weekend of off-the-pitch passion at her Noel Road pad. Best was supposed to be playing for Manchester United against Chelsea at the time and, when it was discovered that he had forsaken 4–4–2 for 1–1–69, journalists and television men besieged Noel Road while local kids chanted: 'We want Georgie', 'Come out, Georgie', 'Georgie Best is on the nest'.

FINSBURY PARK, N4

Alex James's sweetshop, St Thomas's Road

When he retired from football in 1937 Arsenal inside-forward Alex James, the most fêted player of the era, bought a sweetshop opposite the Finsbury Park Empire music hall on a whim. Mrs James was horrified. Not only was she not too keen on doing the work but her husband had secured the shop by handing the owner a large sum of money in cash without obtaining any documents or even a receipt. The shop was not a success. It was too small to hold more than three people, most of whom went in out of curiosity to see James, rather than to buy anything, and was practically devoid of customers outside match days. When the council ordered James to install a toilet to satisfy the needs of his assistant he sold up.

→ Florin Raducioiu at Harvey Nichols, p. 197

Arsenal secretary's address, 32 Pemberton Road, Haringey

To obtain a season ticket for Arsenal around the time of the First World War, when the club had just moved to north London, members of the public simply had to send 21 shillings (£1.05) to the secretary, George Morrell, at his home address, 32 Pemberton Road, Haringey, as an advert taken out by the club in the local papers urged. 'Mr Morrell wants to sell you a ticket,' ran the ad. 'Do not let him be disappointed.'

Other advertisements placed by the club in the press were equally enlightening. One, for a Boxing Day match, read: 'Please note that the popular Bradford team will be at Highbury on Boxing Day. Seats can now be booked.' These days there is a lengthy waiting list for a season ticket, which costs around a thousand times more than it did in the 1920s, and the secretary no longer puts his address in the papers. Morrell was later sacked to save Arsenal money.

Manor House station, Seven Sisters Road

On Dave Mackay's first trip to north London after signing for Tottenham Hotspur on Wednesday 18 March 1959, he took the train from Edinburgh to King's Cross, changed on to the Piccadilly Line and got off at Manor

House tube station. Mackay then nipped on a bus heading along the Seven Sisters Road bound for Tottenham and shot upstairs, quickly followed by the conductor, a Capstan cigarette stuck to his lower lip, who enquired of the future Double-winning wing-half, 'Where to, cocker?'

Eight years later on the evening of an Arsenal *v* Rangers 'friendly' at Highbury, police apprehended hordes of Rangers fans at the station armed with swords and bayonets. By then Mackay had a business, Dave Mackay (Club Ties) Ltd, on Seven Sisters Road – at the Tottenham not the Arsenal end.

Arsenal station, p. 104

HIGHBURY, N5

Arsenal (1913–2006), Avenell Road

Arsenal, playing in Highbury for just over ninety years, were by far the most successful football club London has ever seen. They were the first to win the League Championship, the first to win ten FA Cups, the first to reach the European Cup final and were the best supported for many years until the constraints of the ground as an all-seater stadium meant they needed to move to maintain their status.

Arsenal began as Dial Square in 1886, the most ambitious of the various works teams based at the Royal Arsenal in Woolwich. The club used a number of grounds in south-east London until 1913 when owner Henry Norris, a property developer, decided to move the by now renamed Woolwich Arsenal to the north side of the river. This was not the first time Norris had attempted to carry out a fundamental change to the club's make-up. As he was on the boards of both Woolwich Arsenal with Fulham, he had tried to merge the two clubs in 1910, and one player, a Tom Winship, had been transferred between the two sides without a third party being allowed to bid. The League turned down his plan. This time there was even more opposition, particularly from Tottenham, which in 1905 had objected to Clapton Orient's joining the Southern League on the grounds that 'we are not going to have them on our doorsteps'.

The League had ignored Tottenham then and ignored them now, having never previously prevented clubs changing grounds, and told the two teams that the local population was big enough to accommodate all three sides. The *Tottenham Herald* newspaper was upset and caricatured Norris as a spike-collared Hound of the Baskervilles pillaging the Spurs roost. Even the *Islington Gazette* was hostile. A journalist wrote with some prescience that a 'respectable, decent neighbourhood will be transformed into a rabble-infested den of noise and, I fear, drinking'.

No Longer with the Woolwich

News of the move was greeted with the expected outcry by Arsenal fans in the Woolwich area. After all, they would now have to make a tortuous journey across town to watch their team. There were also many complaints from Highbury locals. A Mr Coventon of Highbury Park urged the council to 'protect us from the utter ruin that a football team would bring'. A Mr A. Bailey of Avenell Road told the council: 'There will be considerable annoyance and inconvenience suffered by the residents in Avenell Road as a result of the erection of lofty stands by the Woolwich Arsenal football club. Can the council please help us on this matter?' Nevertheless many locals were excited at the prospect of League football on their doorstep. The Standen family children made a huge banner to hold up at the first game which read: 'Welcome and good wishes to the team'. And local shopkeepers soon warmed to the prospect of attracting a potential 30,000 extra customers on alternate Saturdays. For Henry Norris the location was perfect. There was a tube station nearby and spectators could be in the West End and the bright lights in about twenty minutes, something which took more than an hour from Woolwich. There was also a bigger fan base here.

For a while it looked as if Arsenal's plans were to be thwarted. The FA decided to hold an inquiry. Another problem was that the land earmarked for the stadium was covered with cricket pitches and tennis courts owned by the Church of England whose London College of Divinity stood alongside. They opposed the move, but when Norris waved a £20,000 cheque at the Ecclesiastical Commissioners the two parties agreed on a 21-year lease and Randall Davidson, the Archbishop of Canterbury, signed for the church. It later transpired that Norris and the archbishop belonged to the same Masonic lodge. To appease the Ecclesiastical Commissioners the club agreed not to play on Christmas Day, Easter or Sundays, and stipulated that intoxicating liquor should not be sold at the stadium – strictures which were dropped in 1925. As for the FA inquiry into the move, the third regarding Woolwich Arsenal, Norris packed the meeting with his supporters. His plans went through.

The club asked fans and locals to suggest a name for the new ground. One man from Camden Town came up with 'Avesbury Park', mixing Avenell Road, Highbury and the ubiquitous footbally 'park' suffix. Others put forward 'The Fortress' and even 'Gun Park'. No such name was ever adopted and the ground became officially 'The Arsenal Stadium', known popularly as 'Highbury'.

When builders started work on the stadium a low brick wall ran the length of Avenell Road. Opposite at No. 85, lived a doctor, A. P. Hazell, who was a communist and allowed the Bolsheviks to use 85 Avenell Road as a mailing address to outwit officers from the Metropolitan Police who sought to intercept mail and pass on information to the Tsarist secret police in Russia. A few years before Woolwich Arsenal arrived in North London a regular visitor to the address had been V. I. Lenin himself, calling at No. 85 to get his post.

The first game at Highbury was against Leicester Fosse, a Second Division fixture, on 6 September 1913, which the home side won 2–1. A year later the club dropped the 'Woolwich' prefix.

When professional football resumed after the First World War the Football League announced they would expand the First Division to take twenty-two instead of just twenty clubs. Maybe the two relegated teams – Chelsea and Tottenham – would be reprieved? Not as far as Norris was concerned. He persuaded the management committee that Chelsea should stay up, as the High Court had ruled one of their defeats had been fixed, but that Tottenham should go down. As for the teams who had finished above Arsenal in the Second Division, Wolves and Barnsley, their claims should be ignored in favour of Arsenal (who had finished fifth) on account of Arsenal's 'long service to League football', a brash claim given that Wolves had been in the League longer. Perhaps visiting First Division directors voted for Arsenal because they preferred weekends away in the capital to trips to Wolverhampton or Barnsley? Perhaps the committee president, John McKenna of Liverpool, voted for Arsenal in exchange for Norris's support for his own club over the 1915 match-fixing scandal? Or perhaps he received a discounted house in Wimbledon through Norris's estate agency?

Archibald Leitch, the great stadium designer, who also worked at Everton, Tottenham, Chelsea and Rangers, was brought in to create the Arsenal Stadium. His original work was just three terraces and a grandstand – the East Stand – not the revered structure that came later. Only the east side was covered; the west side was a huge terraced bank known as the Spion Kop, where fights were commonplace. During games four men carried a tarpaulin around the perimeter of the pitch to collect money for the band that appeared before every match to warm up the crowd with a version of the 'Posthorn Gallop'.

Arsenal achieved nothing on the field until the arrival of Herbert Chapman as manager in 1925. Chapman had had considerable success with Huddersfield Town, taking a club from an obscure Yorkshire town to the League Championship, and now he wanted to prove himself in London. Aided tactically by veteran forward Charlie Buchan, Chapman changed Arsenal's formation to exploit the new offside law. With Buchan as captain, the club reached their first FA Cup Final (in 1927), but lost to Cardiff after a blunder by goalkeeper Dan Lewis. Two years later Henry Norris was banned from football for financial irregularities. He had used the club's expense account for his own good and profited from the sale of the team bus. Sir Samuel Hill-Wood, who had once scored ten runs off a single ball at Lord's, joined the board, founding a dynasty that is still involved with Arsenal.

Success came in 1930 with the club's first FA Cup, followed a year later by the Championship, the first time it had gone to a London club. The 1930s was Arsenal's decade. Five Championships and two FA Cups saw them almost match any other club's achievements since football began. Many of the greatest players of the era played at Highbury: Ted Drake, Eddie Hapgood, Cliff Bastin, Joe Hulme and Alex James as well as Buchan. Even the premature death of Herbert Chapman didn't spoil the run.

Herbert Chapman – football emperor

Chapman was not only the first modern-style manager to pick the team (the secretary usually did that) and run the playing side of the club, but a supreme innovator as well. He advocated the use of white balls, floodlighting and physiotherapists. He sent Arsenal out in white socks with blue hoops so that the players could easily pick out a team-mate without looking up, and introduced numbered shirts so that they could rearrange themselves into their positions easily. Off the field, his greatest achievement was the renaming of the local tube station 'Arsenal' (see below).

Chapman first contemplated the idea of going into management once he'd retired as a Tottenham player, sitting in the bath at White Hart Lane after their last game of the 1907 season. With Huddersfield Town in the early 1920s Chapman pioneered the idea of the manager, rather than the secretary or board, picking the team. It worked. Huddersfield had never previously achieved anything, but under Chapman won two Championships and the FA Cup. He left for Arsenal just before they completed a hat-trick of titles and almost repeated the feat in north London, but died suddenly of pneumonia in January 1934.

Yet Chapman was lucky to be allowed to manage any club at all. He had been in charge of Leeds City in 1918 when they were expelled from the Football League for paying players more than the permitted rates. He was barred from attending matches but the injunction was later lifted.

Victoria Concordia Crescit

In 1932 architects Claude Waterlow Ferrier and William Binnie designed the new West Stand in an exquisite, restrained Art Deco style reminiscent of that unveiled at the 1925 Paris Exhibition. The beauty of their stand was evident in the small, subliminal red and white entrance on Highbury Hill that fitted into the skyline like a four-storey house amongst the terraced properties, albeit with an entrance like that of a warehouse.

Four years after the West Stand came the even more remarkable East Stand, then the costliest sports stand ever built in Britain at £130,000. It had Paris Metro-style lamps by the main entrance, marble halls and a bust of the late Herbert Chapman sculpted by Jacob Epstein. There were heated floors in the changing rooms and padded seats in the stands, and from 1948 the ubiquitous motif of a Latin crest – *Victoria Concordia Crescit:* Victory Comes Through Teamwork – reminiscent of the public schools that had created the modern game seventy years before.

Highbury was now a magnificent and unique football ground. Wilf Mannion, the Middlesbrough inside-forward, called it 'swish and awesome. You'd walk in and the commissionaire would doff his cap to you. It was such a difference to Ayresome Park which always seemed to be falling down.' But with war approaching, Arsenal no longer looked so commanding and were nearly bankrupt after spending so heavily on players and new stands. When the club lost at home to Derby the crowd sang: 'No more money in the bank. What's to do about it? Let's put out the lights and go to sleep.' For that match, strangely, half the team was missing. Trying to make their way back from the annual away fixture to Racing Paris, which always took place close to Armistice Day, they had found themselves stranded in France due to fog at sea.

The battle of Highbury

England's 'friendly' match with World Champions Italy at Highbury in November 1934 was the most brutal international in English history and became known as the 'Battle of Highbury' thanks to the level of unrestrained violence. Yet it all started so innocently. Before the game journalists could hardly contain themselves with excitement. An unnamed 'woman reporter' in the *Daily Mirror* gushed over the 'stalwart, olive-skinned Italian footballers going about London causing many a flutter to feminine hearts', and would probably have gasped had she known the extraordinary bonuses the Italian team stood to gain. A win would earn them £150 a man and an Alfa Romeo car. The England team consisted mostly of Arsenal players, seven of whom (a record) were appearing at their home ground. The score at the end of the game was 3–2 to England, but it was for the bawling and brawling, arging and barging that the game was remembered. In the second minute Luisito Monti had his foot broken in a tackle. The culprit was Arsenal's Ted Drake. He was reprimanded by defender Monzeglio, who tried to strangle him, while another Italian, identity unknown, broke Eddie Hapgood's nose. Following the game the FA considered officially withdrawing from all internationals, but instead carried on, later choosing unofficially to sort of withdraw from some, usually when pitted against Macedonia or Croatia.

The Mee generation

After the Second World War Arsenal under Allison's successor, Tom Whittaker, enjoyed a second period of success. They won the league in 1948 and 1953, and the Cup in between. Fans, starved of competitive action during the war, turned up in absurdly large numbers for even the most inconsequential of events, 27,000 attending a reserve game against Burnley, for instance. Arsenal clinched the 1953 Championship by beating the same team 3–2 in the last game of the season. Surprisingly the match was played on the Friday night before the Cup Final so that the crowd would be boosted by the influx of Blackpool and Bolton fans down for the match, so little faith did the Arsenal board have in their ability to sell out the game. According to the club secretary Bob Wall it was some time after the final whistle that anyone knew that Arsenal had won the League – by 0.099 of a goal – goal average rather than goal difference then being in use.

The 1950s brought Arsenal's first serious decline. As the decade wore on the club descended into mid-table mediocrity which continued into the 60s, when they watched in horror as Tottenham won the Double. A new low point came in May 1966 when a crowd of just 4,544 turned out to see an end-of-the-season match against runners-up Leeds. Spectators on the North Bank lit a bonfire and danced round it like Red Indians. Even if the game did have the misfortune to clash with the first televising of a European final, it was clear that there were serious problems at Arsenal under the management of ex-England captain Billy Wright. The club finished that season in fourteenth place. They lost their main goalscorer, Joe Baker, to Nottingham Forest, had few top-quality players on their books and were going nowhere.

Wright was sacked. Astonishingly, his replacement was the club's physiotherapist, Bertie Mee, who had barely played top-class football. Mee asked for a get-out clause so that he could return to physiotherapy after twelve months if management didn't work out. He was an old-fashioned disciplinarian, reserved and quiet, but turned out to be excellent at man-management. He also recruited first-class up-and-coming coaches such as Dave Sexton and Don Howe. Mee gradually built a new team, using home-grown talent such as Peter Simpson, George Armstrong and Peter Storey.

As with Chapman forty years previously, success came slowly: two losing League Cup finals in 1968 and 1969, and only slight improvement in the club's League position. But in 1970 the club won their first trophy for seventeen years – the European Fairs Cup – an achievement that no one could have predicted, especially when they were paired against Johan Cruyff's Ajax in the semi-final.

Even more amazingly the following year Arsenal won the coveted and rare League and Cup Double, repeating Tottenham's achievement of ten years previously. In 1971 Arsenal boasted none of the superstar names that characterised the era, but they did have a *team* in which everyone worked hard and maximised his talent. When the more highly rated Leeds fell away towards the end of the season, Arsenal moved in for the kill. To win the title they needed to beat Tottenham, of all teams, at White Hart Lane or at least draw 0–0. (A score draw would give the title to Leeds.) A tight game was settled at the death when George Armstrong crossed for Ray Kennedy to score the only goal. Arsenal had won the League for the first time since 1953; the first time they had won it without being expected to.

Five days later came the Cup Final against Liverpool. Arsenal had played so many games over the previous few weeks that it was feared they would never last the pace. At the end of ninety minutes the score was still 0–0. Extra-time was the last thing Arsenal needed, and when Steve Heighway gave Liverpool the lead two minutes later the Double dream looked shattered. But Arsenal, not for the last time, overcame the odds. To this day no one really knows who scored the equaliser, Eddie Kelly or George Graham. No uncertainty surrounded the winner. Charlie George, the local lad who had grown up supporting Arsenal from the North Bank, and whose rebellious long hair and 'attitude' made him a role model for every cocky young Gunners fan, played a one–two with John Radford and let fly a thunderous shot from twenty yards. The net bulging, George celebrated originally and simply by lying flat-out on the pitch. Either that or he was too tired to move another muscle. It was a fitting climax to a remarkable season.

Bertie Mee couldn't keep up the momentum. Nor, despite his experience, was he able to handle Charlie George. Arsenal won nothing else under his tenure and he resigned in 1976 with the club only narrowly above the relegation zone. Ten years of mediocre achievement followed under former players Terry Neill and Don Howe. Neill had played centre-half for the club under Mee and turned to management at a relatively young age, first with Hull, then Tottenham, whom he almost took down. There were mixed feelings at Highbury when it was announced that he was taking over. During one of his first team talks Neill took out of a bag a handful of toy cowboys holding pistols and rifles. 'This is us,' he told the astonished group of players. Then he produced another bundle from the bag. It was of toy Red Indians. He threw them down on the table next to the cowboys. 'And that's the opposition. We'll destroy them just like that.'

They didn't quite. There were plenty of finals and semi-finals under Neill's guidance but only one trophy, the FA Cup in 1979. Yet there was no shortage of quality on the field. For instance, in goal was the formidable figure of Pat Jennings who had starred for over ten years for Tottenham and has managed the near unique achievement of winning over both sets of fans in perpetuity. Jennings deliberately signed for Arsenal to get back at the Spurs directors, not one of whom thanked him for thirteen years' illustrious service when he was released, for just £45,000, at the end of Tottenham's 1976–77 relegation season. In midfield was one of the era's greatest talents, Liam Brady, and up front the mouth-watering partnership of lean Irish striker Frank Stapleton and powerful and fearless Malcolm Macdonald. Yet under Neill Arsenal never seriously challenged for the title, and soon turned into a selling, not a buying, club. When Brady and Stapleton left for 'bigger' clubs the fans began to wonder if Arsenal would ever reach the heights again.

Neill was sacked in December 1983. His replacement, Don Howe, fared worse, despite being the coach who had guided Bertie Mee's side to the Double in 1971. Howe lasted only two and a half years in the post during which time Arsenal made no headway. When he quit in March 1986 reports circulated that the board were looking to replace him with Terry Venables. How Arsenal supporters must give thanks every night that nothing of the sort happened.

The ministry of defence

Don Howe's replacement was another former Highbury star, George Graham. His appointment turned out to be one of the most brilliant decisions the Arsenal board ever made. Graham, a member of the 1971 Double team, ushered in a new era of success, becoming one of the greatest managers football has ever seen. Even though contemporaries such as Bob Paisley and Alex Ferguson won more trophies, they started with bigger budgets and took over clubs in a better position.

Graham built teams on a shoestring. He would spend a few thousand pounds on players from the lower divisions and achieve more with them than rivals who splashed out millions on superstars. He knew that even though football is about scoring goals, there is a simple truism that says: the team that fails to concede cannot lose. Consequently he built the meanest defence English football has ever seen, with John Lukic (and later David Seaman) in goal behind Lee Dixon, Nigel Winterburn, Tony Adams and Steve Bould (and later Martin Keown). When these players let in a goal they saw it as a personal slight that should not be repeated – and wasn't very often, thanks to an offside trap system that became so infamous it featured as a dance routine in the film *The Full Monty*.

Under Graham's management Arsenal won the League Cup in 1987 and the Championship in 1989 in the most dramatic fashion witnessed in the history of the League. Needing to win at least 2–0 to take the title ahead of Liverpool, who had already won the FA Cup, Arsenal scored through Alan Smith early in the second half, but with the final whistle approaching looked unlikely to score a second goal. When Liverpool midfielder Steve McMahon signalled to his team-mates that only one minute was left, Arsenal were galvanised anew. Goalkeeper John Lukic found Lee Dixon who launched it long. Smith controlled it and lobbed it forward for Michael Thomas to run on to. Somehow Thomas evaded all challenges, paused by the Liverpool keeper, and flicked the ball in at the right-hand corner before somersaulting in joy. Within minutes hordes of north Londoners had filled

Avenell Road dancing in delirium. 'We have laid a foundation of belief at Highbury,' explained George Graham. 'If you lose hope or lose belief, you may as well get out of football. Tonight was a fairytale, the unpredictable that makes us all love football.'

Two years later Arsenal secured the League again, this time less frenetically, losing only one League game all season. They won both domestic cups in 1993 and the European Cup Winners' Cup the following year. Then it all came crashing down for George Graham. In March 1994 a Danish television reporter, filming an interview with the manager, asked him: 'Didn't you receive a secret payment on the Jensen transfer?' Graham was forthright in his dismissal of such a claim. 'Me, take money? Hey you'd better be careful, that's a serious accusation.' Yet it turned out that of the £1.57 million transfer of John Jensen from Brondby to Arsenal the Danish club had received only £900,000. What happened to the other £670,000? The agent involved, Rune Hauge, had given it to Graham, who had banked the money in the Channel Islands. He later claimed that it was an unsolicited gift. When Arsenal discovered the shocking news they first tried to preserve the secret and arrange for Graham to 'retire' at the end of the season, but then realised the stupidity of such a course of action. The story leaked out in the *Mail on Sunday* in December 1994, and though Arsenal immediately announced they would not be sacking Graham, sack him they did the following February. The FA subsequently banned him from football for a year.

The 1994–95 season was a tough one for Arsenal. Not only did they lose their manager in unfortunate circumstances, they flirted with relegation, lost the European Cup Winners' Cup Final to a fluke shot from the halfway line by an ex-Spurs player, and ended it by making the wrong choice of new manager. Bruce Rioch came with a sergeant-major approach that annoyed the club's top players, particularly Ian Wright. Rioch lasted only one season – 1995–96 – despite a reasonable record on the pitch and the signing of the player who would go on to become the club's greatest ever, Dennis Bergkamp.

The French connection

With Rioch gone, there were stories in the papers about a barely known French manager taking over. Asked about the rumour at the AGM, chairman Peter Hill-Wood announced: 'I don't want to keep anyone in the dark. It's been one of the worst kept secrets of the year. It's just that we did give an undertaking. It may sound odd too when everyone knows who is coming but I can't say formally.' At this point an exasperated shareholder asked: 'An undertaking to whom, Mr Chairman?', to which the hapless Hill-Wood responded: 'An undertaking to Mr Wenger' whereupon everyone in the room collapsed in laughter.

Surprisingly Arsene Wenger turned out to be as successful as George Graham, but with a different outlook on the game. Where the latter's teams had been built around a formidable defence, Wenger's were primed to attack, underpinned by fast-flowing florid football. Arsenal won the Double in Wenger's first full season (1997–98) and, even though they could not break the domination of Manchester United over the next few years, they repeated the feat in 2001–02, and won the Cup again the following season and in 2005. Most remarkable of all was the 2003–04 season. Arsenal achieved what football experts had always regarded as impossible, going through an entire League season in the top division undefeated, a feat achieved not just through the amazing goal scoring of Thierry Henry but thanks to the power of players such as Lauren, the creativity of Robert Pires on the flanks and the intelligence of Dennis Bergkamp.

The natty professor

⊕ Myths and mistaken theories surround all managers, and never more so than with Arsenal's sophisticated Frenchman. No sooner had he arrived than Wenger was dubbed 'the Professor'. What gave rise to this epithet was a picture of the manager standing in front of what looked like massed tomes on a bookshelf. In fact the volumes were bound collections of old Arsenal programmes rather than the works of Plato or Spinoza.

⊕ Another myth perpetuated by the press was that Arsenal were serial wrongdoers with players more likely to get sent off than those of other clubs. Each time an Arsenal player was sent off, they counted: 'Wenger's fifty-third red card', 'Wenger's fifty-fourth red card' and so on. But the journalists weren't comparing like with like.

The other managers hadn't been in their jobs as long, so could hardly have amassed as many red cards during their reign. Wenger was a rarity in the top division in staying in charge for at least ten seasons. ⊛ Wenger's teams won seven trophies from 1998 to 2005 but it could have been many more. The regular selection of players palpably inferior to the likes of Bergkamp, Henry and Overmars mystified the fans, as Arsenal finished League runners-up three years running in 1999, 2000 and 2001. In the FA Cup semi-final of 2004 Wenger astonished the football world by dropping his world-class striker Thierry Henry for the tepid tyro Jeremy Aliadiere. Arsenal were easily outclassed by Manchester United and the so-called 'invincibles' suffered one of their few losses of the season and with it the chance of another Double. For the 2007 League Cup Final, their best chance of a trophy in what was for the club a bad season, Wenger put out a reserve side against Chelsea – and lost.

The Wenger era was also marked by the club's decision to leave Highbury, where there was no room to expand, for a new stadium that could accommodate 60,000 seated spectators. After several options were considered, a site only a few hundred yards to the west was chosen. Unfortunately, to the chagrin of the football world and those who appreciate quality architecture, Highbury, the most beautiful stadium in the country, was demolished (save for the listed façades) to be redeveloped into apartments.

→ The new Arsenal stadium, p. 105

Arsenal off the bench (1)
⊛ When George Jobey received an injury during the first ever match at Highbury, a 2–1 victory over Leicester Fosse on 6 September 1913, there were no dressing rooms or running water in the ground. Trainer George Hardy didn't want the player to have to walk to get treatment so he borrowed a cart from the

milkman to wheel the injured man up Highbury Hill to his house where he could be examined.

✪ The first live radio commentary from a football match took place at Arsenal's ground in January 1927, when the home side drew with Sheffield United 1–1. The commentators helpfully divided the pitch into numbered sections for their discourse using a guide printed in the *Radio Times*. Arsenal was also the first ground to allow in television cameras (in 1936, for a match against Everton).

✪ At the end of the 1928 season Portsmouth travelled to Highbury needing to win to stay up. Bookmakers reported an unusual increase in the number of punters betting on an away victory, and during the game itself Arsenal, in front of a paltry 15,416 crowd, made little attempt to compete, losing 2–0. Portsmouth stayed up. By an amazing coincidence the team to go down instead of them were Tottenham.

✪ Len Shackleton, the highly talented striker who became known as the 'Clown Prince of Soccer', arrived at Highbury aged sixteen in August 1938 hoping to join what was then the most successful team in the country. He was met at King's Cross station by centre-forward Jack Lambert, shown to his digs on Highbury Hill, and taken round Arsenal Stadium the next day. Shackleton later described making his way through the 'giant stands, the spotlessly clean terracing reaching, to my eyes, into the clouds, the emerald green turf'. But he was annoyed at being handed a set of overalls and told to follow the motor-mower over the pitch clipping any blades of grass the machine had missed, and even more upset when manager George Allison told him he was too slight in build. 'You'll never make the grade as a footballer'. Shackleton became one of the greatest crowd pullers of all time. When he returned to Highbury playing for Sunderland after the war, he dribbled into the Arsenal penalty area at one point during the match and sat on the ball.

✪ Arsenal's match against Brentford in May 1939, the last at Highbury before the outbreak of the Second World War, was filmed for the thriller *The Arsenal Stadium Mystery*. In the movie

Arsenal play a fictitious amateur side, the Trojans, one of whose players drops dead during the match after being poisoned. *The Arsenal Stadium Mystery* starred several Arsenal players and staff (only manager George Allison had a speaking part) who were paid £50 a week during the three weeks of filming. Well-known actors featured included Leslie Banks and Esmond Knight.

✪ During the Second World War Highbury became a first aid post and air-raid patrol centre. The windows of the dressing rooms were boarded up and a clearing station was set up inside. A 1,000lb bomb fell on the pitch during one raid, and the North Bank roof was destroyed by incendiary devices. As for the players, Cliff Bastin, who had been excused war service after failing the army's hearing test, served as an ARP warden at Highbury. Benito Mussolini's fascist Italian Radio claimed otherwise, reporting falsely in 1941 that he had been captured in the battle for Crete.

✪ Not every Arsenal player has treated the bust of Herbert Chapman reverently. In the 1960s John Barnwell used to put a cigarette behind the sculpted ear when he arrived at the club in the morning and retrieve it when he left after training.

✪ In May 1966 Highbury staged the world heavyweight boxing contest between Henry Cooper and Cassius Clay. One of those who helped erect the ring was Charlie George, then an apprentice. The 46,000 crowd watching Clay win the contest included the Hollywood stars Lee Marvin and Burt Reynolds.

✪ Leeds manager Don Revie offered Arsenal's Frank McLintock a bribe before the two teams met at Highbury in May 1968. 'You and Barbara should have a nice holiday this summer,' the Leeds manager thoughtfully suggested to the Scottish centre-half. 'You could go anywhere in the world you wanted as a guest of Leeds United. Just take it easy out there tonight.' McLintock was mortified and shouted back, 'You come up to me and ask me to take it easy! Are you fucking crazy?'

✪ In summer 1992 Arsenal began to build a new North Bank stand. While work proceeded the site was disguised by a huge mural the width of the stand dotted with innumerable painted faces of happy smiling football fans. When it was pointed out that no black people had been depicted Arsenal painted some on. Detractors were pleased and muttered, probably unkindly, that the mural generated more atmosphere than the stand it had replaced.

Arsenal station, Gillespie Road

It was Herbert Chapman, Arsenal's formidable between-the-wars manager, who pushed for the London Electric Railway to rename Gillespie Road station 'Arsenal'. Chapman had first mused over the idea when visiting the ground with Leeds City in 1913. The station was renamed Arsenal (Highbury Hill) on 5 November 1932, and later became Arsenal. The name change has given the club a remarkable amount of free publicity, but has not been accepted by all members of the transport authorities and recalcitrant drivers of trains taking fans to the ground on match days still often announce:'The next station is Gillespie Road.'

After an Arsenal–West Ham game in May 1982, the most violent in the club's history, an Arsenal fan was stabbed to death in the tube station. According to some reports a calling card had been left on his body which read:'Congratulations. You have just met the ICF', referring to the visitors' InterCity Firm hooligan followers (→ p. 79).

HIGHBURY, N5

Drayton Arms, 66 Drayton Park

Before Arsenal moved stadium from Highbury to a new site across the Great North Railway, the Drayton Arms had a policy of letting in only home fans. To gain entrance on match days they had to use a side door where an unseen figure hidden behind a speakeasy-type grille would ask them to recite the entire Arsenal 1971 Double-winning team as the 'password' to gain entrance.

→ **Markham Arms, p. 200**

HOLLOWAY, N7

Arsenal (2006–), Hornsey Road

Whereas Arsenal's Highbury home of 1913–2006 was an architectural masterpiece of gorgeous cream-coloured stone and stylish brick work with exquisite flourishes and Art Deco touches, the club's new address, the horrendously named Emirates stadium, is just a football ground. It may seat around 60,000 spectators in comfort, be within a goal-kick of the old Highbury home and allow Arsenal to compete financially with the best clubs in Europe, but as a venue it is a jumble of ill-conceived concrete massing laden with all the predictable early-twenty-first century corporate trappings – glass sheeting, stainless-steel panels, lifts, underground car parking – but lacking in soul, style and most of the qualities that have made many football grounds so loved over the decades.

Arsenal realised they had a problem at Highbury after the publication of the Taylor Report of 1990. The report, produced in the wake of the Hillsborough disaster in which ninety-five fans were crushed to death on the terraces behind a goal, recommended that clubs in the top division should have all-seater stadiums. At Highbury this meant that, although 57,000 had been sitting and standing in comfort up to that point, capacity would be reduced to fewer than 40,000. Many of those who wanted to watch the club would not be able to, and such low attendance figures would not allow Arsenal to compete financially with other major clubs who could accommodate more fans.

Whereas Manchester United's Old Trafford stadium, for instance, could easily be extended to hold greater numbers of seated fans Highbury couldn't. The club would have to move. Various options were considered. There was available land some two miles south at King's Cross, three miles north at Alexandra Park (where they could perhaps share with Tottenham), alongside the Millennium Dome, and more dramatically on the site of the old Bishopsgate Goods Yard off Brick Lane. Arsenal vice-chairman David Dein favoured the least popular plan of all, a move to a revamped Wembley Stadium, where Arsenal played Champions League home games in much discomfort around the turn of the century.

Discussions meandered, those concerned unhappy with all the proposals, until Arsenal fans Anthony Green and Antony Spencer made an ingenious discovery. Convinced that the club could find land nearer their current home in Highbury, they made an aerial study of the vicinity and spotted the large industrial and waste-disposal estate off Ashburton Grove, only a few hundred yards to the west, lost between the Great Northern Railway and the Northern City Line.

Amid the shabby office blocks and depots were a few shops and a couple of pubs and caffs. There was no access between this decrepit wasteland and genteel Highbury Hill to the east where Arsenal played because of the wide gully in which the railway lines run. The envisaged site was slap bang in one of London's most hellish areas. The community that had grown here during the twentieth century was among the most violent in the city, as its most famous native – John Lydon (Johnny Rotten), an avid Arsenal fan – described in his autobiography. After a policeman was shot on Queensland Road, next to the site of the proposed stadium, one day in the early 1960s, Rotten's younger brother, Jimmy, ran home with the loaded gun and the policeman's helmet, which he had found on a patch of waste ground. Slum clearance in the 1980s removed the decrepit tenement blocks but left the area even more isolated.

Yet Green and Spencer realised they had found what could be an ideal site even though it was inaccessible from Highbury and away from the routes used by fans journeying to and from the stadium. They approached Arsenal's board who were amazed that land with such potential existed so near home. Arsenal soon changed their plans, and in November 1999 announced their intention to move the short distance to Ashburton Grove.

The news was greeted with hostility by those who thought the club was trying to grow too big, and that the scheme was not in Islington's best interests. Many of the existing eighty-three businesses, responsible for some 1,100 jobs, were unhappy at the idea of being forced to relocate, and feared they could go out of business. There was concern that traffic congestion would increase to unacceptable levels, that the new waste-transfer station Arsenal announced they would build in Lough Road, near Highbury Corner, to replace the condemned one at Ashburton Grove, would make life intolerable in a residential area, and that the replacement of the existing firms by one huge concern – Arsenal – would make most normal trade and business hard to conduct. There was also local opposition from those concerned that Arsenal were planning to buy up unattractive industrial sites cheaply to sell them on for residential use for a handsome profit.

Meanwhile, the political machinery whirred into action as the club prepared its planning application. Islington council approved the plan in December 2001, and it was ratified over the following weeks by London Mayor Ken Livingstone and Transport Secretary Stephen Byers despite a local campaign of opposition. A protest from two pensioners living in a tower block near the ground, who tried to get the High Court to reject the plans claiming their 'human rights had not been taken into account', was thrown out. But when disgruntled local businesses complained about the way compulsory purchase orders had been issued, the Deputy Prime Minister, John Prescott, ordered a public inquiry, thereby delaying work for a year, although without threatening the likelihood of the venture.

Building eventually started in February 2004 and the stadium, designed by HOK Sport, was completed at a cost of £430 million in time for the opening of the 2006–07 season. It seats 60,432, making it the third largest in the country, with only Wembley and Old Trafford being bigger. But sadly for Arsenal fans the first few years at the new stadium saw the increasing decline of the club. The first game to be at the Emirates was a testimonial for Dennis Bergkamp in July 2006. In the season that followed, an Arsenal team in transition after the departures of Bergkamp and Robert Pires, and the decline in stature of Thierry Henry and Freddie Ljungberg, finished a disappointing fourth.

The ingenuity which had seen Wenger collect trophy after trophy around the end of the twentieth century had deserted him. Where Arsenal had recently featured such dynamic players as Patrick Vieira, Thierry Henry and Dennis Bergkamp, the team was now full of soporific second-raters such as Denilson and Alex Song. Arsenal consistently came *close* to challenging for honours, but wimped out in the face of bigger, better teams (Chelsea, Liverpool and Manchester United). The nadir under Wenger was reached in December 2008 when Emanuel Eboue was booed by his own fans after robbing a team-mate of the ball and passing to an opponent. Wenger probably didn't see the incident.

Arsenal off the bench (2)

✪ Only Arsenal and Port Vale of the ninety-two League teams are not named after an area.

✪ As with many of football's new grounds, the official name given to the new Arsenal stadium – 'the Emirates' – stemmed from a sponsorship deal. Many Arsenal fans were embarrassed to be associated with a company that had previously sponsored Chelsea and that was part of the name of a foreign country. Many objected to any corporate involvement with the stadium's name, believing that that should be left to lesser clubs such as Bolton (who play at the Reebok stadium).

However, the various Arsenal fan groups and celebrity supporters given a voice in the media have not been able to agree on an alternative. Ashburton Grove, the name of the road where the new stadium is located, can no longer be contemplated as Arsenal wiped the street off the map to build the stadium – deliberately, it appears, to prevent it becoming an obvious alternative name to the Emirates. Tom Watt, the actor and radio presenter who has been one of Arsenal's most visible famous fans in recent years, has incongruously suggested keeping it as Highbury even though the new ground is clearly located in Holloway, a name that has been discounted as it is also that of a notorious prison. But there is one ideal alternative: Drayton Park. It is the name of the smaller neighbourhood in which the stadium is located, and sounds like a traditional home of football, as in Celtic Park, Hampden Park, St James's Park et al.

✪ One of the best seating areas at the new stadium is at Club Level which contains 7,000 places sold on licences lasting from one to four years. For the 2006–07 season these ranged in price from £2,500 to £4,750, yet they had all gone by May 2006. When the first match took place, so vacant was the Club Level area at the restart of play for the second half that those unable or unwilling to buy seats at such an inflated price were led to believe that purchase must have come with a rider stipulating that the buyer was not allowed to watch the first ten minutes of the second half of any match, having instead to spend them consuming 'free' refreshments in the hospitality areas behind.

✪ Two bridges were built over the railway lines that separate the new and old grounds so that those coming from Arsenal tube station and the Highbury area could be spared a lengthy walk. However, promises that the facilities at the two nearest stations – Holloway Road on the Piccadilly Line, and Drayton Park on the overground from Highbury and Islington – would be improved never materialised. This has led to the absurdity of both stations being closed on match days even though more than 20,000 extra spectators are now attending Arsenal matches.

✪ By late 2007 the talk around Drayton Park was about the ownership of the club after the main Arsenal powerbroker of the previous twenty-five years, David Dein, sold his 14.5 per cent stake in the club to a billionaire Uzbek businessman, Alisher Usmanov, for £75 million in August of that year.

Dein had always been one of the more respected football tycoons and had presided over an era of astonishing success at Highbury. But he lost much credibility in backing Usmanov when he talked up the oligarch's knowledge of the club's history. When he was asked to name Arsenal's 2002 Double-winning side, Usmanov paused before searching through his briefing notes and offering a correct Vieira, Bergkamp, Sol Campbell and Wiltord, but a wrong Gilberto and Lehmann, and somehow forgetting the man who made it all possible, Thierry Henry. Next time, if there were a next time, he would be better briefed, but few would be impressed.

Holloway school, Hilldrop Road

Charlie George, Arsenal's most popular player in the 1970s, was expelled from this school at the age of fourteen and a half by the deputy head, Louis Watt, father of Tom Watt, the former *EastEnders* actor who is one of the club's leading celebrity fans. One of the PE coaches at the school in the 1960s was Bob Wilson, whom the young George knew through training at Arsenal and whom he called 'Bob' rather than 'Mr Wilson' to the amazement of fellow pupils.

→ Bob Wilson at Rutherford school, p. 133

SOUTH TOTTENHAM, N15

South Tottenham station, High Road

The train bearing the 1901 Tottenham team and the FA Cup, which the club had just won for the first time in a replay at Bolton on 27 April, arrived at the station at half past midnight, only a few hours after the end of the game. Outside the station the north London streets were thronged with fans celebrating the unlikely Tottenham victory, for the club was then in the Southern League, the equivalent of today's third tier, and had just beaten Sheffield United, champions of England only three years previously.

→ The 1901 FA Cup Final at the Crystal Palace, p. 184

TOTTENHAM, N17

Hotspur Football Club (Tottenham Hotspur) (1882–85), Marsh Lane

Tottenham Hotspur, London's second most successful club, were founded in summer 1882 when the Hotspur Cricket Club decided to set up a football team. Those involved were mostly old boys of Tottenham Grammar School or St John's Presbyterian School and initially they met under a gas lamp at the corner of Tottenham High Road and Park Lane.

The name 'Hotspur' came from Harry Hotspur, the nickname of Sir Henry Percy, rebel son of the Earl of Northumberland, whose family owned land locally and who was immortalised as a hardy soldier by Shakespeare in *Henry IV Part One*. Harry Hotspur was wont to say, 'By heaven, methinks it were an easy leap/To pluck bright honour from the pale-faced moon', a catchphrase which has not been heard as part of the fans' terrace chants to date.

To get to the pitch on Tottenham Marsh for their first recorded game, a 2–0 defeat to the Radicals, the Hotspur players had to cross the Great Eastern Railway, carrying the goalposts. The game may have taken place on 30 August, or possibly 30 September, 1882. Details have been lost, and knowledge of it only came to light at all when the club's accounts for the period were later discovered. Indeed the only records from the Hotspur club's early days are six pages torn from the original club book. In between games the railway authorities allowed them to store the equipment at Northumberland Park station.

In 1884 Hotspur became Tottenham Hotspur to end the confusion with another club, London Hotspur. They played their first competitive match a year later, beating St Albans 5–2 in the London Association Cup. Tottenham cancelled the last game of that season so that they could travel en masse to the Kennington Oval to watch Blackburn play Queen's Park in the FA Cup Final.

Soon the club had a new and more comfortable meeting place than a street corner by the Tottenham High Road: the YMCA building at Percy House. When a councillor went to check on the noise coming from the basement one day he was hit in the face by a ball and the organisation ejected Tottenham from the premises. The club moved its affairs to Dorset Villas, where use of the building came with an attached condition, namely that players and officials attended church every Wednesday. After two years of pious devotion some players were seen playing cards during a service and Tottenham were expelled from this venue as well. They then set up a new headquarters at the Red House, 748 Tottenham High Road, an address which at the time had no connection with their ground but later became the offices at their long-term home, White Hart Lane.

Playing on the marshes was in itself a problem. This was common land and anyone had a right to play there. Consequently the club could not charge for admission despite crowds of 4,000. They soon found a new ground nearby (see below).

Tottenham High Road

Bill Nicholson was happily married to his wife, Darkie, for over sixty years. She was a lovely lady, so down to earth. You'd see her cycling along Tottenham High Road and she'd give you a wave, or stop for a chat. She was totally different from Nick.

Alan Mullery, *The Autobiography*, 2006

Tottenham Hotspur (1885–98), south side of
Northumberland Park, west of Trulock Road

Tottenham Hotspur moved to a new ground where they could charge admission in 1885, playing their first match against Stratford St Johns. Most of their games in those days were friendlies, and not all were particularly successful. For instance, on 13 October 1888 Tottenham lost at home 8–0 to the Old Etonians.

It was at Northumberland Park on 10 November 1887 that Tottenham first played the team that were to become their biggest rivals: Arsenal (then Royal Arsenal). The game started late and was abandoned with fifteen minutes to go due to bad light, with Spurs winning 2–1. No other records were kept so the goalscorers remain unknown.

In 1892 Tottenham attempted to join the new Southern League, which would soon be of a standard almost in line with that of the Football League's Second Division, but received only one vote – their own. Instead they entered the lower-ranking Southern Alliance, where they played Erith, Slough, Windsor and Eton, Polytechnic, Old St Stephens and Upton Park.

Three years later Tottenham turned professional after a row over a pair of boots. A player called Ernie Payne joined Spurs from Fulham and turned up for his first match only to find his kit had disappeared. One of the Tottenham officials gave Payne ten shillings to go and buy a pair of boots, but when Fulham discovered what had happened they reported Spurs to the London Football Association for making 'financial inducements'. The London FA found Tottenham guilty and suspended them for two weeks. Spurs felt the FA's attitude over payments was unacceptable and in December 1895 turned professional. They now gained admittance into the Southern League that had earlier rejected them.

In 1898 the Northumberland Park ground was closed after fans attacked Luton players. During the visit of Woolwich Arsenal in April the following year spectators climbed on to the roof of the refreshment hut, which collapsed. It was time to find a bigger ground with better facilities, the club decided. A spare piece of land was found next to the White Hart pub and Tottenham moved to what has been their home since.

Tottenham Hotspur (1899–), 748 Tottenham High Road

Tottenham are the epitome of the badly managed, underachieving 'big' club forever dining out on past glories. Despite becoming the first team to win the Double of League Championship and FA Cup in the twentieth century, they have not won the League since, or even come close. Despite being the first British club to win a European trophy, they have only once played in the main European competition of the European Cup/European Champions League. Theirs has been a tale of missed opportunities and misguided intentions as the club's supporters have sought success with style over success *per se*, unable to grasp the notion that success can itself breed style as with Don Revie's Leeds or Alex Ferguson's Manchester United.

Seventeen years after forming under a gas lamp on Tottenham High Road, Tottenham Hotspur moved to a new, bigger ground at the rear of the White Hart pub. Conveniently, the club was already using part of the site, at 748 Tottenham High Road, for its offices. The surrounding land was a plant nursery, and contained greenhouses and sheds. It was owned by Charrington's Brewery, which allowed Spurs to use it provided they attracted a crowd of at least 1,000 for every match, a condition which they have managed to meet ever since.

The first game here saw Tottenham beat Notts County 4–1 in a friendly on 4 September 1899. The crowd numbered 5,000 and they watched from stands that had been moved from the previous ground. A year later Tottenham were champions of the Southern League, but more laudable was their winning of the FA Cup in 1901. After a 2–2 draw at the Crystal Palace (→ p. 184) against First Division Sheffield United, who had recently been champions, in front of a then world record attendance of more than 110,000, a replay was held at Bolton a few days later. Only 20,740 saw Spurs win 3–1 and back in London a crowd of 5,000 was watching the reserves play Gravesend at White Hart Lane. Special arrangements had been made to deliver a telegram to the ground every ten minutes with news from the replay. The final telegram reporting that Spurs had won the Cup was brought on to the pitch by a delirious official, even though the reserve match was still in progress. There were wild scenes of celebration, and on the main stand the Southern League championship flag was replaced with a stuffed cockerel bearing blue and white ribbons. Spurs are still the only non-League side since the Football League was formed to win the FA Cup.

Cock and ball

Winning the FA Cup allowed Tottenham to incorporate luxurious facilities at the ground. In 1904 they built a recreation club for the players, claiming: 'Here, the comforts of a home are provided and the men may read, write, play billiards or cards, as fancy takes them. Needless to say the club is greatly appreciated.' That year a reporter from C. B. Fry's magazine went to White Hart Lane to watch Sam Mountford take the team training. 'If a man wants to drink or smoke, no prohibition will prevent him,' Mountford said. When asked about the players' diet, he explained that 'they are never allowed to tire of any new dish'.

Election to the Football League came in 1908, and Spurs won promotion to the First Division at the first attempt in 1909, the year they adopted the cockerel and ball as their emblem. In 1913 Tottenham's status as North London's only major club ended when Woolwich Arsenal announced plans to move to Highbury. Spurs were mortified at the prospect. The *Tottenham Herald* newspaper ran a cartoon of Arsenal owner Henry Norris as the Hound of the Baskervilles about to attack the Tottenham cockerel and eat its food.

Tottenham could do nothing about the arrival of the South London team, and were powerless six years later to prevent Arsenal pipping them to an extra spot in the First Division. It was an extraordinary story. When football was stopped because of the First World War Spurs were bottom of the table. At the resumption of the game four years later the FA decided to increase the size of the top division. It looked likely that Spurs and Chelsea, who should have gone down, would earn a reprieve. Instead fierce lobbying by Arsenal's Henry Norris saw Arsenal win promotion at the expense of Tottenham, while to compound the ignominy Chelsea stayed up.

Nevertheless Spurs were good enough to win the Second Division in 1920 and the FA Cup again the following season. They reached the semifinal a year later and, back in the First Division, came second in the League behind Liverpool. By the mid-1920s Tottenham had become the most successful professional side London had ever seen, superior to Arsenal and Chelsea. But they were soon eclipsed once more by their neighbours who, under Herbert Chapman, a former Tottenham player, won the Championship and Cup a number of times in the 1930s, a decade during which Tottenham languished in the Second Division.

The power and the glory

Things improved immensely for Tottenham at the end of the 1940s. The catalyst was the appointment of Arthur Rowe as manager in 1949. Rowe devised a 'push and run' style of play which involved quickly laying the ball off to a team-mate and running past the marking tackler to collect the return pass. It was so successful Tottenham not only won the Second Division in 1950 but clinched their first Championship the next season. Tottenham couldn't capitalise on their new lofty status, however, and decline set in for the rest of the decade until the appointment of the dour Yorkshireman Bill Nicholson as manager in 1958.

Nicholson, who had played in Rowe's push-and-run teams, made an extraordinary start in his first game on 11 October. With defender Tommy Harmer restored to the team against Everton, they were 6–1 ahead at half-time and went on to win 10–4. Nicholson made inspirational signings and built a team laden with talent. There was the ultimate hard man in Scot Dave Mackay, a wonderful schemer in John White, and a master tactician in Danny Blanchflower. In autumn 1960 Tottenham won the first eleven League games of the season and went on to lift the Double of Championship and FA Cup in glorious style; not even Herbert Chapman's Arsenal, Stan Cullis's Wolves or Matt Busby's Manchester United had achieved that.

Six months after clinching the two trophies Bill Nicholson splashed out almost £100,000 on Jimmy Greaves, the most exciting young striker in the game. Greaves went on to become the club's record goalscorer but was unable to score the goals that could secure a championship medal. In the season after the Double Tottenham won the FA Cup again, while coming third in the League, and the following season an improvement to runners-up position was surpassed when the club became the first English side to win a European trophy – the European Cup Winners' Cup. Again Tottenham failed to consolidate their League success. Instead they became cup specialists (briefly) – even 1980s chairman Irving Scholar once admitted 'Spurs are really a Cup side' – while frustrating their fans by never rising above third place after 1963, even when the quality of their team on paper looked a match for anyone.

Unlike Matt Busby or Bill Shankly, Bill Nicholson failed to substitute one winning team with another. He failed to find equivalent-quality replacements for Danny Blanchflower or John White, the latter tragically killed on a golf course by lightning at the age of twenty-six. Even though more trophies came in the second half of Nicholson's tenure they were all cups: the FA Cup in 1967, the League Cup in 1971 and 1973, with the UEFA Cup in between.

Bill Nicholson resigned on 29 September 1974 following four consecutive League defeats and a few months after Tottenham lost to Feyenoord in the UEFA Cup Final, a match marred by crowd trouble which resulted in a life ban from Europe (overturned in 1980). Nicholson was sickened by the violence which marred that final and felt the modern game was running away from him. The reality was that his new batch of players – Neighbour, Holder, Naylor – were uninspiring and unmemorable.

Under Terry Neill Tottenham narrowly avoided relegation in 1975, and when Neill left for Arsenal, where he had been a player, Keith Burkinshaw took over. It was too late to redress the decline that had set in and in 1977 Tottenham went down, something that would have been unthinkable a few years previously.

Spurs bounced back immediately. They were rejuvenated by the young midfield prodigy Glenn Hoddle and boosted by the then startling signings of two Argentinian internationals, World Cup-winner Ossie Ardiles and squad player Ricky Villa. At that time there were no foreign superstars in the League, and some 10,000 fans turned up at the ground at a club open day in August 1978 to see the novelty of these two players training. The reporter from the *Guardian* couldn't contain himself and wrote: 'It was as if the janitor had gone out to buy a pot of paint and returned with a Velasquez.' Not that the new acquisitions were immediately successful. Their home debuts against Aston Villa on 23 August 1978 ended in a 4–1 defeat. A few weeks later they played in the Spurs team humiliated 7–0 by Liverpool. There were plenty who sneered at the signing of not just foreigners but Latin Americans in particular. Tommy Docherty said they'd be off at the first fall of snow, but when Tottenham played Bristol City on an ice rink of a frozen pitch Ricky Villa, according to his manager, 'stood up better than anybody else'.

Eventually Ardiles's and Villa's presence paid off. Surprisingly, the Spurs board stuck with the manager who took them down in 1977. Keith Burkinshaw rewarded them by becoming the second most successful manager in their history. The board allowed him time, unflustered by mid-table finishes back in the top division. By the beginning of the 1980s Burkinshaw's hard work was beginning to pay off. Tottenham were a formidable outfit. In attack they had a vibrant partnership of the ginger Scot Steve Archibald, and the silken-tongued and smooth-passing Garth Crooks. Behind them were Hoddle, Ardiles and the hard-working Steve Perryman. A new era of success followed with successive FA Cup wins in 1981 and 1982, the former won by Ricky Villa after a mazy run towards goal. There were consistently high League placings (regularly above Arsenal for once) and the enviable capturing of the UEFA Cup in 1984 at a time when the competition was almost on a par with the European Cup. But Burkinshaw quit at the height of his success, sickened by the board's decision to sell some of his best players while wasting vast sums on advertising. His parting shot remains a classic: 'There used to be a football club over there.'

Burkinshaw's replacement, Peter Shreeve, was a poor choice. He took Tottenham nowhere and was sacked after two seasons. His successor, David Pleat, was a considerable improvement and quickly built a high-octane team. Tottenham thrilled football fans in 1987, finishing third in the League, reaching the FA Cup Final and showcasing, in Clive Allen, one of the most prolific goalscorers in modern football. Typically things soon started to go wrong, though. David Pleat was caught kerb-crawling in autumn 1987 and was forced to resign. His team turned out to be the last great Spurs side.

Just a spoonful of sugar

There was much triumphing when Terry Venables, former player and larger than life personality, took over in November 1987. Venables was treated like a returning hero but he hadn't always been so fêted by the Spurs fans. When he joined the club in 1966 from Chelsea, where the manager, Tommy Docherty, could no longer tolerate a 23-year-old acting as if he were the boss, Tottenham fans saw him as a poor replacement for the late John White. To them he was a Chelsea dilettante who would not be prepared to get stuck in and they nicknamed him 'Terry Vegetables'.

Now Venables was back, as manager. The Tottenham fans and media heralded him as a tactical genius who would soon lead the club to new heights. They glossed over the way he had abandoned the so-called 'Team of the Eighties', Crystal Palace. They ignored the fact that his pampered Barcelona had become the only team ever to lose a European Cup Final to an army side.

There were comparisons with his great friend and former team-mate George Graham, then manager at Arsenal. Venables announced that he had come to Spurs to win the First Division: 'I need it. I desperately want to do it, and I know it has to be next season.' But it was Arsenal not Tottenham who won the title in 1989. At Tottenham Venables failed to deliver. Departing quality players were replaced by second-raters: Terry Fenwick for Richard Gough; Bobby Mimms for Ray Clemence.

In Venables's first season Tottenham finished thirteenth. They went out of the FA Cup embarrassingly to lowly Port Vale. Under his tutelage there were no championships or European trophy to rival those won by Graham at Highbury. Spurs' League position declined from top-four finishes under the previous two regimes to mostly mid-table anonymity. In four seasons with Venables as manager there was only the FA Cup success of 1991 to silence the sceptics.

Behind the scenes Tottenham were a byword for administrative and financial turmoil. In 1982 diehard fan Irving Scholar, a Monte Carlo-based property tycoon, had bought the club. He was shocked at the level of financial incompetence he found: big debts, wads of banknotes lying about the ticket office. Scholar put considerable effort into developing the club's business strategy, its marketing wing and merchandise side. He wiped out the debt, raised the money to build a new stand, and in 1983 made Spurs the first League side to register with the stock market.

It was of little help. Scholar tried to rearrange the structure of the club so that Tottenham on the pitch was just one part of a grand leisure business, whereas in reality the playing fortunes of Tottenham Hotspur dictate the success (or otherwise) of all the off-the-pitch ephemera – the shirts, duvet covers and cuckoo clocks. Despite the administrative changes and the rewards of playing in the top flight season after season Tottenham could still not get their bureaucracy running smoothly. On 27 August 1988, while the rest of the football world were getting their season under way, Spurs had to call off their home game against Coventry City because they could not get a safety certificate for their newly built stand. In 1990 Scholar naively approached the corrupt publishing tycoon Robert Maxwell, well known for his crooked dealings, for financial help. Maxwell loaned the board £1.1 million to buy Gary Lineker. For a while it looked as if Maxwell was going to buy the club, a move which Spurs fans vehemently opposed. Fortunately for them the Mirror Newspapers mogul died at sea in mysterious circumstances in 1991.

A new administrative overlord did appear. Astonishingly it was Terry Venables himself. In June 1991 Venables went from boss to baron and took over the club with the help of Alan Sugar, the computer magnate, who staved off imminent bankruptcy. Sugar became the largest shareholder of the plc and non-executive chairman, while Venables promoted himself to non-executive managing director and chief executive. He intended to spend less time with the team from now on and more time running the business side of the club.

Tottenham had just won a major trophy, the FA Cup. What they needed was stability. If they couldn't avoid selling their best players like Waddle and Gascoigne to finance the club at least they could appoint a manager to create a dynasty à la Alex Ferguson at Manchester United. Instead the Venables/Sugar partnership got off to a terrible start with the appointment of the squeaky-voiced Peter Shreeves as team manager. He had briefly served as stand-in manager after Keith Burkinshaw resigned in 1984 but had proved to be sub-standard and been sacked.

Now Spurs finished fifteenth, and Shreeves was replaced with Doug Livermore and Ray Clemence for the 1992–93 season. Soon things were so bad that fans began clamouring for the return of the good old days under Shreeves. And things started to go seriously wrong off the pitch too. Sugar and Venables often clashed, and at a board meeting on 6 May 1993 Sugar turned sour. His first target was the barrister Jonathan Crystal, who had criticised the club's purchasing of Sugar's Amstrad computers. As Crystal poured himself a cup of tea, Sugar turned on him with the kind of unambiguous clarity that has made him infamous in business: 'We ain't spunking money on fuckin' lawyers. You ain't going to spunk any more of my money up the wall,' he raged. He then continued more noisily, 'You fucking cunt, you fucking cunt, you fucking arse-licking cunt' – a reference to Crystal's perceived obsequiousness when dealing with Venables.

Sugar had by now realised what most Tottenham fans have yet to grasp, namely that Venables is more mess than Messiah, and demanded

Venables's resignation. Sugar told journalists: 'I should have done more due diligence on him. He had no business acumen at all. He started to dabble in things beyond his comprehension.' The Spurs fans, always quick to back the wrong horse, rounded on Sugar. Some even tried to barricade him in his Essex mansion. 'I feel like the man who shot Bambi,' he wailed.

Sugar brought in yet another new manager – Ossie Ardiles. His first and only full season was disastrous, and only a 2–0 away win at Oldham in May 1994 staved off relegation. On 17 June, a few days after Arsenal won the European Cup Winners' Cup, Tottenham were again caught up in financial woe. This time the FA charged them with misconduct for making allegedly irregular payments to a number of players between 1985 and 1989. The FA fined the club £600,000, expelled them from the FA Cup and deducted them twelve league points in the following season. And Tottenham needed the points. During the 1994 season they had won only four home games. It was a brutal punishment and Alan Sugar immediately announced an appeal. The outcome was that the points deduction was halved to six, the fine increased to £1,500,000, but the Cup ban remained. Eventually the points deduction and the Cup ban were both lifted, but not the fine.

That July Ardiles staged a transfer coup to match his own signing in 1978: the purchase of German World Cup-winning striker Jürgen Klinsmann. This was a man notorious for falling to the ground when an opponent ventured near him. He scored on his debut and promptly 'dived' in celebration, immediately winning over thousands of sceptics. However, in true Spurs fashion the benefits of Klinsmann's arrival were nullified by Ardiles's absurd decision to play him as part of a five-man forward line. Goals went in with carefree abandon at both ends, but a little too many at the back and a little too few at the front. Ardiles's Subbuteo-style system soon foundered and he was removed that November. Yet another change of manager.

Under Gerry Francis, who took over in November 1994, the playing style was reversed. Gone was the attacking flair, and defence, not usually a Tottenham priority, became the driving force behind the team. It worked for a while as Tottenham reached the semi-final of a cup from which they had initially been banned. However, a 4–1 defeat to Everton at the last four stage led Klinsmann to announce his departure. Sugar was furious, seeing the player's decision as an act of betrayal. Klinsmann simply wanted one last chance to win a championship medal and didn't relish the prospect of playing beyond the telegram-from-the-Queen age to do so at Tottenham. When he asked Sugar if he could keep a 'Klinsmann 18' shirt as a memento, he was told to pay for it in full.

To Francis money was evidently something to be wasted on second-rate players. And so £3.75 million went on Ramon Vega, £2.6 million on John Scales and astonishingly £4.5 million on Chris Armstrong. The team went nowhere and Francis quit in November 1997.

Why Tottenham don't do very well

In *Association Football and the Men Who Made It* the authors Alfred Gibson and William Pickford raved in 1908: 'Than the famous Spurs there is probably no more popular club in England. Do they not play pretty and effective football? Are they not scrupulously fair? Are they not perfectly managed?' The answer has to be: No.

✪ After Tottenham won the UEFA Cup in 1972, back in the days when it was the hardest of the European trophies to win, manager Bill Nicholson came into the team's dressing room at the end of the game. But rather than celebrating euphorically he told the Spurs players: 'I've just been in the Wolves dressing room. I told them they were the better team. You lot were lucky. The best team lost tonight.' Two years later Nicholson, the most successful manager in Tottenham's history, resigned, admitting he'd lost the support of his players.

✪ Leaving Tottenham for the last time in August 1977, after being released because the board thought he was finished as a player, goalkeeper Pat Jennings made his way through the car park. He walked past all the directors, not one of whom even acknowledged his presence despite his ten years' sterling service during which Spurs had won four major trophies. A few weeks later Jennings signed for Arsenal with whom he played in four cup finals.

✪ In the mid-1980s the club passed up the chance of signing David Rocastle from Arsenal before George Graham became manager. Having not learned their lesson, a couple of years later they turned down the opportunity to sign Lee Dixon from Stoke. No such caution, however, prevented them from taking on Steve Sedgeley, Ramon Vega or Chris Armstrong.

⊗ 1–0 up at half-time during the League Cup semi-final against Arsenal in 1987, and carrying a 1–0 win from the first leg, the club announced over the tannoy arrangements to buy tickets for the final. The Arsenal players hearing this in their dressing room needed no greater incentive and turned the game around, and went on to Wembley.

⊗ In June 1996 Alan Sugar showed that despite his sound judgement on matters of business and apprenticeship his knowledge of football was paltry. Commenting on the arrival of Dennis Bergkamp at Arsenal he claimed: 'There's no way he's going to have the same impact as Klinsmann. If Bergkamp thinks he is going to set the world alight he can forget it. There is no way it is going to happen.' At Arsenal Dennis Bergkamp won the League three times and the FA Cup four. At Tottenham Klinsmann won nothing. Bergkamp has gone down in football lore as one of the greatest players to grace the game. Klinsmann may have won the European Championship, World Cup and thrilled millions but he wasn't exactly in the Dennis Bergkamp league.

⊗ Despite an almost complete absence of silverware in sixteen years since the 1991 FA Cup, Tottenham fans mostly refuse to acknowledge winning the 1999 League Cup as it was achieved under an 'Arsenal man', George Graham.

⊗ Tottenham, alone of the ninety-two League clubs, deployed until recently a continental-style management system in which a director of football chooses which players to buy and the manager selects from a squad he has little control over. The system, introduced at the beginning of the twenty-first century, was singularly unsuccessful for a club that once regularly won trophies. It was shown not to work in the summer of 2007 when manager Martin Jol identified a need for a creative midfield player, a left-winger and a proven centre-half. Instead the directorate of football at

White Hart Lane bought him an unknown German youngster for midfield, a pubescent left-back, a tyro centre-half who couldn't cope in the Premier League, and an overpriced striker who couldn't be accommodated in the team. The outcome was less than impressive, but it was Jol who took the blame with the sack.

Grossing out

Francis's replacement was the unknown Swiss Christian Gross. The rationale behind his appointment seemed to be little more than 'Arsenal have prospered under an obscure continental [Arsene Wenger], obviously Tottenham will now do likewise.' Gross soon showed his prowess in making people laugh, if not in making his team play better. He turned up at his first press conference brandishing a tube ticket and promising to bring 'zree zings to ze club – 'ard verk, 'ard verk, 'ard verk'. By the end of the season Spurs looked as if they might be relegated despite the unexpected return of Jürgen Klinsmann. Only a 6–2 victory at Wimbledon in May kept them up.

By September 1998 Christian Gross had used his tube ticket for the last time. David Pleat returned as caretaker manager, but Gross's permanent replacement caused the greatest shock to Spurs fans in the club's history. It was none other than George Graham – 'Gorgeous George' – the sharp-suited, tactically brilliant, no-nonsense former boss at Arsenal whom he had managed to six major trophies before being sacked for accepting a financial gift. The Tottenham fans were devastated. Some wrongly castigated Graham as a 'long ball' merchant whose idea of entertainment was to watch a defender hoof the ball fifty yards in the sky and the strikers chase after it. The reality was that George Graham's sides had been as attack-minded as Tottenham's. His midfield had bristled with quality. His Arsenal teams had scored more goals than Spurs. Except that Graham understood that no matter how many a team score, if they concede more they will lose. Eventually they will get relegated. They will be playing back on the marshes watched by a couple of passing dog-walkers rather than in a smart stadium in front of 40,000 fans. With George Graham in charge of Tottenham success would surely follow – but it would forever be tainted in the eyes of the supporters with Arsenalness.

Graham made an immediate impression, or as the *Daily Express* put it: 'Graham already looks and talks the part of the Tottenham manager. Compare his suave sophistication on the White Hart Lane touchline with the eccentric appearance of David Pleat, who looked as if he had been dragged from the river-bank clutching a fishing rod minutes before kick-off.' Graham soon began curing Tottenham of their traditional sicknesses. The club's lengthy injury list magically shortened overnight when 'unfit' players learned that they had to report in for training regardless. The players began to play for the shirt. They worked hard. They ground out results. They turned into a football team. The fans were slightly, very slightly mollified, singing: 'Man in a raincoat's blue and white army'. (They couldn't quite bring themselves to sing his name.)

Sure enough, in his first season George Graham brought them a trophy – the League Cup. Of course the fans were not entirely satisfied and moaned instead about Graham's sale of their favourite, the flamboyant fancy-dan David Ginola. Sugar, who had continued to be subjected to abuse, by 2001 had had enough and sold up to the leisure group ENIC. Meanwhile, George Graham was undermined and sacked in spring 2001.

For reasons unknown and inexplicable, perhaps seduced by his playing record, for it could not have been by his managerial abilities, Tottenham fans heralded the arrival of Glenn Hoddle as boss. They sang lustily 'We've got our Tottenham back.' Hoddle's first significant act was to lose to Arsenal in the FA Cup semi-final in spring 2001. He lacked the nous to take the club further. When they reached the League Cup Final in 2002 they lost easily to Blackburn. After finishing tenth in 2003 Hoddle wasted the club's meagre resources that summer buying two substandard strikers: Helder Postiga (19 appearances, 1 goal) and Bobby Zamora (16 appearances, 0 goals). By mid-September Hoddle was gone. The players publicly criticised his management style and communication skills. There were no more songs about getting 'our' Tottenham back.

David Pleat took over as caretaker (again) until a full-time successor could be found, but Spurs couldn't even get the process for that right, let alone the choice of personnel. In June 2004 there was a perplexing restructuring of the backroom staff as Tottenham excessively appointed *three* heavy-duty foreigners to head the management team, introducing a continental-style system that has been of little benefit to the club. Frank

Arnesen arrived as sporting director, with ex-France manager Jacques Santini (not one of those who had taken the national team to their recent trophies) as head coach and Martin Jol 'assistant to the manager' as later echoed by the *nebisch* Gareth in the sitcom *The Office*.

Jol never stood much chance. Within weeks he had been undermined by the appointment of Dominique Cuperly to a similar role. Arnesen persuaded Jol to stay, but he was soon gone himself, as was Santini. Jol became manager, but he was hamstrung by a system that ranked him below sporting director Damien Comolli. Jol, well someone, did bring about improvements to Tottenham's League position. Top-four status throughout 2004–05, which would have seen Tottenham enter the European Champions League, possibly at the expense of Arsenal, vanished on the last day of the season when the club's game against West Ham was ruined after a number of their players contracted gastroenteritis. Spurs lost much credibility by trying to get the game played after Arsenal's so that they would know what result they needed to finish higher. The Premier League refused to postpone the game and Tottenham lost to West Ham, thus ending the season fifth – with no Champions League football to look forward to.

'There always seems to be a good reason why "next year" will be the one when the team really clicks.' So wrote Alex Flynn and H. Davidson in 1996 in *Dream On*, their book on a year in the life of Tottenham Hotspur. This sentiment has been present at the club since they somehow missed out on all three domestic trophies in 1987, and it reappears at the end of every season with increasing monotony, doing so particularly at the end of 2006–07 when a repeat of the previous season's fifth place was followed by much media harrumphing of how Tottenham were about to break into what was looking like a closed shop at the top of the League at Arsenal's expense. Yet during the first fifteen League games of 2007–08 Tottenham won only twice while Arsenal remained unbeaten. Jol was undermined at the beginning of the season when Levy and Comolli were caught meeting Seville's manager, Juande Ramos. Tottenham kept on losing and the inevitable happened: Jol was sacked and Ramos appointed.

Surely with a manager as capable as Juande Ramos in charge Tottenham would soon be back up the table challenging for fifth spot? In his first season Ramos secured a trophy – the League Cup. It was not quite the Double of days of yore but it was more than Arsenal were capable of. However, the Spaniard's tenure was a false dawn. The start of the 2009 season saw Tottenham manage only two points from their first eight games. Ramos was ousted along with sporting director Damien Comolli. Yet another new manager, or rather a dog-eared one in the shape of the inimitable Harry Redknapp. Spurs climbed the table, reached the League Cup Final (this time losing) and began to look like a proper team again.

Tottenham off the bench

✪ Tottenham's stadium was originally known as the High Road Ground. The club favoured calling it Percy Park, in honour of their founding spirit, Sir Henry Percy, also known as Harry Hotspur. Another suggestion was Gilpin Park. After the Great War it became known as White Hart Lane, even though the title is a misnomer as the road of that name is some distance away.

✪ In 1908 on the ship returning from a tour of Argentina a fancy-dress contest was held and two of the Tottenham squad, dressed as Robinson Crusoe and Man Friday, accompanied by a parrot, won. They took the parrot back to the club, but when Arsenal beat Spurs to a place in the First Division in 1919 the bird immediately dropped dead, thereby giving rise to the footballing expression 'sick as a parrot'.

✪ The club's cockerel and ball emblem first appeared in 1909 when a former player, W. J. Scott, cast a copper centrepiece to perch on the new West Stand. Harry Hotspur, after whom the club was named, wore spurs while leading his troops into battle, as did fighting cockerels.

✪ During the First World War the Ministry of Munitions requisitioned Tottenham's ground to make 11 million gas masks.

✪ In 1935 the German national team played England for the first time, not at Wembley but at White Hart Lane. A week before the December match the Trades Union Congress asked the FA to ban the game to prevent thousands of Germans marching through London displaying the swastika. The FA refused to do so and the Germans arrived *en masse* but played down the Nazi stuff. They even brought with them a six-foot-long laurel wreath commemorating the war dead of 1914–18, which they placed on the Cenotaph. But their sentiments weren't entirely honourable. With the imminent war in mind many of them were armed with binoculars and cameras taking photos that would aid pilots of fighting planes bombing London a few years later. For the only time at a British football ground the swastika flew, which was somewhat ironic given Tottenham's long-standing Jewish support.

✪ In November 1945 White Hart Lane played host to a remarkable match between Arsenal, bombed out of their Highbury home, and the touring Moscow Dynamo side. The game was a friendly but it took place at a time when there were no matches against European teams, and attracted considerable interest from the press and public. So thick was the fog the crowd booed and slow handclapped as the game wore on. Refereeing was impossible. Though George Drury was sent off for fighting, he stayed on the field and simply spent the rest of the match on the other side of the pitch away from the ref.

At half-time the Russians went into the dressing room, picked up their tea, flung it across the room in disgust, and took out the vodka. The farce continued into the second half in which Moscow fielded twelve players. After the game Stanley Matthews, who had guested for Arsenal, was chatting to a fan who expressed surprise that Matthews was there at all, having not been able to spot the great winger on the pitch in the pea-souper. Moscow won 4–3.

✪ Arriving to play at White Hart Lane for the first time in 1957 at the age of seventeen, Jimmy Greaves was eyed up and down by the doorman. 'I know what you're thinking,' declared Greaves. 'You know you're getting older when the players look younger at the start of every new season.' The sour-faced attendant quickly replied: 'I know I'm getting older when the Popes look younger.'

✪ During Tottenham's 1962 run to the European Cup semi-finals in their only season in the competition, assistant manager Harry Evans sat the players down and told them that the club had reached a 'crossroads'. He explained that 'one road will take us to glory and success, but the other leads to a dead end'. The room went quiet, and captain Danny Blanchflower looked in deep thought. 'That's not a crossroads,' he finally said, 'it's a T-junction.'

✪ John White, the club's revered early 1960s midfield creator, was killed by lightning on Crews Hill golf course in Enfield on 21 July 1964. Sheltering from a thunderstorm, he had taken refuge under an oak tree. It's possible that it was his wedding ring that conducted the electricity. Bill Nicholson and White's widow had to identify the body.

✪ In 1986 Izzy Brown, a New Jersey shopping mall magnate, turned his attention to buying the club, announcing predictable plans to turn White Hart Lane into a leisureplex and shopping mall. Brown chomped his way through the share option, buying at the bargain price of 54p. In classic American franchise fashion, he announced that he had no particular interest in Spurs, but that he simply wanted to buy a First Division club, and Tottenham were the only one for sale. Brown was unable to secure more than 14 per cent of the issue and disappeared from view.

Further north

BARNET

Barnet, Underhill Stadium, Barnet Lane

One of the most successful of the new breed of clubs that have risen from non-League obscurity since automatic promotion to the League was introduced in the mid-1980s, Barnet have enjoyed near-uninterrupted League status despite the proximity of mass-supported clubs such as Arsenal and Tottenham, and despite playing at what is one of the smallest grounds in the League.

A club called Barnet was formed in 1888 but disbanded three years later for breaking FA rules. Rivals Barnet Avenue took over the name in 1903, and four years later Barnet Alston began playing. In 1912 Alston and Avenue merged to become Barnet and Alston, and simply Barnet from 1919.

Barnet won the first post-war Amateur Cup in 1946 and the Athenian League seven times in all before 1965, when they turned professional. In their new guise Barnet joined the high-standing Southern League which they immediately won. Barnet also profited from the introduction of the FA Trophy in 1969. They reached the semi-final during the Cup's first year and lost in the final two years later. In the mid-1970s the club featured a number of famous names at the end of their careers including Marvin Hinton, Bob McNab and even Jimmy Greaves.

Under the management of the colourful Barry Fry, in the following decade Barnet elevated themselves to the point where accession to the Football League looked imminent. A succession of near misses culminated in promotion in 1991, but Barnet have yet to escape the cycle of promotion from the fourth tier to the third, followed by inevitable relegation back to the fourth.

Barnet off the bench

✪ In October 1946 Underhill was the setting for the BBC's first live televised match when twenty minutes of the first half of the game against Wealdstone and thirty-five minutes of the second half were shown before it became too dark.

✪ The club's League days have been dominated by two extrovert characters: serial manager Barry Fry and chairman Stan Flashman. Fry was a 'Busby babe' who was once George Best's drinking partner. The late Flashman was the country's leading ticket tout who claimed he could obtain entrance for almost anything, from cup finals to Buckingham Palace garden parties. Flashman became chairman in 1985, buying the club for £50,000, and he presided over Barnet's rise into the League. He was also responsible for sacking Fry some twenty times (and reappointing him, inevitably) although Fry often took no notice of him. One who did take notice of Flashman was striker Harry Willis. After playing poorly in one game he was sitting in the dressing room when Flashman came in and thundered: 'Willis, you were hopeless today. You'll never play for Barnet again.' Fry interjected: 'Yes he will, Stan. He's playing against Watford in the Herts Senior Cup on Friday.' Flashman retorted: 'If you turn up on Friday, Willis, I'll break your legs with a cricket bat.' According to Barry Fry the club smuggled Willis into the ground, which was fortunate as he scored a hat-trick in a 5–2 win.

4   North-west London

No League club plays in the wealthy north-west London neighbourhoods such as Hampstead and St John's Wood, but through the good fortune of being host to the national football stadium, Wembley (despite its lack of charm and amenities), this has become one of the most famous areas of the capital.

CAMDEN, NW1

Euston station

When Arsenal decided to give a trial to the Workington winger 'Midget' Moffatt in 1923, they sent a telegram inviting him to London, with details of the train he should take. When the 11.30 train arrived at Euston station, however, there was no sign of the player, and the annoyed Arsenal manager, Leslie Knighton, headed off to Highbury to begin the day's work. When he arrived at the ground the doorman told him there was 'a little tiny chap asleep in the dressing room'. Moffatt had taken an earlier train and gone straight to what he hoped was the ground – at Woolwich – unaware that the club had moved to Highbury. In Woolwich there was no trace of a football club, and no one could understand his accent apart from a road sweeper who took pity on the Scot and drove him all the way to Highbury in his van, the first time Moffatt had been in a motorised vehicle. Arsenal signed the 5ft outside-right, much to the displeasure of the club's capricious owner, Henry Norris, who had outlawed signings shorter than 5´ 8" and immediately sold Moffatt on to Luton before he played a League game.

Officials from Arsenal and Bolton met at the Euston Hotel, a sumptuous building which adjoined the station prior to 1960s redevelopment, when the London club were trying to sign the Lancashire side's star centre-forward, David Jack, in autumn 1928. Bolton wanted Arsenal to pay at least double the existing record fee of £6,500, and as negotiations were going nowhere officials from both clubs agreed to meet at the hotel. For Arsenal's directors it was the chance to set in motion a fiendish plan. They arrived half an hour early, found a friendly looking waiter, and placed two pound notes in his hand. Herbert Chapman, the Arsenal manager, explained to the man: 'I shall drink gin and tonic. Mr Wall [the Arsenal secretary] whisky and dry ginger. When our guests arrive you are to serve them whatever they ask – in trebles. Meanwhile, Mr Wall's whisky and gingers will contain not a drop of whisky, and my gin and tonics will contain no gin.'

Bolton's directors arrived off their train on time and before long were merrily bantering with their north London counterparts whose mildly drunken bonhomie was a masquerade. Soon Bolton were accepting all Arsenal's demands and selling Jack for just £10,000, well short of their original asking price, but still the highest fee ever paid for a player at that time.

Chelsea, shockingly, temporarily purloined London as their personal fiefdom on 30 April 1970 after winning the FA Cup in a replay at Old Trafford, as if they were the official London team. After journeying south with the trophy, they disembarked from the 12.44 to find more than a thousand fans at the station to greet them and thousands more lining the route from Euston to Fulham Town Hall where the official reception was to be held.

Walking through the station concourse in the late 1970s England World Cup hero Geoff Hurst was stopped by three tramps. One said to him: 'You're what's his name, that golfer, aren't you?' The second one countered: 'No, you're that footballer, ain't you?' The third realised it was Geoff Hurst. 'I remember I was away when you scored that hat-trick in the World Cup Final.' 'Somewhere nice?' asked Hurst. 'Portugal? The Costa Brava?' 'Nah,' replied the tramp, 'Pentonville.'

→ Peter Storey goes to jail, p. 86

Rutherford school, Penfold Street, Marylebone

Bob Wilson, a young up-and-coming goalkeeper on Arsenal's books in 1963, was also a teacher at Rutherford, and when he was called up to play for the first time reporters and photographers descended on the school. 'Arsenal Call Up Amateur Schoolmaster' ran the headlines the next day alongside pictures of 'Mr Wilson' in the playground.

A few days later, on 26 October, Wilson made his debut against Nottingham Forest. Only hours earlier he had refereed a school match at Wormwood Scrubs. When that game ended he had rushed off to Highbury but hadn't dared tell anyone how he had spent his morning in case the manager decided he wouldn't be fresh and dropped him. The game ended in a 4–2 win for Arsenal. Wilson signed as a professional for the club in February 1964 and starred in the Double team of 1971. Arsenal players had been bemused by their educated team-mate since he joined the club. 'He was the only one of us who could do joined-up writing,' Double-winning Frank McLintock once joked.

White House Hotel, Albany Street

One of football's most surprising transfers, that of World Cup-winner Alan Ball from Everton to Arsenal, took place at the hotel on 22 December 1971. Ball left Merseyside after Everton manager Harry Catterick summoned him to his office to announce that he was being dropped after a home defeat to Derby and that the club was prepared to release him. Ball, with his white boots and column in *Shoot*, was a major star at that time and even considered to be a fashionable dresser, this being a few decades before he took to wearing an old man's flat cap. But Arsenal were a surprising choice as his new club. They didn't sign major internationals in those days, despite being reigning champions and Cup holders, yet now they were prepared to pay out a record British fee of £220,000 to secure Ball, even though he was ineligible for the European Cup. Ball told the press: 'I am sure I will fit in quickly at Arsenal. They are a workmanlike side who play for each other, and that will suit me fine.' The transfer was only partly successful: Ball continued to play top-class football but won nothing at Arsenal.

A year later Arsenal sold George Graham, whom Ball had replaced, at the same hotel. Graham later recalled that Bertie Mee handled the transfer with 'absolute class.' The manager told him: 'George, we are accepting bids for you and we have set a price of £120,000. Three clubs have offered the asking price – West

Ham, Everton and Manchester United. I have organised a room at the White House Hotel so that you can meet the three managers at your convenience.' Graham chose Manchester United, where he later captained them to relegation.

→ Roasting at the Grosvenor House Hotel, p. 24

CRICKLEWOOD, NW2

Hendon (1926–), Claremont Road

One of London's most successful non-League teams, Hendon began as Christ Church Hampstead in 1908 and soon became Hampstead Town. Progress through the local leagues led them to apply to join the Isthmian League in 1963. They were rejected, but were accepted into the Athenian League in 1914. In 1926 Hampstead Town moved to their current home, Claremont Road, and seven years later changed their name to Golders Green even though the council wanted Hendon Borough. Another switch of name, to Hendon, came in 1946.

The club's greatest years soon followed. In 1951 Hendon reached the Amateur Cup semi-final but they missed a last-minute penalty and lost the replay. Four years later Hendon made it to the final at Wembley, where 100,000 saw them lose 2–0 to Bishop Auckland. In 1960 came Amateur Cup success at last, this time at the expense of Kingstonian. This was rewarded three years later with promotion to the Isthmian League. Hendon prospered at this level, securing the title and Amateur Cup in 1965. A third Amateur Cup triumph was achieved in 1972 against Enfield, and two years later Hendon took five-times FA Cup-winners Newcastle to a replay in the third round. Two seasons later came a first win against League opposition – Reading.

Since the creation in 1986 of the League pyramid to help part-time clubs rise up the divisions Hendon have failed to capitalise on their earlier standing and have yet to make it into the Conference (the fifth division) or its successors.

Mezzaluna, 424 Finchley Road

When former Arsenal manager George Graham walked into the restaurant in spring 1995, a few months after his sacking from Arsenal for taking a bung, he was greeted by a party of friends that included Terry Venables, then England manager, who presented Graham with a cake in the shape of a football pitch and quipped: 'This is an unsolicited gift.'

→ **George Graham takes a bung, p. 25**

Welsh Harp Ground, North Circular Road at Welsh Harp Reservoir

The Chelsea youth team trained at the Welsh Harp Ground in the mid-twentieth century at a time when they had one of the best reputations in the country for nurturing young players. This came about through an advert the club placed in the press asking schoolboys who thought they had sufficient talent to apply to the club for a trial. Thousands responded and the number was whittled down to thirty-two, from which a junior team, Tudor Rose, was selected. The Chelsea youth team manager was Dickie Foss, who used to greet new players with a beer and the quip: 'I only drink twice a day – when I'm thirsty and when I'm not.' Chelsea's youth system paid off, for in 1955 manager Ted Drake took the club to their first Championship using a number of players – 'Drake's Ducklings' – who had graduated through the youth ranks.

Tommy Docherty signed Peter Osgood for Chelsea as a teenager after watching him for forty-five minutes in a trial game at the Welsh Harp Ground. 'I knew I had to sign him there and then,' Docherty later explained. 'We did the deal at half-time and the fee was £15 – the best bit of business I did. Osgood was different class, up there with Gianfranco Zola and the rest among the very best in Chelsea's history. It was an insult to his ability that he won only four England caps.'

→ **West Ham's Manor Park training ground, p. 70**

HENDON, NW4

Hendon Hall Hotel, Ashley Lane

The England team used this hotel as a base during the 1966 World Cup, and stayed here throughout that decade before playing matches at Wembley, or before flying off from London airport for overseas games. In May 1964 before an away match in Portugal the team booked into the Hendon Hall. Desperate for something to do outside the confines of the hotel, a group of players including Jimmy Greaves, Bobby Charlton and Gordon Banks sneaked out to the local pub. They returned at midnight only to find that manager Alf Ramsey had placed each player's passport on his pillow. The guilty men spent a fretful night wondering what would happen to them. In the morning they were summoned before Ramsey, who told them: 'Gentlemen, I didn't tell you not to go for a drink, I just expected you not to go . . . we are going to win the World Cup.'

Just before England began their 1966 World Cup campaign there was one small matter to sort out: Bobby Moore's contract. The England captain was refusing to sign again for West Ham, and without a club he would be ineligible under FIFA rules to play in the finals. After some debate Moore agreed to sign a temporary contract just for the month of July, which would cover him for the tournament. The West Ham manager, Ron Greenwood, rushed over to the Hendon Hall Hotel with the forms and Moore put pen to paper just in time to claim eligibility.

The players' attempts to relax while staying here occasionally ended in farce. One night reserve goalkeeper Ron Springett, the squad's practical joker, discovered that Nobby Stiles had bought his wife, Kay, some lingerie. When Stiles went to the bar, Springett nipped into his room, 'borrowed' the item, and waited for the midfield maestro to return upstairs. Eventually Stiles did and once he had settled down in the room he was sharing with Alan Ball, Springett, having slipped into the little number, came cavorting in only to find Stiles on the phone to Mrs Stiles at the time trying to explain what had happened to the present he had bought her.

An hour before kick-off for the opening game of the '66 World Cup – England *v* Uruguay – the referee, Istvan Zsolt, came into the Wembley dressing room and announced he would be checking the players' ID cards. This was a precaution the authorities had introduced to prevent countries fielding players banned from taking part or from 'borrowing' superior players from those who hadn't qualified. Alas, Harold Shepherdson, the England trainer, had left the players' credentials at the Hendon Hall Hotel. With everyone in a panic a dispatch rider was sent to collect them. The courier had to ride on the wrong side of the road to get back to the ground before kick-off.

On the evening before the World Cup Final, manager Alf Ramsey took the players out of the hotel to watch the film *Those Magnificent Men in Their Flying Machines*. Alan Ball recalled how as the curtain came down, 'the entire picture house rose to us and applauded. One of the lads then said to me: "We can't lose it for these people."'

→ *The Arsenal Stadium Mystery*, p. 102

Wingate (1946–72), Hall Lane

Jewish sportsmen founded a club to play at senior amateur level immediately after the Second World War as a way of combating anti-Semitism. The founders, who included a future mayor of Finchley in Frank Davis and a Jewish army major, Harry Sadow, named the club, strangely, after a non-Jewish army chief, Major-General Orde Wingate, who had worked with Jewish soldiers in the Holy Land during the war. The club rose through the non-League ranks, and even made it into the Athenian League in 1964. They played at Hall Lane, a ground the England team occasionally trained on when they were staying at the nearby Hendon Hall Hotel (see above) before matches. The Hall Lane stadium was bulldozed when the M1 was extended in the 1970s. Wingate then shared with Finchley and in 1991 merged with them as Wingate-Finchley, playing at Summers Lane. Ex-Chelsea players Tommy Cunningham and Clive Wilson took charge early in the twenty-first century. The club are now in the Division One North of the Isthmian League.

KILBURN, NW6

Queen's Park Rangers (1891–96, 1915–17), Kilburn Cricket Club, Harvist Road

QPR moved to the Kilburn Cricket Club's ground near Kempe Road in 1891, a time when they wore green rather than blue and white hoops, and entered the West London League. When they played Paddington, with whom they had once been merged, watched by a crowd of more than a thousand, there was much nastiness, which resulted in QPR refusing to play the return match. They won their first trophy, the West London Observer Cup, in 1893, beating Fulham in the final, and entered the FA Cup for the first time in 1896. That year QPR were off on their travels, this time to the Kensal Rise Athletic ground, but they returned here during the First World War and stayed until the land was turned into allotments in 1917. It was then that club officials heard that a site was available on Loftus Road following the disbanding of the Shepherd's Bush club.

→ Loftus Road, p. 261

WILLESDEN, NW10

Neasden FC

Football's famous spoof club was created by *Private Eye* magazine in the early 1970s to satirise the ever farcical world of football and the cliché-ridden, hyperbole-driven inarticulacy of those in the game.

Neasden was chosen because the area was then considered to be typically bland, uncultured London suburbia, too near central London to offer the *rus in urbe* charms of the so-called Metroland suburbs, but too far from anywhere interesting to be popular with educated folk. The names of those involved with the fictitious club are fatuous but appropriate. The manager is Ron Knee (at West Brom in the 1970s a whole slew of managers were called Ron – Ronnie Allen, Ron Atkinson, Ronnie Allen (again), Ron Wylie, Ron Saunders and Ron Atkinson (again) – always described as 'ashen-faced and tight-lipped'. The leading player is 'Baldy' Pevsner (no relation to the respected architectural writer Nikolaus Pevsner) and the goalie, Wally Foot, evidently a nod to the *Eye*'s legendary investigative reporter Paul Foot, a fanatical Plymouth supporter, is one-legged (unlike the late Foot). The fans – all two of them – are Sid and Doris Bonkers, and the club's ground is located on Tesco Road, a name that looked ridiculous when first used but turned out to be prescient given the later deals between second-rate clubs such as Bolton and supermarket chains.

The brains behind Neasden is long-standing *Eye* journalist Barry Fantoni, who evidently was well acquainted with Bernard Joy's long-lost 1954 tome *Forward, Arsenal!* in which the author describes early twentieth-century Arsenal player Archie Gray as 'Archie "Baldy" Gray, an ashen-faced man, thin-lipped . . .'

Queen's Park Rangers (1886–88), Welford's Fields, immediately south of Kensal Rise station

Queen's Park Rangers, football's most travelled team with around twenty grounds to their name, played their first games at Welford's Fields (now covered by houses) a year after forming at Droop Street, Queen's Park. They were then known as St Jude's Institute and their first headquarters was the nearby St Jude's Church. In 1886 the club merged with Christchurch to become Queen's Park Rangers, but some of the Christchurch players were not keen on the new club and hived off to form Paddington, a club that has failed to achieve even the somewhat modest success of QPR and no longer exists in the same form.

Queen's Park Rangers played at Welford's Fields for two years before moving to the London Scottish Ground in Brondesbury, a site whose location remains unknown, although there was an enclosed arena and QPR could charge admission for the first time. Because the Brondesbury pitch was kept in poor condition, the club were soon off to a succession of new grounds: Home Park, Kensal Rise Green, the Gun Club on Wormwood Scrubs and Kilburn Cricket Ground (→ p. 137).

Queen's Park Rangers (1896–1901, 1902–04), Kensal Rise Athletic Ground, Whitmore Gardens

After five years playing on Harvist Road (→ p. 137) QPR headed a little way north for the start of the 1897 season, taking out a ten-year lease at the Kensal Rise Athletic Ground. This was their best ground to date, enclosed in a large site, and within a year the club had turned professional to the consternation of the London FA, which still abhorred professionalism, considering it a northern aberration. The first game for the now pro QPR was a 6–0 victory against Brighton United in the Southern League which later had to be wiped from the records when the losing team withdrew from the League along with Cowes.

Despite the fact that the lease had years to run, the landlord evicted QPR from the ground in 1901 and football's most travelled team was off again, this time to North Kensington (→ p. 259). Things didn't turn out successfully there so QPR returned here in 1902 for two years.

Queen's Park Rangers (1904–07), Agricultural Showground, between Coronation Road and Twyford Abbey Road

QPR's tenth home in twenty years was the Agricultural Showground, a huge site covering 100 acres that the owners had to sublet to break even. QPR played in an oval-shaped section called the Horse Ring, and for their first game here in the Southern League in summer 1904, at a time when the Southern League was considered to be equal in status to the Second Division, were watched by a sizeable crowd of 12,000. At the end of the 1906–07 season the Royal Agricultural Society gave QPR notice to quit. The club investigated a number of locations and ended up at the Great Western Railway's new Park Royal stadium 400 yards to the south (see below). The site of the Agricultural Showground later became part of the Guinness complex, which itself has now gone.

Queen's Park Rangers (1907–15), Park Royal stadium, south side between the railway and Coronation Road

When the Royal Agricultural Society sold their Showground (see above) in 1907 QPR had to move out, and they relocated to the Park Royal Ground, 400 yards to the south. The new stadium which was a replica of Middlesbrough's Ayresome Park had its own railway station and a capacity of 60,000, not that Rangers came close to filling it. QPR won the Southern League in 1908 and met the Football League champions, Manchester United, in the first ever Charity Shield, which was played at Stamford Bridge. They resigned from the Southern League as they were expecting to win a place in the higher-ranked Football League's Second Division, only to find themselves pipped by Tottenham who had finished seven places lower. After protracted negotiations the Southern League reluctantly agreed to readmit QPR, but they had lost several major players during the period of uncertainty. QPR won the Southern League again in 1912 but did not manage to join the Football League until after the First World War. In 1915 the government commandeered the Park Royal ground for the army, and Rangers returned to Harvist Road (→ p. 137).

Tales of the North Circular

After the great 1930s Arsenal goalscorer Cliff Bastin retired in 1947 he opened a café on London's ever-growing North Circular Road. Three years later Bastin was approached by a young would-be writer, Brian Glanville, who wanted to write his biography, and the two men discussed football and Bastin's career in a room above the café. The biography was written and privately published with £400 from Glanville's father – which is what an original copy with the dust jacket will fetch now.

Arsenal were lucky to get Bastin at all. When manager Herbert Chapman tried to sign him from Exeter his grandmother warned him: 'Cliff, don't go to London!' as she believed the capital city was a 'Sodom and Gomorrah full of snares and pitfalls for innocent young West Country lads'. When Bastin did enter Highbury stadium for the first time he was stopped by a commissionaire who asked him curtly: 'What do you want?' Bastin explained that he was trying to meet up with the other players, but the commissionaire looked him up and down and added, 'You're a bit young son. But don't worry. One day you may be good enough to play for Arsenal.'

Bastin's 178 goals were an Arsenal record until Ian Wright overtook the total in 1997. The Second World War cut short his career, but hearing problems meant he was unable to join the army. Instead he became an air-raid warden at the ground. In 1941 Italian radio falsely claimed they had captured Bastin at the Battle of Crete.

Sixty years later the orbital road has grown out of all proportion, as have footballers' wages. Arsenal left-back Ashley Cole was driving on the North Circular in his Baby Bentley when he found out on his mobile that the club he had supported since boyhood and for whom he now starred wouldn't increase his pay from £55,000 to £60,000 a week. He nearly swerved off the road. 'He is taking the piss, Jonathan,' Cole yelled down the phone to his agent. 'I was so incensed. I was trembling with anger. I couldn't believe what I'd heard. I suppose it all started to fall apart for me from then on.'

Further north-west

HARROW

Harrow School, High Street

The famous public school, attended by such luminaries as Lord Byron and Winston Churchill, was instrumental in devising modern football. Here in the school grounds there was more space for games than in central London public schools such as Charterhouse or Westminster, but as the large playing field had poor drainage the ball soon became heavy on the swampy ground, which meant that only boys adept at dribbling prospered.

Harrow's rules acted as a model for the FA's first set of regulations. Typical was Rule One which stated that 'The choice of Bases is determined by tossing: the side that wins the toss must have the choice of Bases, the side that loses has the right to kick off.' That wasn't the only rule that now looks odd. There was one which stated that, if a game was drawn, the length of the pitch would be doubled for the replay, and if the umpire (not referee) was at a loss to make a decision he could refer the incident to the committee of the 'Philathletic Club'.

Old Harrovians were behind the founding of the Sheffield Club, the world's oldest, in 1855. To persuade the northerners not to handle the ball the Harrow men gave them white gloves and a florin for the players to hold in their gloved hand. (It was not a payment, something that was then considered distasteful.)

When the Football Association was founded in 1863 Harrow could not be persuaded to join. 'We cling to our present rules,' they responded, 'and should be very sorry to alter them in any respect.' Consequently Harrow have not become a force in the game. However, the school's Cock House competition did provide the model for the FA Cup (→ p. 4), and it was a former Cock House participant, Charles Alcock, a founding member of the FA, who devised the first tournament in 1871–72.

WEMBLEY

Bobby Moore statue, outside Wembley stadium

If anyone deserved to be honoured with a statue outside the national stadium it was Bobby Moore, the 1966 World Cup-winning captain, whose authoritative playing and calm demeanour made him a worthy role model and icon of the game. Indeed one of the reasons behind England's failure to win another honour in the forty years since the '66 victory could be the run of uninspiring captains in Moore's wake (epitomised by such lightweights as Gerry Francis, David Platt and David Beckham) and the desperation to imbue the undeserving with heroic status à la Moore on the flimsiest evidence (Bryan Robson and Alan Shearer).

Moore was lucky to be playing in the final at all. Not only was there a problem with his registration which would have made him ineligible (→ p. 136) but Alf Ramsey considered dropping him before the final and playing Norman Hunter instead.

Wembley Stadium, Olympic Way

The world's most famous stadium, home of the FA Cup Final and England internationals, including the 1966 World Cup Final, was built not for football but as part of the attractions that made up the 1924 British Empire Exhibition.

The land on which the stadium stands had previously been leased by the Metropolitan Railway, which wanted to develop it as an amusement park. In 1901 the company's owner, Sir Edward Watkin, began to construct what he hoped would be a rival to Paris's Eiffel Tower. The project had to be abandoned when the foundations moved, and the 200-foot stump came to be known as Watkin's Folly. The field which also contained an 18-hole golf course was used for some of the first displays of flying and was cleared in 1920. Architects John Simpson and Maxwell Ayrton working with Owen Williams, who later designed the M1, created a stadium greater than anything ever seen before, the façade crowned with twin towers based on Edwin Lutyens's work in New Delhi. Edward, Prince of Wales, gave the stadium the royal seal of approval in a speech that described it as 'a great national sports ground' which the Football Association was considering as a home for the Cup Final. This announcement attracted funding including, remarkably, more than £100,000 from Glasgow council. The stadium was built in 300 days, which compares most favourably with the length of time taken in the rebuilding programme staged in the first decade of the twenty-first century. To test the strength of the terraces before it opened, an infantry battalion and hundreds of locals were invited in, and asked to stamp and jump up and down.

Scorey draw

The Empire Stadium as Wembley was then known opened on 28 April 1923 with the Bolton Wanderers *v* West Ham United Cup Final. The Football Association decreed that the match need not be all-ticket as the ground could hold around 117,000 fans, and so anyone could turn up on the day and probably get in. But this led to chaos on a scale that has rarely been seen since at a football match. More than 200,000 entered, many illicitly, those in the stadium with tickets being pushed aside by those without as men climbed on one another to gain a view. One of those who broke in was Dennis Higham who, eighty-four years later, prior to the 2007 Cup Final, the first at the rebuilt Wembley, appeared in the *Independent* newspaper as probably the last surviving attender of the first match. He had become a bank manager and taken part in the Second World War D-Day landings, but still felt guilty about bunking in back in 1923.

The Bolton Wanderers team had some difficulty getting to the stadium at all. Caught in a traffic jam, they abandoned their vehicle, made their way across some fields and a railway line, and arrived at the ground to find two West Ham fans armed with spades digging a hole under the fence. This was most convenient, for it provided an easy route in. All the players now had to do was climb another fence, past a disbelieving policeman. The mayor of East Ham was less fortunate. He had paid a guinea for a good ticket and went in with a group of friends who found their seats already occupied. After arguing his friends' case he returned to his seat only to find it too had been taken by someone else. He was then thrown out.

At two o'clock, an hour before kick-off, the pitch was entirely covered with people. The police sent for reinforcements and an officer called George Scorey on a white horse, Billy, saved the day by clearing the crowds. Elsewhere extraordinary little dramas were being played out. One attendant was so inundated with money from people trying to get in that he lay on the mound of banknotes to hide them from prying eyes. Other spectators were so vexed by the chaos they were offering staff money to get *out*.

Once the game started, it took only two minutes for David Jack to open the scoring for Bolton. They went on to win 2–0 in a game without a proper half-time break, the two teams simply swapping ends and restarting immediately. After the match West Ham, despite losing, attended a dinner in Golders Green from which they were transported to a reception at the Princess Alice Hotel, Forest Gate, way over on the other side of London, in a fabulously ornate illuminated tramcar decorated with various shields and bizarrely the Star of David.

It wasn't until a year later that the second match was played at Wembley. This was an England–Scotland international on 12 April 1924, which ended 1–1. Later that month George V officially opened the British Empire Exhibition that had brought the stadium into being. As England internationals were not regularly played at Wembley before the Second World War and the FA Cup Final occurred only once a year, by 1927 only a handful of games had been played here. Football alone could not support the stadium commercially in its early days, and when the company running it went into liquidation it looked as if the stadium would be demolished.

A scrap metal merchant, Arthur Elvin, then stepped in and bought Wembley. Only three years previously he had been working as an assistant in a tobacco kiosk at the British Empire Exhibition, and he had bought up and cleared out the pavilions when the exhibition closed. After becoming managing director of the new Wembley Stadium Ltd in 1927 Elvin persuaded the board to build an indoor sports arena. It went up in 1934 and was known as the Empire Pool (now Wembley Arena).

Elvin introduced greyhound racing at Wembley. The initial races attracted a crowd of 50,000, the money from which buoyed the stadium commercially for decades. (It ceased in 1998.) Elvin also brought speedway to the stadium, which became home of the Wembley Lions, occasionally attracting huge crowds such as the 85,000 who turned up for the 1937 World Championship. To get more football played here Elvin turned to the amateur game, whose clubs would be only too keen to play at such a stadium – something that they couldn't contemplate via the FA Cup route in those days. On Saturday 29 September 1928 Ealing met Hastings and St Leonards in Wembley's first amateur match. The west London club played a few more matches here, including a victory against Ipswich, who did return fifty years later to win the FA Cup, but crowds of around fifty meant the idea was not worth pursuing.

Hungary for change

In 1953 Hungary came to Wembley for an international and played England off the park in a remarkable 6–3 win, the first by a foreign country at the stadium. If the idea of a bunch of foreigners from a mysterious communist country who had barely been playing football a few decades coming to England and trouncing those who had invented the game was barely possible to contemplate, how much more worrying was the 7–1 drubbing in Budapest six months later? Once failure at the subsequent three World Cups brought the realisation that English football had fallen well behind that of a number of countries, one way of making amends would be to win the trophy when the tournament was played in England in 1966.

With football not the subject of great hype in those days and the televised game in its infancy there was only limited interest at first. For instance, the first group game, England v Uruguay, attracted a crowd of just 87,148, a paltry number well short of capacity, something unthinkable now when media frenzy would probably result in many outside the ground trying to buy tickets from touts. The uninspiring match ended in a 0–0 draw, but then England rarely win their opening game in a tournament (Portugal '86, Ireland '88 and '90, Switzerland '96, Portugal '00, Sweden '02, France '04).

England's wasn't a tough group. Mexico were dispatched 2–0 and France, not then a football power, were beaten by the same scoreline. The quarter-final, however, was particularly nasty, the first of many such encounters against the eternally bad-behaved Argentinians. Trouble erupted when the Argentina captain, Antonio Rattin, was sent off for what the West German referee, Rudolf Kreitlein, later explained was 'a look in his eyes'. According to Kreitlein, 'I did not need to speak his language. The look on his face was enough to show that he thought that he was in charge of things. Only one of us could referee the game, and it was not going to be him. His arrogance and defiance caused great disruption.' In the mêlée Bobby Charlton, of all people, was booked – the only time in his career – and Rattin refused to leave the field. England left-back Ray Wilson was heard to say, 'I hope he sends them all off' and had to be escorted away by police. As Rattin finally walked off he wiped his dirty hands on a corner flag displaying the Union Jack, which many took as a sign of contempt for the home nation. When the Argentine side came off at half-time a few minutes later, one of them shoved an orange into the face of Harry Cavan, a senior FIFA official. The players also urinated in the dressing-room corridor and tried to smash down England's dressing-room door. The result of the match was 1–0 to England.

England were now in the semi-final, without having let in a goal. Portugal, their opponents, had only narrowly got through, having been three down to North Korea in their quarter-final before Eusebio intervened. This time the formidable Mozambican failed to sparkle and England won 2–1. Over the next forty years England failed to beat Portugal in any of the six competitive matches between the two nations.

All chewed up

With only minutes to go before England's World Cup semi-final against Portugal on 26 July 1966 goalkeeper Gordon Banks realised when he got on the pitch that he had no chewing gum. Banks could not play without a masticatory aid as he would not be able to concentrate so manager Alf Ramsey instructed his assistant, Harold Shepherdson, to get some gum, preferably Beech Nut, for the worried keeper.

'Where on earth am I going to get that from?' asked the unimpressed assistant as he made his way to the dugout. 'How the hell should I know?' responded Ramsey. 'I'm a football manager not the bloody owner of a sweetshop.' Jackie Charlton came to the rescue. He recalled that there was an off-licence at the end of Stadium Way and gave Shepherdson directions. With time for kick-off approaching and Gordon Banks waiting nervously, Alf Ramsey's assistant tore out of the stadium, headed down the road in the opposite direction from the fans arriving at the last minute, found the shop, breathlessly asked for several packets of gum, and ran back.

Ramsey, meanwhile, had urged the referee to delay the kick-off so that his goalkeeper wouldn't be without his gum, but M. Schwinte, the French referee, wasn't inclined to be too sympathetic. Fortunately the band which had been playing for the crowd, took so long to leave the pitch that Shepherdson was able to get back in time to deliver the gum to the anxious Banks. The semi-final kicked off with a happy England goalkeeper, who produced an excellent display that helped England reach the World Cup Final.

It is now

The 1966 Final still ranks as the most controversial of the eighteen played by the end of the first decade of the twenty-first century, thanks to one incident: in extra-time a Geoff Hurst shot hit the bar and rebounded – maybe over the line, maybe not. The Swiss referee, Gottfried Dienst, consulted the Azerbaijani linesman, Tofik Bakhramov, before ruling that it was a goal – even though it probably wasn't.

Ramsey picked the side which had got them through the previous two rounds which meant there was no place for the era's greatest English goalscorer, Jimmy Greaves, but he may not have been fully fit anyway. The big four English clubs sides of the period were represented on the field, apart from Burnley, and there were players from what now look like unlikely sources such as Blackpool and Fulham. England's opponents, West Germany, had superior players, including the unimpeachable Franz Beckenbauer who could play in practically every position.

The Germans looked more dangerous at the start. Haller gave them a twelfth-minute lead, which meant England were behind for the first time in the tournament. But the home side equalised six minutes later thanks to Hurst. With only twelve minutes to go Peters scored from a Hurst cross. As the final whistle approached, it looked as if England were going to hold on but in the last minute Jackie Charlton was adjudged, perhaps harshly, to have committed a foul on the edge of the area, and Emmerich's free-kick found Weber, who shot slowly past a despairing Banks.

Surprisingly, it was the English not the Germans – the last time for many decades – who looked fitter as the game went into extra-time. It was then, in the 102nd minute, that Hurst scored his controversial goal. To silence any complaints resounding down the years he wrapped it up in the final seconds with a rasping shot that completed his hat-trick, still the only one ever scored in a World Cup Final. The moment was captured for ever in Kenneth Wolstenholme's immortal words: 'Some people are on the pitch. They think it's all over [and as Hurst scores] – it is now!'

Great Wembley matches

⊕ Bolton Wanderers 2 – West Ham United 0, FA Cup Final, 28 April 1923. Perhaps as many as 200,000 filled the stadium and spilled on to the pitch for the first ever Wembley match – that was lucky to go ahead at all.

⊕ England 1 – Scotland 5, Home International Championships, 31 March 1928. Quality passing on a level never before seen enabled a tiny Scottish forward line that included Hughie Gallagher and Alex James to tear through the England defence. They became immortalised as the 'Wembley Wizards'.

⊕ Blackpool 4 – Bolton Wanderers 3, FA Cup Final, 2 May 1953. Stan Mortensen scored a hat-trick, the only one ever achieved in an FA Cup Final, in a game that has gone down in history as the Stanley Matthews Final, thanks to the match-winning presence of the ageless winger.

⊕ England 3 – Hungary 6, International, 25 November 1953. Olympic champions Hungary hadn't lost a game in three years and were favourites to win the forthcoming World Cup in Switzerland. England still thought themselves superior to continental opposition and had never been beaten at home by a team from outside the British Isles. England didn't help their cause by handing first caps to two players, one of them an amateur, but it probably didn't matter given how far beyond England the Hungarians were, and Puskas, Kocsis and Hidegkuti raked up a 6–3 victory. According to Geoffrey Green of *The Times*, 'England were strangers in a strange world', while Frank Coles of the *Daily Telegraph* wrote that 'this was the most brilliant display of football ever seen in this country'. Six months later in Budapest England went down 7–1.

⊗ England 9 – Scotland 3, Home International Championships, 15 April 1961. Jimmy Greaves hit a hat-trick past the Scotland goalkeeper Frank Haffey in England's biggest ever victory in the world's oldest international fixture. Back in the Scottish dressing room one wag broke the ice by asking no one in particular, 'What's the time?' and wittily answering himself, 'Nearly ten past Haffey.'

⊗ England 4 – West Germany 2, World Cup Final, 30 July 1966. The only time in nearly eighty years of the competition's history that England won the tournament. It was their only appearance in the final to date.

⊗ Manchester United 4 – Benfica 1, European Cup Final, 29 May 1968. No English team had ever won the trophy, but if any side were to break the duck it had to be Manchester United, semi-finalists on three previous occasions. In the final United strangely played in blue, and without the inspirational Denis Law who was injured drew 1–1 after ninety minutes. After extra-time United ran out 4–1 winners with George Best and Bobby Charlton scoring. It was the last trophy either man was to win.

⊗ England 1 – Poland 1, World Cup qualifier, 17 October 1973. England needed a win against an unrated Poland to reach the World Cup finals, but after Jan Domarski scored in the fifty-fifth minute the task became harder. An Allan Clarke penalty gave England hope but, despite an extraordinary number of chances, the home side failed to find a winner. The hero was the Polish goalkeeper, Jan Tomaszewski, who made four outstanding saves. The villain was Derby's Kevin Hector who missed the easiest of chances in the dying minutes. But the fault was Ramsey's. He should never have given a player as pedestrian as Hector a debut in so important a game.

⊗ Wimbledon 1 – Liverpool 0, FA Cup Final, 14 May 1988. Brian Moore on ITV billed it as 'the Crazy Gang *v* the Culture Club', but the reality was that a team of brutes and bruisers who had been in the League only thirteen years lifted the trophy at the expense of the near invincibles who had won the European Cup four times in the previous eleven seasons.

⚽ England 2 – Scotland 1, European Championships, 15 June 1996. One of only two wins in competitive matches under Terry Venables's management for an overhyped England side that beat a second-rate Scotland side thanks to an outstanding goal by Paul Gascoigne. After scoring the Rangers midfielder lay on the grass while team-mates Steve McManaman, Teddy Sheringham and Gary Neville helped him re-create that special moment in the 'dentist's chair' of a Hong Kong nightclub when the England players had drunk themselves senseless a few weeks earlier. The stunt was so cleverly executed it suggested hours of practice had gone into it, instead of into taking penalties. Failure to score from the spot led to England's elimination from the tournament soon after.

One of the many myths surrounding that World Cup win in 1966 was that the nation rejoiced as one at England's victory. In reality there were many in England who were unimpressed. Denis Law, linchpin of Manchester United, spent the day playing golf in Chorlton, three miles from Old Trafford, unable to face the world should England win – and probably ignorant of the fact to this day. The Richardson brothers, London's most powerful gangsters, also missed the game. They were not short of patriotism but had suffered the ignominy of being arrested on charges of torture on the morning of the match by an uncaring police force.

Others, though, enjoyed the day. Journalist James Mossop recalled how 'the expectancy was incredible. Walking up Wembley Way [sic] to the final, you knew this was a very special day. I remember a little band of old men on the road who were busking, and they were playing "There Will Always Be An England". I thought that was wonderful, it seemed so patriotic yet innocent in a way. Everyone was caught up in it. It was like the word cynical hadn't been invented.'

As the years passed and the England national team deteriorated ever further under a succession of ever more uninspiring managers or 'chief coaches', the '66 final has become an ever greater legend. England remain almost unique among successful football nations in reaching a major final just once. Supposedly inferior countries such as Hungary and Czechoslovakia/the Czech Republic have six finals between them.

The toppling of the towers

In 1967 Wembley hosted the League Cup Final for the first time. It continued as the setting for the FA Cup Final, England home matches, and sundry play-offs and lesser finals until autumn 2000 when the ground closed for redevelopment. The FA had long deemed Wembley unsuitable for twenty-first-century football and announced it would have to be rebuilt. Cities in the North and Midlands argued that the national stadium should be situated in Manchester or Birmingham, but failed to explain how crowds of around 80,000 could smoothly get to and from the various suggested sites, given the poor public transport available compared to Wembley with its multitude of stations as well as easy access to motorways.

The famous architect Norman Foster was chosen to create the new ground, but the inspired design of his work for the Willis Faber building in Ipswich and the Hong Kong and Shanghai Bank in China, for instance, was not evident in this project – though culture secretary Chris Smith described Foster's vision as 'stunning'.

When the public saw the plans for the new stadium there were gasps, not of admiration but of horror. The exquisite twin towers that had featured in so many fans' and players' dreams were to be demolished in a callous display of needless destruction. Their replacement was a gigantic McDonald's-style arch that now soars over the western side of the capital but adds nothing to the London skyline.

The rebuilding work itself was marred by delays, political squabbling, debate over whether there should be a running track around the pitch, accusation and counter-accusation, suing and counter-suing, which resulted in the new Wembley opening two years late, at a cost that almost broke the billion-pound mark, despite the absence of a roof.

Seven years after the last final at the old Wembley, the FA Cup Final returned for the May 2007 meeting between Chelsea and Manchester United. Chelsea won a game much less dramatic than the first final back in 1923. It was too early at that stage to say whether there was any point to the new Wembley, but after the crucial qualifying game for the European

Championships against Croatia many questioned the worth of the seven-year rebuild. The pitch had been rendered practically unusable by a recent game of American 'football', and despite the lavish spending there were still not enough toilets or any chance of getting a beer cheaply and quickly at half-time. Even more astonishingly, despite seven years' preparation, the authorities had made no attempt to address the problem of how to get the tens of thousands of spectators out of the ground easily and quickly by perhaps introducing a continental-style system of whisking fans away in fleets of mini-buses to one of the many railway stations within a two-mile radius of the ground, instead forcing huge numbers of people to queue for ever to enter the tube at overburdened Wembley Park.

Perhaps rather than building a new stadium the FA should have created some new fans. Before the match the Croatian national anthem was booed, just as foreign anthems have been for decades, the new toilet sinks were soon stuffed with uneaten burgers and many in the crowd were so inebriated that they had no idea at the end whether England had gone through or not.

Wembley off the bench

⚽ At the 1933 FA Cup Final the players wore numbers for the first time, a slightly confusing 1–22 rather than the 1–11 that would later be adopted, but more meaningful than the squad numbers now used.

⚽ In 1953 Bobby Charlton played at Wembley for the first time, appearing for England schoolboys, and was amazed at the quality of the pitch: 'Wembley was so beautiful. It was just made for me. I used to love passing the ball, and it used to go where you meant it to go. True as anything. It was like a billiard table.'

⚽ Bert Trautmann, a German captured during the war and interned in a British prisoner-of-war camp, played in the 1956 Cup Final for Manchester City despite sustaining a broken neck.

⚽ After the Queen handed Bobby Moore the World Cup following England's victory in 1966, a plainclothes police officer, Bob Geggie, shadowed the England players around the Wembley turf on their lap of honour, keeping a close watch on the trophy. The cup had been stolen from an exhibition in Westminster a few months earlier (p. 43) and now the FA was taking no chances. Unknown to Geggie, an ordinary constable, Peter Weston, was positioned near the changing rooms with a replica of the trophy. As a toothless, delirious Nobby Stiles jigged with the trophy in one of the most joyous scenes of that day, PC Weston wrested the real cup from him and gave him the replica instead to continue his celebrations.

✪ Before playing for England against Holland on 9 February 1977 the mercurial striker Stan Bowles accepted £200 from Gola to wear their boots. Later that day he was offered £300 to wear Adidas boots. Bowles took that money too and turned out for the match wearing one boot from each company.

✪ Scottish soccer fans, who had long had a love–hate relationship with Wembley, ripped up much of the turf and smashed the goalposts to celebrate a 2–1 victory over England in the 1977 Home International.

✪ At the 1981 Cup Final against Manchester City Tottenham fans brought in a banner bearing the tasteful slogan 'Hold on to your knickers, it's the Year of the Cock'.

✪ In charge of the Rest of World team to face a Football League XI in August 1987 for the Football League's centenary celebrations was Terry Venables, the man who would later take England to the European Championship semi-finals. Venables was astonished to find that the Rest of the World's dressing room had few accessories and that he himself had to fork out £80 to buy a first-aid kit and sponge. At the end of the game the Football League officials refused to reimburse him, until he threatened to leak the story to the press.

✪ After England lost 1–0 to Germany in a World Cup qualifier at Wembley in October 2000, the last to be held there before its lengthy rebuilding, England manager Kevin Keegan, who had just seen his hapless team lose 1–0, resigned – in the toilets.

⚽ By 2009 the reputation of the new Wembley stadium had been sullied by a series of barely usable playing surfaces caused by the desperate need to hire out the venue regularly to raise the money to pay for it. Of course had the FA left the perfectly adequate traditional Wembley with its immaculate pitch and iconic twin towers in place the problem wouldn't have existed in the first place.

5 South-east London

Three major clubs dominate the game in south-east London: Charlton Athletic, Crystal Palace and Millwall. Between them they have won one major trophy in the first century and a third of competitive football. Charlton were briefly a force before and after the Second World War, and won the FA Cup in 1947. Crystal Palace, named after the long-gone glass exhibition hall that originally stood in Hyde Park and was moved to Sydenham in the nineteenth century, are serial promotion challengers/relegation strugglers between the top two divisions. Millwall have spent only one period in the top flight, in a year when they somehow finished above Manchester United, but are once again struggling, weighed down it seems by their troublesome history.

SOUTHWARK/BERMONDSEY, SE1

Daily Express, 245 Blackfriars Road

A *Daily Express* photograph of West Ham's Paul Ince posing in a Manchester United shirt in 1989 turned the midfield player into a pariah at the east London club. Ince had been keen on a move away from West Ham since his mentor, John Lyall, had been sacked in June 1989, and he agreed to pose in the United shirt before signing for the northern club on the understanding that, if the deal taking him to Old Trafford fell through, the photo would be destroyed. Instead, an awful mishap occurred: the negative found its way to the *Daily Express* building and appeared in the paper prior to the start of the following season. Ince remarkably played one game for West Ham before joining United and when asked about the incident disingenuously responded: 'It wasn't really my fault. I was only a kid, I did what my agent told me to do, then took all the crap for it.'

→ Ashley Cole plans to leave Arsenal, p.141

Old Kent Road

Paul Vaessen, scorer of Arsenal's winner against Juventus in Turin in the 1980 European Cup Winners' Cup semi-final, was stabbed six times on this notoriously violent south-east London road in 1986 after a drug deal went wrong. Vaessen was taken to Guy's Hospital. As chance would have it, another ex-Arsenal player, Gary Lewin, was training to be a physio there at the time and was greatly shocked to see his former team-mate so badly injured. Vaessen was in intensive care for four days, after which he discharged himself to go back on the street to look for drugs. In August 2002 a friend found Vaessen dead in the bathroom of the house the former Arsenal man shared with his brother.

→ Tottenham High Road, p. 113

Southwark Crown Court, English Grounds

George Best was given a suspended prison sentence at Southwark Crown Court in 1984 after he failed to appear at Bow Street magistrates court on a drink-driving charge. Before the Southwark hearing Best's counsel reasoned that it might help his client if Jeff Powell of the *Daily Mail* and Hugh McIlvanney of the *Observer* appeared as character witnesses. But as the journalists explained to the fallen star in the court canteen prior to the hearing, if they took the stand Best might become the first man to be hanged for a driving offence. After the sentence Best turned to McIlvanney and said, 'Well, I suppose that's the knighthood fucked.'

→ The High Court, p. 15

Waterloo station

The teenage Terry Venables used to meet a scout, Jimmy Thompson, at the station in the early 1960s, just before he joined Chelsea, and was forced to take part in an absurd cloak-and-dagger ritual. The eccentrically dressed Thompson in his bowler hat and pin-striped trousers, and always carrying a furled umbrella, would hide in case a rival scout was hoping to nab the gifted young midfield player from under his nose, and would try to attract Venables's attention with whispers and signals. On one occasion the two met at a busy London hotel where Thompson led Venables through a succession of corridors and passageways in case anyone was following. Venables had to endure similar paranoia from Thompson at home. Should the doorbell ring while the scout was at the Venableses' he would flee to the bathroom lest a rival spotted him.

→ Arsenal and Bolton at Euston station, p. 132

BLACKHEATH, SE3

The smart south London suburb had three teams – Blackheath, Percival House and Blackheath Proprietary School – at the initial meeting of the Football Association in Covent Garden in 1863 (→ p. 11). Although Blackheath's Francis Maude Campbell had been elected treasurer, there were constant arguments between the main Blackheath club and the other founders of the FA over the question of hacking – kicking a player in the shins. Campbell passionately argued that to eliminate hacking would 'do away with all the courage and pluck from the game. I will be bound over to bring over a lot of Frenchmen who would beat you with a week's practice.' He failed to win the argument and at the FA's sixth meeting on 8 December Blackheath withdrew. They later developed as a rugby club.

CATFORD, SE6

Mountsfield Park, Carswell Road

Charlton Athletic devised an ill-fated scheme to move the club, then in the Third Division (South), to the home of non-League Catford Southend, in 1923. Charlton's directors believed that by playing in Catford rather than

Charlton they would increase their support base, much as relocating to Highbury had done for Woolwich Arsenal. Once Charlton had moved the club's name would change from Charlton Athletic to the rather unappealing Catford Southend, and to complete the embarrassment Charlton would play in the lesser club's colours. Charlton's directors assured worried fans that even though the Catford club's ground, the Mount, was inferior to the Valley, it would be enlarged – to hold 80,000 spectators.

Work began on upgrading Mountsfield Park in spring 1923 so that it would be ready by the following November. Charlton appeared in Catford for the first time and began attracting crowds twice the size of the 4,000-odd who had been turning up at the Valley. However, the novelty soon wore off, and attendances plummeted back to 4,000, and then down to just 1,000, fewer than those who had been watching Catford Southend and lower than the number watching Charlton's reserve games at the Valley. The venture flopped and after six months in Catford, Charlton returned north.

The club did, however, play in south London again in the 1980s when the Valley's future was in doubt, on that occasion at Selhurst Park (→ p. 186). The Catford club suffered a worse fate and folded in 1927.

CHARLTON, SE7

Charlton Athletic origins (1905), Warspite Road, west side

It was unlikely when a group of teenage boys formed Charlton Athletic in June 1905 that the club would prosper. Local football fans were well catered for at Woolwich Arsenal, only a few miles east, and across the river at Millwall, who moved south to New Cross in 1910 and attracted new fans from the vicinity. On top of that this was rugby territory. Which probably explains why Charlton remained amateur until 1920, by which time Woolwich Arsenal had moved to north London.

Charlton's first ground was Siemens Meadow, a rough patch of grass next to the Thames by the now demolished Siemens Telegraph Works. There they played for a year, but then had a number of different grounds in quick succession: Woolwich Common (1907–08), Pound Park (1908–13) and Angerstein Lane (1913–19, see below).

Charlton Athletic (1913–19), Angerstein Athletic Ground, Horn Lane, just north of Aldeburgh Street

Charlton moved to their first proper home, the Angerstein Athletic Ground, capacity 4,000, for the start of the 1913–14 season. Now that Woolwich Arsenal had moved to north London there was a bigger fan base to draw on. However, Charlton had to share the ground with another South Suburban League club, Deptford Invicta. When Charlton reformed at the end of the Great War they couldn't return to the Angerstein, as it had been used for storing petrol. They soon found a new ground though, which became the Valley, their long-term home.

Charlton Athletic (1919–85, 1992–), the Valley, Floyd Road

According to popular legend football and politics don't mix, but in Charlton's case politics saved the club. When they were exiled from their own ground in the 1980s, it was the decision of determined fans to stand for office in Greenwich council on a 'Back to the Valley' ticket that led to a resurgence in support for the club and saw them return to their traditional home in 1992. Promotion to the Premiership followed to make the fairy tale complete, and by the time they were relegated in 2007 the club had enjoyed twelve seasons in top-flight football over the previous two decades.

Like their south-east London rivals, Crystal Palace and Millwall, Charlton have achieved only the briefest success. However, they are the only one of the teams located south of the Thames to have won a major trophy (the FA Cup in 1947). Charlton are also the only south London club to have come close to winning the Championship (ten years previously).

Unlike most clubs Charlton Athletic were not the product of a church or works team. They came into being in 1905 through the efforts of a group of sports lovers keen to promote a football club – much like the Save the Valley campaigners eighty years later. After playing at various local sites Charlton moved to the Valley, then a derelict chalk pit known as the Swamps, in 1919. At that time they played in the Kent League. Their first game was against Summerstown on 13 September 1919, and officials passed a collection box around the crowd to get some extra money. Charlton soon turned professional, and were elevated to the Southern League in 1920. There they played for just one season before promotion to the Football League's newly created Third Division (South).

Although the Valley had been enlarged, in 1923 the directors announced the extraordinary news that the club would be moving four miles south to merge with non-League Catford Southend. The Valley would be redeveloped as an entertainment complex. (The first of several controversial schemes proposed and cast aside for this land.) Charlton did play in Catford for six months but returned in 1924. The scheme was dropped.

Charlton gained promotion to the Second Division in 1929, but were relegated back to the Third in 1933. That year they made one of their most important recruitments – Jimmy Seed – as manager. Seed had played in the Tottenham team that won the 1921 FA Cup, and he took Charlton on an unprecedented and unequalled ascent – three successive seasons in which they won the Third Division (South), followed by promotion to the top division, culminating in second place in the League in 1936–37, a bizarre season in which Manchester City were champions.

Crowds flocked to the Valley, which had grown into the biggest ground in the country. For one FA Cup tie in 1938 there were 75,031 in attendance. And not only was the ground big, but just before and after the war Charlton were the best team in England. After finishing second in 1937, they were fourth and third before professional football closed down because of the war. When play resumed, they reached the FA Cup Final two seasons running – in 1946 and '47 – losing the first but winning the second, their only trophy to date. Yet Charlton's directors inexplicably refused to allow Seed to invest the bountiful gate receipts in new players, and by the 1950s criticism of his waning regime was coming from an unlikely source. A young full-back took it on himself to revolutionise the club's training methods. After studying the most advanced new coaching techniques of the time, then being deployed in Austria, he approached Seed to adopt some of these innovations, but was immediately rebuffed.

The maverick upstart was none other than Malcolm Allison, who coached Manchester City to the Championship the following decade. Seed didn't welcome Allison's ideas and as the latter told Jimmy Greaves, 'Jimmy Seed was happy continuing with the traditional methods of training, which amounted to little more than the players doing a few laps of the cinder track, some exercises, then into the dressing room for a shower and a Woodbine. We used to have to run in and out of a copse of trees. It was impossible for the trainer to keep his eyes on all the players. If he was alert he might spot blue cigarette smoke filtering through the trees.' Allison was considered such a troublemaker with his constant gripes about the club's outmoded training methods that Seed placed him on the transfer list. 'What makes you think you know so much about football?' the manager asked Allison as he walked out of the ground for the last time, on his way to his new club, West Ham. 'Talking to you,' Allison replied. When Seed left in 1956 it seemed that the invisible thread that had kept the club at the top had broken. Relegation swiftly followed.

Around that time there was another planned move, this time far away across the Thames Valley to Slough. It came to nothing, as did a plan to merge with Romford on the other side of the Thames. But Charlton spent nearly thirty years, from 1957 to 1986, languishing in the Second Division with the occasional spell in the Third. The golden years of English football, around the time of the World Cup success, and the era of Best, Marsh and Bowles, passed Charlton by. To compound matters, the owners let the ground decline to the point where it became practically unusable. In 1977 capacity was cut from 66,000 to 20,000, and four years later to 13,000.

Charlton hit the headlines for the right reasons in 1983 when somehow they lured one-time European Footballer of the Year, Allan Simonsen, to the Valley. Simonsen scored nine times in sixteen games, but the club couldn't afford his wages and he was soon sold. Behind the scenes problems were mounting. The threat of bankruptcy after debts had risen to £1.5 million was staved off at the last minute in 1984, but property developer John Fryer, who had cleared the deficit, took the opportunity afforded by the council inspector's condemnation of the East Bank as unsafe to leave the Valley. On Saturday 21 September 1985 just 8,858 saw Charlton play what nearly everyone assumed would be the last match here. The club moved to Crystal Palace, seven miles away at the southern end of the metropolis, for the rest of the 1985–86 season.

If the move to Catford had been unpopular, what of this one that was twice the distance? Surely the club would rot away? Yet at the end of the season Charlton remarkably finished second and were back in the top flight for the first time in thirty years. While the Valley did rot away, homeless Charlton prospered. With their lack of big names and internationals, the side were never likely to set the First Division alight but they managed to stay clear of automatic relegation. A nineteenth-place finish meant a play-off fight with Leeds, fourth in the Second Division, to determine who would take the last slot at the top the next season. The football world tipped mighty Leeds over No Fixed Abode Charlton, but it was the Addicks who went through.

Somehow Charlton survived amongst Liverpool, Arsenal and Manchester United. Bolstered, a group of fans began contemplating a return to the Valley. John Fryer had retired as chairman in 1987 due to poor health. Pro-Valley executives were now on the board. One of these, Michael Norris, reached an agreement with the builders Laing to buy the freehold of the site. Rumours abounded of a new scheme, that the old ground might be redeveloped and Charlton move to North Greenwich. However, the prohibitive cost of decontaminating the polluted land there made the notion of rebuilding the Valley more attractive. Thousands of supporters cleaned the ground, burning the debris in a huge bonfire on the pitch, and proposals were submitted to Greenwich council for an all-seater stadium at the Valley. But then disaster struck: the Town Hall rejected the idea.

The fans, rather than giving up as many people expected, formed a political wing, the Valley Party. They ran candidates throughout the borough at the next elections and won 14,838 votes – 10 per cent of the electorate chose them – in 1990. Greenwich council changed its mind and work began on the club's return to their traditional home. As things rarely run smoothly in SE7, the euphoria at the election success was tempered by relegation in May 1990, but for once footballing considerations were not paramount. What mattered to the club's supporters was that they would again play at their own home, not somebody else's. Charlton left Selhurst Park in April 1991, briefly shared with West Ham until the Valley was ready, and returned in triumph in December 1992.

Under the management of Alan Curbishley, who began as joint manager with Steve Gritt and then took sole charge in 1995, Charlton slowly prospered. They won a thrilling 1998 play-off final against Sunderland on penalties after Clive Mendonca had scored a rare Wembley hat-trick. Charlton went down straight away but won the Second Division championship the following season to return to the top flight. Although no trophies came Charlton's way under Curbishley, it was the fact that they could compete at all – regularly staying in touch with wealthier, better-supported clubs by hard work and guile – that was important.

Alas when Curbishley decided to stand down in summer 2006, having become one of the longest-serving bosses in the game, all the good work that had gone into reviving the club was thrown away. It was not the appointment of Iain Dowie in May 2006 that was the problem but the panic that led to his sacking the following November after a bad start. Then, to compound matters, Les Reed was promoted to the boss's chair. Acknowledging that his appointment was a surprise, Reed then embarrassed himself by claiming he had come up through a route not unlike that taken by 'Arsene Wenger, José Mourinho, Rafael Benítez, Sven-Goran Eriksson and Carlos Alberto Parreira'. True, but whereas those men are internationally renowned winners, Reed won one game in six weeks. The man the press dubbed 'Les Miserables' and 'Santa Clueless' was soon out. Surprisingly, the appointment of Alan Pardew – probably the most inspired of the few Englishmen managing at a high level – after he had been recently and unfairly sacked by West Ham, couldn't save the club from the drop in May 2007, and sinking further in 2009.

Charlton off the bench

❊ The club's nickname, the Addicks, dating from the time of the First World War, is a take on the local pronunciation of haddock, and came about because a Charlton fishmonger, Arthur 'Ikey' Bryan, used to reward the team with meals of haddock and chips when they won.

❊ There was nearly a Hillsborough-style disaster when Charlton played Bolton in the FA Cup in March 1923. The barriers gave way and dozens of fans were sent tumbling on to the pitch. There were no serious injuries but many sued for compensation.

❊ The legendary Charlton goalkeeper Sam Bartram signed for the club after the regular keeper, Alex Wright, died in a freak bathing accident. His first game was a 6–0 defeat for the reserves, but he became one of Charlton's greatest players, staying in the team for twenty-two years. Bartram played by himself during one fog-plagued game in the 1930s. In the thickening gloom the goalkeeper began to see fewer and fewer figures, and as he recalled in his autobiography, 'the game went unusually silent but I remained at my post, peering into the thickening fog from the edge of the penalty area'. Bartram wondered why the play was not coming his way, until after some time 'a figure loomed out of the curtain of fog in front of me. It was a policeman, and he gaped at me incredulously. "What on earth are you doing here?" he gasped. "The game was stopped a quarter of an hour ago. The field's completely empty."'

⚽ During the Second World War, when it was hard to come by quality footballers, Charlton were duped into playing a chap called Tim Rogers, thinking he was the ex-Arsenal and Newcastle man. This Rogers, however, was simply a soldier on leave who fancied a game. In the programme for the match that followed manager Jimmy Seed was forced to apologise. 'I have now found out we were hoodwinked, although his inept display was sure evidence of his inability. We will leave it at that.'

⚽ When Charlton reached the Cup Final in 1946 ties were played over two legs, so they became the only team to get to the final after losing a game en route.

⚽ In the late 1950s Charlton considered renaming themselves London Athletic.

⚽ Rare for a top club, Charlton have a seat on the board of directors for a fans' representative. Any season-ticket holder can put themselves forward for election, and votes are cast by all season-ticket holders over the age of eighteen.

KENNINGTON, SE11

The Oval, Kennington Oval

One of the world's greatest sports stadiums – a top Test Cricket ground for over a century – the Oval was the original venue for the FA Cup Final, and the setting for England's first home international match.

The first FA Cup Final took place here on 16 March 1872. The finalists were Wanderers, a team of roving ex-public schoolboys, and the Royal Engineers. Two thousand spectators attended, the field had no markings, the goals no nets, and the crossbar was simply a length of tape. Royal Engineers were hampered by an injury to Lieutenant Cresswell, who broke his collar bone after ten minutes. No substitutes were allowed in those days, so Cresswell returned to the pitch, but Wanderers took advantage of the injury and scored the only goal of the game.

The scorer was A. H. Chequer who was hiding his real name of Morton Peto Betts. He had originally registered to play in the competition with Harrow Chequers as Betts, and switched to Wanderers when Harrow scratched. But the goal was mostly down to the skill of an eighteen-year-old ex-Westminster school pupil called Robert Vidal. He later earned the nickname 'The Prince of Dribblers' after running the length of the field from the kick-off and scoring without an opponent touching the ball three times in one match. Fittingly, the winning Cup Final captain, Charles Alcock, was the individual who had devised the competition a few months earlier.

Two years previously, on 5 March 1870, the Oval had been the setting for the first England international, a match against Scotland. It is not, however, included in the official records as a proper international because the FA chose not only the England team but picked the Scotland team as well – from the Scottish players playing for clubs in and around London such as Old Etonians, No Names and Civil Service.

It wasn't until 8 March 1873 that England played their first proper home international fixture, and this also took place at the Oval. Play had to be held up several times when the excited crowd spilled over the rope on to the pitch. England won 4–2 thanks to Captain Kenyon-Slaney of the Household Brigade in attack.

Nine years later the Oval FA Cup Final saw the first appearance by a team from the industrial North: Blackburn Rovers. They lost 1–0 to the Old Etonians, who featured Lord Kinnaird (→ see box below). Before the game Etonian fans stopped his carriage as it approached the ground, unclipped the horses and carried it the last dozen yards to honour the noble hero playing in his eighth final.

Northern teams playing professionally would soon dominate the competition, and the trophy went north for the first time the following year with another Blackburn team, the short-lived Blackburn Olympic. The Olympic players prepared carefully in the week leading up to the final with a strict diet of a glass of port and two raw eggs at 6 a.m., breakfast of porridge and haddock a few hours later, dinner of mutton, high tea of porridge and a supper of half a dozen oysters – an interesting comparison with the modern-day staple of chicken and pasta. The winning goal was scored for the first time by a worker, rather than a gentleman, a cotton spinner no less, by the name of Costley.

Blackburn Rovers returned to the Oval to play the Scots, Queen's Park, in the 1884 final. 'A northern horde of uncouth garb and strange oaths', the *Pall Mall Gazette* described the Lancastrians. After the 1888 final between West Brom and Preston an FA official wrote: 'No words of ours can adequately describe the present popularity of football with the public – a popularity which though great in the metropolis – is infinitely greater in the large provincial towns.' Following the 1892 final the Surrey Cricket Club urged that no more matches be played here because it spoiled the turf. Thus little football has taken place here since, although the highly principled amateur side, Corinthian Casuals, used it as their home venue in the 1950s.

→ **Wembley, p. 143**

The good Lord

No one has ever matched the FA Cup Final record of Lord Kinnaird, the late-nineteenth-century football pioneer who played in an astonishing nine finals (out of the first twelve). Three times Kinnaird was on the winning side with Wanderers and twice with Old Etonians. Indeed he was so pleased with winning his fifth Cup that he celebrated by standing on his head in front of the pavilion crowd at the Oval.

'Tityrus', editor of the *Athletic News*, called Kinnaird a 'leader, and above all things, a muscular type of Christian . . . As a player, in any position, [he] was an examplar of manly robust football. He popularised the game by his activity as a footballer among every class. His blue and white quartered cap was as familiar on the field as the giant figure of W. G. Grace with his yellow and red cricket cap.' But it wasn't all glory for the man born Arthur Fitzgerald Kinnaird. Playing in goal for Wanderers in the 1877 Final, he suffered the indignity of scoring the first major own goal in football history when he accidentally stepped backwards over his own goal-line holding the ball. For years the records failed to note the embarrassing incident, and it later transpired that Kinnaird had used his influence as a member of the FA council to doctor them.

NEW CROSS, SE14

Millwall (1910–93), The Den, Cold Blow Lane

No football stadium ever had a more appropriate address than the Den at Cold Blow Lane, Millwall's home for much of the twentieth century. And no club has had more fearsome a reputation thanks to the catalogue of violence meted out to interlopers over the decades to the chilling refrain from the home fans of 'We are Millwall . . . no one likes us, we don't care.'

The club were formed as Millwall Rovers by workers at the Morton jam factory in the Millwall part of the Isle of Dogs in 1885. They played at a number of local venues until 1910, when they crossed the Thames and moved to a rhubarb patch near New Cross bounded on three sides by the railway. The club lost much of their original support in crossing the river as Millwall locals felt that the team was no longer theirs even if it retained the name of the area. Nevertheless Archibald Leitch, the king of stadium designers, drew up plans for a ground that would hold 30,000, though when it opened against Brighton on 22 October 1910 only one stand had been built and there was open banking on three sides. The guest of honour at the opening ceremony was Lord Kinnaird, who had played in nine FA Cup Finals and had chosen *both* line-ups in an early England–Scotland match. So great was the congestion outside the ground that the noble lord was forced to climb over the wall – best suit and all – to get in. He then went to the wrong end, performed a brief ceremony, and led the players on to the pitch. Before kick-off a brass lion, inscribed in Gaelic 'We Will Never Turn Our Backs to the Enemy', was presented to the club.

The new ground quickly became known as the Den as it was home to a team that had been nicknamed the Lions. It was set among the meanest streets of London, dotted with the nastiest pubs, filled by the most uncompromising fans, and it soon acquired a reputation as the most unwelcoming in the country, eventually becoming associated with a longer history of violence than any other stadium in the country (see below).

At the outbreak of the First World War the Den was also used as an army recruitment centre, plastered with adverts urging the 'MEN OF MILLWALL ... Don't be left behind. Let the Enemy hear the Lions' Roar. Join and be in at THE FINAL and give them a KICK OFF THE EARTH', patrolled by a character in striped pyjamas called Darkie Beal who would wander through the crowd on match days playing the banjo, raising money for the war relief fund.

As Millwall Athletic the club joined the Football League in 1920. They dropped the 'Athletic' in 1925 and three years later won the Third Division (South) Championship, and with it promotion to the Second Division. A creditable seventh place followed in 1933, but after manager Bob Hunter died they were relegated. In 1937 Millwall became the first Third Division side to reach an FA Cup semi-final, losing to Sunderland, and the following year they won the Third Division title again. But Millwall just couldn't get beyond the Second Division, and in 1948 went down again. They struggled in this early post-war period, even dropping to the Fourth Division for a while, but after their return to the Second Division in 1966 they set a remarkable record of fifty-nine home League games undefeated.

In 1972 they almost achieved the ultimate promotion prize – elevation to the First Division. Twenty minutes from the final whistle of Millwall's end-of-season match against Preston the crowd suddenly erupted into a cacophony of celebration believing Birmingham were losing at Sheffield Wednesday and that Millwall, who were 2–0 up, would therefore be promoted. Millwall mainstay Harry Cripps ecstatically jigged round the pitch, delightedly telling the Preston players, 'We're in the First Division.' But journalists in the press box knew the reality, that Birmingham were leading, not losing. So did Millwall manager Benny Fenton, but he could not get the news to his players above the hubbub. More celebrations followed the final whistle, while those who knew that Birmingham had won and that it would all be down to the match against Orient the following Tuesday headed off quietly. When the crowd found out the truth, euphoria turned to silence. Worse came a few days later: Birmingham won at Orient and Millwall stayed in the Second Division.

When promotion to the top eventually came – in 1988 – it was a complete surprise. As manager John Docherty described it: 'The full enormity of what we had achieved struck home that night as we celebrated with the players and fans. When Frank McLintock and I went into the Royal Archer with the Championship trophy, I think most of our fans thought it was a cardboard cut-out! They couldn't believe that we wanted to have a drink with them and let them hold the trophy, but for me, that sort of moment is what the game is all about.'

With Tony Cascarino and Teddy Sheringham in attack, and the no-nonsense Terry Hurlock in midfield, Millwall briefly rose to the top of the First Division, but slipped after Christmas and finished tenth – one place above Manchester United. The following season they went down and have never returned to the top flight. In 1993 Millwall left the Den, hoping to leave behind the ignominious reputation that was so indelibly linked with the ground.

Den of iniquity

Despite stiff competition from Leeds, Cardiff and Chelsea over the decades no club has quite matched Millwall for nastiness and violence. Their gang, the Bushwackers, named after the American Civil War group who went around ambushing people, was once described by the Metropolitan Police as the most dangerous in the country – even worse than West Ham's InterCity Firm.

That Millwall should bear so invidious a reputation stems from their lack of middle-class support. Other football clubs, even in violent cities like Liverpool and Manchester, attract fans from a wide section of the population, with the civilised supporters acting as an unstated peer pressure bulwark against the feral, beer-fuelled extreme elements. But Millwall have always been based in run-down parts of London that defy any measure of respectability, and the crowding in one place of so many people leading lives of casual violence has long spilled over on to the terraces and stands.

✪ The first recorded incident of trouble at a Millwall match came at one of their East Ferry Road grounds on the Isle of Dogs in the late nineteenth century after the club doubled the entrance fee to 6d to keep out the riff-raff. Those who felt they were being barred decided to storm the barrier and refuse to pay any entrance money at all.

✪ The Den was temporarily closed in 1920, 1934 and 1950 after crowd disturbances. In 1947 it was shut when a spectator threatened the referee.

✪ When Mickey Purser was chairman in the 1960s he would often find his Old Kent Road garage stoned after bad results.

✪ Away from home Millwall games often attract trouble. In March 1966 Millwall were losing 6–1 to Queen's Park Rangers at Loftus Road when someone in the stand threw a penny at Millwall centre-forward Len Juliens. It hit him on the head and drew blood, but Juliens picked up the coin and flung it back into the crowd. A QPR official warned over the tannoy that the match would be abandoned if there was any more trouble, whereupon around thirty young Millwall fans invaded the pitch and staged a sit-down in an attempt to get the game abandoned. Order was restored by Millwall manager Billy Gray, who took the microphone to urge the 'hotheads' to acknowledge Rangers as 'the better team on the day' and leave the field. In the next game at the Den smoke bombs were thrown at the Cold Blow Lane end of the ground.

✪ When Plymouth ended Millwall's fifty-nine-game unbeaten home run in January 1967 the fans stoned the Plymouth coaches.

✪ Millwall supporters wrecked a train coming back from Norwich in 1967, resulting in most of the carriages having to be taken out of service.

✪ Referee Norman Burtenshaw was knocked down and claimed that he had been rendered unconscious when spectators rushed on to the pitch at the end of a match against Aston Villa on 14 October 1967. The club were fined £1,000 and ordered to raise the height of the wall running around the pitch. The referees' association threatened a boycott of the Den.

✪ March 1978 saw a riot at the Den during a Cup match against Ipswich. Fighting began on the terraces, and continued on the pitch and in the streets amid a welter of bottles, knives, iron bars and lumps of concrete. Dozens of innocent people were injured including 72-year-old Joe Hale, blood pouring from his head wound.

✪ 13 March 1985. The worst violence yet as Millwall fans went on the rampage at Luton Town's Kenilworth Road ground and thirty-one policemen were injured. The referee halted the game in the fourteenth minute and took the teams off for twenty-five minutes as fans spilled on to the pitch to escape overcrowding. Journalist James Murray phoned his copy to the paper as he watched the mêlée: 'I stood in disbelief as I watched the riots and I felt like crying. Children around me clung to their parents in fear; women and pensioners vowed never to go to a football match again. Seats were torn out of the stand and hurled on to the pitch. They became weapons for the invading fans who hurled them again at police. The scenes before me were ones of open bloody warfare.' Interestingly, of the thirty-one who appeared in court the following morning, many claimed to be fans of London clubs other than Millwall.

Since the move a few hundred yards north to the New Den there have been fewer serious incidents, but little respite from the air of menace pervading Millwall's ground.

PECKHAM, SE15

Famous as Del Boy and Rodney's home in the TV sit-com *Only Fools and Horses* and more recently in the news as an area brutalised by a series of random meaningless murders, Peckham is known in football terms only for being the much trumpeted birthplace of Manchester United and England centre-half Rio Ferdinand.

For many people, Ferdinand, even more than John Terry, Frank Lampard, Ashley Cole, Sol Campbell, Joe Cole or David Beckham, is the epitome of the brash, arrogant, over-hyped Premiership player, handicapped with a daft name, haircut and accent, and even dafter clothes. And Ferdinand has done little to dispel this image. He boasts of growing up on an estate near where ten-year-old schoolboy Damilola Taylor was horrifically murdered in 2000. He is keen to mention how he went to the same school as another famous murder victim, Stephen Lawrence. He was once filmed having sex with a girl in Ayia Napa. Not only has he committed a string of driving offences and been convicted of drunk-driving, but he also became the game's most notorious drugs casualty when he failed to turn up for a random test in 2003, alleging he was preoccupied with buying bed linen, which earned him an eight-month ban from football and thus absence from the 2004 European Championship. Ferdinand then rewarded the loyalty of Manchester United, who stood by him in this, his most difficult hour, by quibbling over his contract, for which he was booed by United fans.

And if that wasn't enough, in 2006 he hosted the moronic *Rio's World Cup Wind-Ups* with its unfunny practical jokes against team-mates, such as the bogus Scouse policeman who stops the more-Manc-than-thou Gary Neville for bad driving. 'The two things that really get under Gary Neville's skin,' Ferdinand witters, 'are scousers and policemen . . .' The show surprisingly didn't include the one in which a Golden Generation of overpaid, over-blinged footballers exit a tournament prematurely after failing to beat inferior opposition. Worse still, that year he wrote *Rio: My Story*, a football autobiography so badly received that it is likely to earn a place in the *Guinness Book of Records* for the largest number of hostile reviews. It 'plumbed the depths', according to Howard Wheatcroft in the *Daily Star*. 'The worst soccer book of the season – and there's plenty of competition,' declared Kelvin MacKenzie in the *Sun*. 'He claims he forgot about his drugs test while preoccupied about buying bed linen for partner Rebecca – please! He then accuses a footballer of using the word "coon" during a match but because the player is still in the game will not name him. Double please!'

The most savage critique came in the *Sunday Times*, courtesy of Rod Liddle:

> Now, I ought to admit – I haven't read his book. If I am absolutely honest, I'd rather read my own death certificate. It seems to me entirely likely that reading Rio's book will not only tell you nothing even minutely interesting about anything, anywhere, whatsoever, but may actually act like a sort of literary black hole and suck out from the reader's brain any last vestiges of intellect and even motor capacity, thus requiring the unlucky purchaser to lead the rest of his life as a drooling vegetable. An incontinent slab of turnip, say. And it will serve them right.

On the field at least Ferdinand could point to more success, with a Championship medal after arriving at Manchester United in 2007, which only left football fans worried that winning more trophies might lead to *My Story (Continued)*.

But Ferdinand has more than his fair share of competitors for the title of King Spoiled Brat of the Golden Generation. Ashley Cole, his England team-mate, quit Arsenal when earning the 'slave' wages of £55,000 a week because he wanted £60,000 to keep off the breadline. He joined Arsenal's new most hated rivals, Chelsea, and to compound the felony, later tried to explain himself in an autobiography bereft of any understanding of what is important in football or in life. Then there was Sol Campbell, who left Tottenham because they weren't very good (fair enough), but went to Arsenal (a bit of an insult to the Spurs fans) *without* taking the usual transfer route that would at least have netted his first club a hefty fee. Six years later Campbell was still whingeing – in public, to no less a figure than Radio 4's John Humphrys – that he was getting abuse from the fans for it, and that it had to stop, because it upset him.

→ **Frank Lampard insults grieving Americans, p. 276**

ROTHERHITHE, SE16

Fisher Athletic (1981–), Surrey Docks stadium, Salter Road

A rarity for a football club – they are named after an individual, St John Fisher, a Catholic martyr, rather than an area – Fisher Athletic are a semi-professional side who have flirted with the top of the non-League tier. Fisher were founded in 1908 by Michael Culiton, a local headmaster who wanted to provide sports facilities for local youths. The club competed in various local leagues and rose to a creditable amateur standard in the 1960s. A move to the Surrey Docks stadium came in the 1981–82 season. The eighties were their most successful decade, culminating in an FA Cup first round proper tie against Bristol City (they lost) and promotion to the Conference (the fifth division) in 1987. Recent years have not been so kind and Fisher are ground-sharing with Dulwich Hamlet in the first decade of the twenty-first century while their stadium is renovated.

Millwall (1993–), the New Den, Senegal Fields, Zampa Road

Optimistically hoping that a move to a new stadium would herald better times for the club, Millwall built a new stadium in the early 1990s only a few hundred yards from the existing Den. The idea of a new stadium first came about in 1979 as part of a complex which would include a leisure centre, ice rink, cinemas and supermarket. After several delays by the council the scheme won approval and became the first new all-seater stadium to be completed in England following the Taylor Report that damned English football grounds in the wake of the Hillsborough disaster.

Things haven't gone to plan since Millwall moved here. Not only have the club floundered, failing to return to the top flight, but the nastiness has remained. As journalist Ken Morgan put it after one match in 1994:

To watch Millwall is to journey into a valley of hatred. Tragically their fans remained in the gutter. Walking towards that spanking new stadium to watch Millwall play Derby was a nerve-jangling foretaste of the stomach churning events to come. Venturing past the pub near the ground, all you saw was a sea of scowling vengeful faces bounded by beer-fuelled loathing for any outsider. To talk of hatred in people's eyes is not to exaggerate the most evil stench of wretchedness I have ever encountered.

In May 2002 a Birmingham City win which sent the Midlands team into the play-off final at the expense of Millwall led to trouble erupting outside the ground as fans threw bricks and paving stones. Six police officers needed hospital treatment. The Met considered suing Millwall until club chairman Theo Paphitis explained that Millwall could not be blamed for the actions of those who attached themselves to the club and announced a membership scheme that would ensure only those registered could attend home matches. Scotland Yard withdrew its threat.

In 2004, with considerable surprise, Millwall reached their first FA Cup Final – held at the Millennium stadium, Cardiff, not Wembley – only to lose 3–0 to Manchester United. It meant that Millwall would play in Europe for the first time, but their campaign lasted only one round in which they went out to the Hungarian side Ferencvaros. The manager who had guided them there, Dennis Wise, left soon after, citing his inability to work with the chairman. Steve Claridge, Wise's replacement, lasted just thirty-six days, never taking charge of a competitive match. Constant changes to the board and the management are a regular occurrence at the New Den, preventing any improvement away from the third division.

WOOLWICH, SE18

Arsenal (1887), Plumstead Common

Arsenal's first proper home ground was a large open patch of grass on Plumstead Common which was hilly, uneven and in poor condition, used by the Royal Artillery to exercise its horses. The club first played here on 8 January 1887 as Royal Arsenal and beat Erith 6–1, the Arsenal players identifiable not by the colour of their shirts but by wearing the same type of cap. Royal Arsenal played only eight games on the common – Fred Beardsley, one of the players, stored the goalposts in his back garden – before moving a mile north to the Sportsman ground in September 1887.

Arsenal (1887–88), Sportsman Ground, Plumstead Marshes, Griffin Manor Way

Newly formed Royal Arsenal moved in autumn 1887 from Plumstead Common a mile north to Plumstead Marsh to play at the Sportsman Ground. Unfortunately the land had been used as a pig farm and was prone to regular flooding. As there were no facilities the players had to change at the nearby Sportsman pub.

It was here that Arsenal first played the team that were to become their greatest rivals, Tottenham Hotspur. The game took place on 11 November 1887 but was abandoned with only fifteen minutes to go due to encroaching darkness with Tottenham leading 2–1. Turning up for a home match against Millwall in February 1888, the Royal Arsenal players found the pitch unplayable and realised they had to move again. They found a new ground a few hundred yards away nearer Plumstead station: the Manor Field.

Arsenal (1888–90), (1893–1913), Manor Field, Griffin Manor Way

Royal Arsenal moved to the Manor Field, later renamed the Manor Ground, in the winter of 1888. Success against local teams meant that they began to attract crowds of several hundred spectators who had to stand on wagons brought over from a nearby barracks. The players changed at the Green Man on Plumstead High Street or at the Railway Tavern by the station, and it was also they who collected the gate money.

Like the previous pitches Arsenal used, the Manor Field was not an ideal venue for football and was flooded regularly. Indeed one newspaper described it as a 'perfect quagmire, as water lay in a pool along the touchline'. That was the day the crowd refused to pay at all and stood on the sewer pipe to watch for free. By spring 1889 the team was establishing itself as one of the best in London, at a time when no London side was involved in the new Football League and there was then no Second Division. That April a crowd of 10,000 saw Royal Arsenal beat Old Westminsters in the final of the London Charity Cup at Leyton.

After a game against Millwall in front of several thousand spectators had to be played under several inches of water, the club realised it had to move again. This time they went to the Invicta Ground (→ p. 179), just south of Plumstead High Street, where they played for two years until

1893. By that time Royal Arsenal had gone professional (the first southern club to do so) and become Woolwich Arsenal. This led the landlord to increase the rent, however, so Arsenal moved back here.

As a professional club Woolwich Arsenal were ostracised by the London FA, which objected to the 'northern disease' of professionalism. Woolwich Arsenal were, however, successful in joining the Football League's new Second Division for the 1893–94 season. In the summer of 1893 supporters helped to convert the place into a ground worthy of League football. They built changing rooms and erected a stand, thus turning the Manor Ground into a 20,000-capacity stadium.

It was a shock for the Second Division's northern- and Midlands-based clubs to play here. Not only did they have to travel all the way to London, they also had to get over to Cannon Street for a forty-minute train journey to get to a ground situated next to an engineering works, filled with squaddies. No wonder the *Liverpool Tribune* described Woolwich Arsenal as 'the team who play at the end of the earth', and the *Newcastle Echo* complained about 'an annual trip to hell'.

Success came slowly to Woolwich Arsenal. In their first season in the Second Division they finished ninth. Only 900 saw the club's record 12–0 victory over Loughborough in 1900. Two years later, after the Boer War ended, a raised part of the ground was given the name of Spion Kop in memory of a battle from that conflict. This was long before the name was purloined by Liverpool.

At last in 1903–04 Woolwich Arsenal won promotion to the top flight. Two years later Arsenal reached the FA Cup semi-final for the first time. Yet by 1910 bankruptcy loomed. The club were struggling in the top division, attendances were dwindling, the ground was still too remote. George Allison, who later became the club's manager, was often the only journalist on the train leaving Plumstead for Cannon Street after the match.

Enter Henry Norris, an estate agent who was also chairman of Second Division Fulham. A redoubtable figure with a white walrus moustache, Norris arrived in south-east London with big plans. At first he wanted to merge the two clubs at Craven Cottage: Arsenal had the First Division status and Fulham had the top-quality ground. When the League turned down the proposal, he considered moving Woolwich Arsenal to Fulham anyway and have them play alternately with the home club. That idea also came to nothing. Instead Norris dropped all notions of a merger and concentrated his attentions on Arsenal rather than Fulham. In 1913 he announced plans to move Woolwich Arsenal to Highbury, north London, where he had found six acres of available land alongside the St John College of Divinity.

The fans in Woolwich were furious. A Mr Paul Donaldson wrote to the *Kentish Gazette*: 'Mr Norris has decided that financial gain is more important than protecting our locals' club. He is making a mistake. You cannot franchise a football club. Woolwich Arsenal must stay near Woolwich.' Norris ignored them. He even deliberately underinvested in playing resources so that the club would be relegated which would strengthen the case for a move. Sure enough, Arsenal dropped down, for the only time in their history, in Easter 1913. By then they had only £19 in the bank. They left for Highbury (→ p. 89) the following September.

Arsenal (1890–93), Invicta Ground, Hector Street

Royal Arsenal moved to the Invicta Ground in 1890 after flooding rendered their Manor Field pitch unplayable. The Invicta was their best ground to date as it had a dressing room, terraces and a grandstand that ran behind the east side of Hector Street. Some of the concrete terracing remains there to this day in the residents' gardens. When the club joined the Football League in 1893 after turning professional, the Invicta landlord, George Weaver, of the Weaver Mineral Water Company, decided Arsenal now had more money and could afford a higher rent. Rather than pay the increase, however, the club decided to leave. They bought the Manor Field where they had previously played, and converted it into the Manor Ground.

Royal Oak, 27 Woolwich New Road

After playing their first fixture on 11 December 1886 as Dial Square against Eastern Wanderers, the team that became Arsenal met on Christmas Day two weeks later at this now demolished pub to discuss how to proceed. One of the first items on the agenda was the club's name, for not all the players worked in the Dial Square section of the Royal Arsenal factory. Those present failed to reach an agreement until R. B. Thompson, who had scored Dial Square's first goal in that first game and who was the only player not to work at the arsenal, asked: 'Who outside Woolwich ever heard of Dial Square? Who has not heard of the Royal Arsenal?' The meeting duly agreed to change the club's name from Dial Square to Royal Arsenal, which was a touch arrogant as there were other sports teams at the Arsenal called 'Royal Arsenal'. There was even a works football team – Royal Arsenal Gymnasium FC – who were not happy when Dial Square started passing themselves off as *the* works team.

As for kit, the players decided to wear red as some of them had played for Nottingham Forest before moving to London to work at the armaments factory. They also felt it would be best if everyone wore the *same* colours; in that first match Richard Pearce had turned out in a black and blue hooped shirt that looked like no one else's kit. It would not be easy to afford football gear of any colour, which in those days might have cost an arsenal worker over a week's wages, so Fred Beardsley asked his contacts at Nottingham Forest for help and the Midlands club sent a complete set of red shirts as well as a football. The red shirts meant that for many years Dial Square FC were known as 'The Woolwich Reds', just as Forest were known as 'The Nottingham Reds'.

For their second game the club found a venue away from the Isle of Dogs on the Woolwich side of the river at Plumstead Common. Ironically, Royal Arsenal and, as they later became known, Woolwich Arsenal never played in Woolwich. The Royal Oak pub was demolished in summer 2007 to make way for the Docklands Light Railway extension.

→ Peter Storey's pub, p. 86

The Royal Arsenal, Woolwich Church Street

Workers at Britain's main armaments depot founded Arsenal Football Club in 1886 as Dial Square. Behind the venture were two Arsenal workers, David Danskin and Jack Humble. Danskin, from Kirkcaldy in Scotland, had worked in the Ravenscraig shipyard; Humble had walked the 400 miles from Durham to London to secure his job in the factory. Before the team's first game Danskin had to organise a whip-round to raise half a guinea to buy a football. The works team played their first game as Dial Square, the name of the arsenal factory where most of them worked, but soon became Royal Arsenal.

When the club turned professional in 1891 workers at the Royal Arsenal formed a new company team – Royal Ordnance Factories FC –

who played in an all-blue kit at the Invicta Ground, Plumstead, which the better-known Royal Arsenal side had just vacated. Royal Ordnance were founder members of the Southern League in 1894 and a year later moved to Maze Hill, Greenwich. They resigned from the Southern League in the 1896–97 season after only seven games and folded soon after. By that time the earlier Royal Arsenal team were established in the Football League Second Division as Woolwich Arsenal.

→ **Arsenal in Highbury, p. 89**

Windsor Castle Music Hall, 36 Maxcy Road

It was at Royal Arsenal's annual general meeting held at this venue in 1891 that the committee who ran the club decided to turn professional. They were worried that players were being lured away by full-time clubs such as Derby County who had tried to sign two Arsenal men after an FA Cup tie, and that going pro would stop this. Royal Arsenal became the first professional team in the south and changed their name to Woolwich Arsenal.

One committee member who was worried about the political consequences of the move was Jack Humble, who was also Arsenal's full-back. Humble was staunchly left-wing, a campaigner for shorter working hours and more time for leisure activities such as football, and with his socialist views was loath to see the club become a limited liability company. 'The club has been carried on by working men and it is my ambition to see it carried on by them,' he pledged. The committee duly issued 4,000 £1 shares, which were taken up by 860 people, mostly local munitions workers, and the first board of directors included six engineers and a builder. But there was also a surgeon and the owner of a coffee house, and little chance that the proletariat might remain in charge once Arsenal joined the capitalist world.

Arsenal had other problems to worry about. The London FA, which had threatened to suspend any club that turned pro, immediately ostracised them. So Woolwich Arsenal left the organisation, but as they were now short of fixtures they suggested that the London FA should form a professional southern version of the Football League, a proposal the London FA, predictably, rejected.

Woolwich might have gone bankrupt but for their success in winning admission into the Second Division of the newly expanded Football

League whose clubs played a higher standard of football than those in the London League. None of the Second Division clubs who would be playing Arsenal in Woolwich from September 1893 were from London and they would have to make the tortuous journey from the Midlands and the North. Eventually more southern teams joined the League, and Woolwich Arsenal had local rivals who didn't have quite so far to travel.

Jack Humble remained a director for over thirty years, by which time Arsenal had moved to Highbury, and continued to work at the Royal Arsenal as a gun inspector. He was the last founding member of the football club to keep his connections with the armaments company. He resigned in 1929, an innocent victim of the financial scandal that brought down megalomanic chairman Henry Norris ($\rightarrow$ p. 90).

$\rightarrow$ **George Robey entertains Manchester United, p. 11**

Woolwich High Street
In the late 1880s Arsenal Football Club, newly founded by workers at the Woolwich Arsenal armaments factory, were so short of cash they sent one of their players, Jack Humble, down Woolwich High Street asking shopkeepers if they wanted to become directors. Only one, G. H. Leavey, a tailor, agreed. Shares cost £1. They were trading for £4,600 each by autumn 2007.

UPPER NORWOOD, SE19

Beulah Hill
The stolen Jules Rimet trophy – the World Cup – was found by a dog called Pickles, sniffing in the bushes on Beulah Hill on 27 March 1966, a week after it had been stolen from Westminster's Central Hall. Pickles's owner, Dave Corbett, a Thames lighterman, knew it was the World Cup as soon as he saw the gold trophy featured a 'woman holding a dish over her head, and the words Germany, Uruguay, Italy, Brazil'. Corbett rushed inside to his wife and cried, 'I've found the World Cup! I've found the

World Cup!' He picked up a £6,000 reward. The man who had demanded a £15,000 ransom for the return of the Cup was jailed for two years.

→ The World Cup trophy: real or fake?, p. 9

Crystal Palace origins (1861–1915)

The first Crystal Palace football club was founded in 1861 by workers at the Crystal Palace itself. Known as the Groundkeepers, they were founder members of the Football Association in 1863. They reached the semi-finals of the first FA Cup in 1872, played in claret and blue (like the modern-day side), but were wound up in 1876. Some of the players continued playing and there are records of a Crystal Palace Rovers from 1883.

It was only in 1905 that the modern-day Crystal Palace were formed by the company that owned the Crystal Palace stadium. They also played there originally, but in a ground capable of holding more than 100,000 their first attendance was twelve, half of whom were officials. The new Palace applied to join the Football League Second Division but were rejected. Instead they had to settle for the Second Division of the Southern League. In March 1915, during the First World War, the Admiralty, who had taken over the ground, ordered the club to leave. Palace never returned here but kept the name, playing at first at the Herne Hill stadium (→ p. 186), then at the Nest on Croydon Common (→ p. 186), and finally at Selhurst Park (→ p. 186).

Crystal Palace stadium, Crystal Palace Parade

The venue known simply as the Crystal Palace was built in the 1890s as the home of the FA Cup Final, and was where the match was staged from 1895 to 1914. It took its name from the huge glass exhibition centre that had moved here, to land then known as Penge Common, from Hyde Park after the 1851 Great Exhibition, and which burned down in 1936.

Although located at some distance from central London, the venue was served by two stations, Crystal Palace High Level and Crystal Palace Low Level. Those who arrived at the former were able to enter the ground via a gorgeous vaulted Italianate subway. The stadium held 115,000 but was appallingly designed, and if there were more than 20,000 in the ground few could see satisfactorily. At the first final to be held here, in 1895, 42,650 saw

Aston Villa beat West Brom 1–0, but many were unable to find their places until after the kick-off and missed the only goal of the game. Villa didn't manage to hold on to the trophy for long. It was stolen from a Birmingham shop window on 11 September and never found again.

Billy Tennant, the Wolves goalkeeper in their team's defeat by Sheffield Wednesday in the 1896 final, was amazed to discover at the end of the game that his side had lost. A shot by Wednesday's Fred Spiksley had failed to settle in the goal net and rebounded back into play, and Tennant didn't realise a goal had been given. At the end of the game the Wednesday captain asked, 'When's the replay?', to which he was told, 'There is no replay, old man! We won by two goals to one as you will see when we take the medals!'

In the 1901 final Tottenham Hotspur of the Southern League met First Division Sheffield United in the first football match to be filmed. Tottenham prepared by training in Epping Forest, and on the morning of the game made their way from their Chingford hotel to Upper Norwood by train and horse-drawn coach. United had taken the sea air at Skegness and stayed overnight at the Bedford Hotel in Covent Garden.

The FA was not expecting the huge crowd of 114,815 that turned up – a world record attendance at that time for a sporting event – and in the dreadful crush people spilled on to the pitch at half-time for the chance to breathe some fresher air. At least the caterers were better prepared. The spectators ate their way through 120,000 slices of bread and butter, 100,000 Bath buns, 2,000 smoked sausages, 6,000 pork pies, 200 rumps of beef, 40 lambs, 300 quarters of whitebait, 22,400 lbs of potatoes, 2,000 cabbages and cauliflowers, and 500 lbs of sole. They drank 120,000 bottles of mineral water and incalculable amounts of tea, coffee and alcohol.

Sheffield United, who had won the League only three years previously, were clear favourites to beat non-League Tottenham. In goal they had the redoubtable Willie 'Fattie' Foulke, a 22-stone man mountain with a penchant for throwing troublesome (and usually lighter) opponents into the back of the goal. Yet the Londoners held them to a 2–2 draw, and in the replay a few days later at Bolton's ground won 3–1 to become the only non-League team to win the trophy since the Football League was formed.

During the First World War the Crystal Palace ground was used by the Royal Navy for training and as a transit camp. This left the pitch in too poor a condition to be used for the Cup Final, which moved to Old Trafford, Stamford Bridge and then Wembley.

In 1922 the legendary amateur side Corinthians played here. In the early 1950s an athletics stadium was built on the site but football continued intermittently until 1982. Plans mooted for Crystal Palace FC to move here in the 1990s came to nothing.

Queen's Hotel, 122 Church Road

Teams playing in the Cup Final at Crystal Palace in Edwardian times would stay at the Queen's, a sumptuous south London hotel, where the French novelist Emile Zola exiled himself after fleeing France when the authorities wanted him on trumped-up charges of criminal libel. Sheffield Wednesday stayed here the night before the 1896 final against Wolves. Their line-up had not yet been selected, and defender Ambrose Langley was told he would only play if the ground was on the light side. Langley barely slept, getting up every hour to check the weather, but he did play and helped his team-mates win the Cup.

→ Roasting at the Grosvenor House Hotel, p. 24

EAST DULWICH, SE22

Dulwich Hamlet (1902–), Edgar Kail Way

One of the oldest and most famous non-League sides, Dulwich Hamlet were formed in 1893 and moved here in 1902. They have played in a distinctive pink and blue strip since, and won the Amateur Cup in 1920 and 1932. The club's greatest ever player was not Peter Crouch, who spent some time here in the late 1990s, but Edgar Kail, who scored over 400 goals for Dulwich and won three England caps in the 1920s despite being an amateur. In those days Dulwich Hamlet attracted crowds of up to 20,000 to their fine stadium, since redeveloped by Sainsbury's as a supermarket with a football ground attached, and now attracts around 250.

HERNE HILL, SE24

Crystal Palace (1915–18), Herne Hill stadium, Burbage Road

During the First World War Crystal Palace moved from the palace itself to the Herne Hill stadium, a venue used mostly for cycling, including for the 1948 Olympics. The stadium is one of the few intact former football grounds in London.

SOUTH NORWOOD, SE25

Crystal Palace (1918–24), the Nest, Selhurst Road opposite Selhurst station

Palace took over the ground vacated by disbanded Croydon Common at the end of the First World War when they were still in the Southern League. They became a League club in 1920, when the Football League accepted the entire Southern League as the new Third Division (South), and won the title in the new League's first season. This makes Palace one of only a handful of clubs to win a division at the first attempt. (The others are Preston, Small Heath/Birmingham, Liverpool and Bury.) The club moved out in 1924. Railway sheds now occupy the site.

Crystal Palace (1924–), Selhurst Park, Whitehorse Lane

Selhurst Park has never witnessed a Crystal Palace team return with a major trophy to lift triumphantly to the fans. Few clubs have such potential to become a major team left unfulfilled, but then few have caused as much exasperation to their followers over the decades as Palace.

The club began in 1905, formed by workers at the huge iron and glass exhibition centre known as the Crystal Palace which had originally stood in Hyde Park and later moved to Upper Norwood. There Palace played until 1918 when they moved a few miles south, first to land by Selhurst station, then in 1924 to Selhurst Park.

The Selhurst Park site was first identified as a likely home five years previously, after the secretary had been instructed to 'investigate the possibility of obtaining a lease at Selhurst'. It was then just waste land owned by the London, Brighton and South Coast Railway, and Palace were playing at the Nest opposite Selhurst station. In 1922 the club bought the land and hired Archibald Leitch, the great stadium builder, to design a venue suitable for a side that had just won the first ever Third Division Championship.

Palace lost their first Selhurst Park game 1–0 to Sheffield Wednesday in front of a crowd of 25,000, and more defeats followed, resulting in the club being relegated back to the Third. It took Palace almost forty years to return, during which time they suffered the ignominy of finishing bottom of the entire League (in 1949).

Queen of the Palace

The 1960s was the best decade yet for the club. In November 1961 Johnny Byrne was picked for England – one of only five men to play for the national side while playing in the Third Division – and was soon sold to West Ham for a record British fee of £65,000. In 1964 Palace returned to the Second Division. Five years later promotion to the top division was finally achieved.

Palace looked to be immediate relegation candidates but at least in Gerry Queen they had a real headline-maker, and newspaper hacks were always at hand with a new 'Queen of the Palace' angle. With Bert Head in charge Palace – wearing a sumptuous strip of claret shirts with sky-blue pinstripes, and primrose collar and cuffs – struggled along in the First Division for a few seasons, until in March 1973 new owner Ray Bloye 'promoted' Bert Head to general manager, appointing the flamboyant, super-confident Macolm Allison as coach in his place.

The experts were quick to predict that Palace would soon be a force. After all, Allison had coached Manchester City to an astonishing run of Championship, FA Cup, League Cup and European Cup Winners' Cup in three seasons. He changed the strip to red and blue stripes so that Palace looked like Barcelona, and changed their nickname from 'The Glazers' to 'The Eagles'. But by then Allison was a spent force and at the end of the season Palace were relegated.

Surely this failure was only a blip and Palace would bounce right back? The bookies made Palace clear favourites for Second Division promotion the following season. Allison also predicted that the team would not be in the Second Division for long. At the end of the season he was proved right, but again they went down, not up.

Bloye kept faith with Allison. After all the man was regarded as a Messiah. Back in the Third Division, Palace finished only fifth. That was again where they finished the following season, 1975–76, although at least the campaign featured a glorious Cup run to the semi-finals, with the scalps of mighty Leeds and Chelsea en route. What with Allison's cigars and fedora hat, it was all great fun, and winger Peter Taylor even won four England caps despite playing for a Third Division team. But League football in the third tier and an FA Cup semi-final place were not much to show for one of football's self-styled greatest coaches.

It was a member of the same exclusive club – Terry Venables – who rescued Palace. Venables took them up in his first season, 1976–77, in which the youngsters won the FA Youth Cup, and in the second season back they gained promotion to the top division. As the players from the Youth Cup-winning side began to establish themselves in the first team the press gave Crystal Palace the nickname 'The Team of the Eighties'. A similar epithet had been applied to Burnley a decade earlier and they soon crashed to relegation.

Surely Palace were made of sterner stuff? Briefly they looked world-conquering. The football was fast and flowing with the ball mostly on the ground, in the purist manner, thanks to classy players such as future multi-capped England left-back Kenny Sansom and flying winger Vince Hilaire. Palace even topped the First Division in autumn 1979. But like so many Venables sides (Barcelona '86, Tottenham '90 and England '96), Palace '80 lacked backbone; what Arsene Wenger a few generations later would call 'mental toughness'. Far from winning the League, Palace slipped to thirteenth. In the summer the Venables transfer merry-go-round began. Kenny Sansom left for Arsenal, where he became the best left-back of the 1980s, and was replaced by Clive Allen, an energetic young striker who would go on to score an extraordinary number of goals, but not at Palace. The club lost nine of their first ten games and Venables bailed out to QPR. Failing to learn any lessons from the recent past, Palace reappointed Malcolm Allison as coach – fresh from a disastrous second spell at Manchester City. Palace ended the 1981 season bottom.

There was more drama off the pitch. Around the time of their relegation, Ron Noades, formerly chairman of Wimbledon, had bought the club. Noades sacked Malcolm Allison, and appointed Dario Gradi as the fourth manager that season. Gradi, a thoughtful, conscientious operator who went on to work wonders at Crewe, was not given time at Selhurst Park. Noades was too quick to hire and fire, and made a succession of ill-conceived choices as manager: Steve Kember, Alan Mullery (hated for his Brighton links) and Dave Bassett, whose reign was brief to the point of near non-existence – four, just four, *days*. Meanwhile, the long-suffering Palace fans were left wondering how a side top of the entire League well into the 1980 season could finish fifteenth in the Second division in 1981–82 and 1982–83.

The future's bright, the future's claret

In summer 1984 Noades made a wise move. He appointed 29-year-old former England winger Steve Coppell as manager and, surprisingly, allowed him time to do the job. Improvement came slowly, but in 1989 Palace returned to the top division. Theirs was a team packed with high-class players. Up front were Mark Bright, a solid, no-frills centre-forward, and Ian Wright, a livewire goalscoring machine with an astonishing bag of ball tricks, who had come into football late. In goal was the dependable Nigel Martyn, and there was skill aplenty in midfield thanks to John Salako and Andy Gray. They helped the club reach their first FA Cup Final, a run that saw them shock football by knocking out soon-to-be crowned champions Liverpool in the semi-final only a few months after a 9–0 League defeat to the same club. The final against Manchester United was unusual and unforgettable. It finished 3–3, but Palace lost the replay 1–0.

Good times for once at the Palace. The following season, 1990–91, the club reached their highest ever League placing: third; only Arsenal and Liverpool finished higher. But then it all came crashing down. Noades failed to strengthen the team to capitalise on this lofty finish. Worse still, in a BBC documentary in September 1991 he was heard stating that 'black players at this club lend the side a lot of skill and flair, but you also need white players in there to balance things up and give the team some brains and some common sense'. Ian Wright vowed never to play for Palace again and soon left for Arsenal, where he became the greatest English goalscorer of the decade. In 1993 Palace were relegated to the second tier, the beginning of what has become a continual pattern of struggling in and relegation from the first, soon followed by promotion from the second before the inevitable struggle begins all over again.

This seemingly endless cycle of mediocrity has been enlivened by more bizarre signings and appointments: Dave Bassett returned in 1996, despite that earlier short, short tenure; Steve Coppell came again and again. (The fans knew it was all too much for Coppell when they heard him explain that 'At the end of the day, it's all about what's on the shelf at the end of the year.')

In March 1998 Ron Noades sold his Crystal Palace stake to computer tycoon Mark Goldberg. Although Goldberg mouthed the usual predictable cant about transforming the club into a European force within five years, he failed to make the appointments that might have brought this about. Instead, with the club looking doomed to relegation for the third time in six seasons, he appointed as joint managers ex-Swedish international Tomas Brolin and recent Italian signing Attilio Lombardo. If it wasn't bad enough having a chubby, Samantha Fox lookalike in a managerial position, how much more ridiculous could it be to have someone, Lombardo, alongside him who could not speaka da English too well. Frank McLintock put it succinctly. 'I understand Lombardo getting the coaching job, but what is Brolin's role? Catering manager?'

The Italo-Swedish partnership was never going to save the club from relegation, and sure enough at the end of the 1997–98 season Palace were down again, after only one year. They had won just two home games and finished bottom. After this débâcle Goldberg's recipe for revival was to appoint Terry Venables as head coach. There was a brief flourish on the pitch, but then the finances went into disarray. The club had paid £448,796 to an unknown agent for the signing of three Argentinians, only one of whom arrived, and Ron Noades, by now chairman of Brentford, was still owed an undisclosed amount.

Goldberg put the club into administration and ousted the most expensive employees (Venables and Lombardo), along with forty-four members of staff. Palace slumped, and the fans were livid. As Chris Winter, who has written extensively on the sordid Selhurst saga, noted in his entertaining diary:

I write this on Easter Monday, 1999. The Eagles are in the middle of the worst crisis ever known at the club, caused by the unholy alliance of Mark Goldberg, Terry Venables and Ron Noades. At the moment Palace are being run by administrators and have made long-serving staff redundant. Half the first team squad have been sold or loaned to other clubs to cut the wage bill ... The fans have had to swallow months of half truths and absurd fantasies ...

Going Dowie

Another new owner arrived in July 2000: Simon Jordan, a mobile phone tycoon and life-long fan. There were more comings and goings of managers, but, finally, in 2003–04 Iain Dowie transformed Crystal Palace from relegation candidates at Christmas into play-off contenders in April, helped by the phenomenal goalscoring exploits of Andrew Johnson. Despite finishing sixth in the table it was Palace that went up, but Dowie, like so many of his predecessors, found that the Palace eagles fail to soar in the top flight. Even Johnson's twenty-one goals were not enough. Down went Palace again after a final day 2–2 draw at Charlton, of all places. The 2005 drop was their fourth relegation from the top division in a dozen years.

In May 2006 Ian Dowie left Palace by 'mutual consent', claiming that he wanted to be closer to his family in the North. The chairman, Simon Jordan, waived a £1 million compensation fee. A few days later it was announced that Dowie had indeed moved North . . . all the way to the Valley, Charlton, SE7. Jordan was furious. He sent a minion to serve Dowie with a writ. The High Court later ruled that Dowie had 'deceived' Jordan when negotiating his way out of his contract at Palace and ordered him to pay £300,000 in legal costs. Dowie appealed against the verdict.

Palace failed to return to the top division quickly. Perhaps the yo-yo years are now over? The appointment of Peter Taylor as Dowie's successor made many question whether the club really did want success, and in October 2007 Taylor was ousted after an uninspiring sixteen months. With Neil Warnock in charge, Palace almost won promotion at the end of the season but slipped to fifteenth in 2009.

Crystal Palace off the bench

⚽ Selhurst Park had a variety of uses in its early days. An England–Wales international was held here in 1926, and around the same time England amateur matches and other sports including boxing, bicycle polo and cricket were staged.

✪ Palace have been the most generous of neighbours. Charlton Athletic were invited to share the Selhurst Park ground from 1985 to 1992 when the Valley became unusable, and as soon as Charlton left, their place was taken by Wimbledon, who alleged they had been forced out of their traditional SW19 ground by Merton council.

✪ Finishing third in the League in the 1991 season behind Arsenal and Liverpool should have earned Palace entry to the UEFA Cup. However, in the summer UEFA rescinded its ban preventing Liverpool playing in Europe, and the Merseyside outfit took the one UEFA Cup place available, at the expense of Palace.

✪ Palace managed a unique last four place in all three competitions in the 1994–95 season. They reached the semi-finals of both cups and were in the bottom four of the Premiership, which led to their relegation.

✪ Selhurst Park was the setting for one of the most notorious incidents in football history on 25 January 1995. Manchester United's French striker Eric Cantona was sent off for a bad tackle, and as he walked to the dressing room was taunted by Palace fan Matthew Simmons. Cantona was so incensed that he hurled himself over the barrier and aimed a kung-fu kick at Simmons. Perhaps it was lucky for Cantona that this was at Palace. 'If Cantona had jumped into our crowd he'd never have come out alive,' Alex Rae of Millwall once claimed. The Frenchman was banned for seven months. The nation's football journalists later showed their lack of concern at the example set by his thuggery and made him their player of the year in 1996.

Further south

Croydon Crown Court, Altyre Road

At Croydon Crown Court in March 1995 Eric Cantona won his appeal against his jail sentence for assaulting a fan and was ordered to do 120 hours of community service instead. When the judge announced his decision, there was applause from Cantona's supporters and several girls burst into tears. The usually taciturn Frenchman then revealed at a hushed press conference what he thought of the recent events: 'When seagulls follow the trawler it is because they think sardines will be thrown into the sea,' before walking out. The world was perplexed. Some – mostly Manchester United fans – were impressed, and Scottish winger Gordon Strachan summed it up succinctly when he lamented that 'If a Frenchman goes on about seagulls, trawlers and sardines, he's called a philosopher. I'd just be called a short Scottish bum talking crap.'

Croydon Magistrates' Court, Barclay Road

Eric Cantona, the Manchester United forward, was sentenced to two weeks in jail at Croydon Magistrates' Court in March 1995 after pleading guilty to assaulting a Crystal Palace fan, Matthew Simmons, who had supposedly abused him as he walked off the Selhurst Park pitch. Cantona's counsel maintained that Simmons had gone to 'considerable trouble' to insult his client, 'rushing forward eleven rows from his seat in the main members' enclosure to the side of the pitch'. Cantona appealed and spent only twenty-four hours inside before being bailed and ordered to do 120 hours of community service.

→ Football at the High Court, p. 15

Croydon Park Hotel, 7 Altyre Road

Before Cantona's first court appearance the Manchester United party stayed at the Croydon Park Hotel. In the morning midfield general Paul Ince knocked on the accused's door and found him wearing a jacket and white shirt with long pointed collar 'unbuttoned so that you could see his chest. "Eric, you can't go to court like that," I told him, and he says, "I am Cantona, I can go as I want."'

6 South-west London

South-west London is dominated in football terms by two neighbourhoods: Chelsea and Fulham. The main roads connecting both places – King's Road and Fulham Road – are synonymous with luxurious London living and still exude memories of the late 1960s and early 70s when football and Swinging London merged with the so-called Chelsea Set and players such as Peter Osgood and Alan Hudson frequented venues patronised by the likes of the photographer David Bailey, the clothes designer Mary Quant, the Rolling Stones, and showbiz fans Richard Attenborough and Leonard Rossiter. To the east the grand stucco-clad terraces of Belgravia have been popular in recent decades with the better-paid players from both clubs.

BELGRAVIA, SW1

Carlton Hotel, 90 Belgrave Road

Cash-strapped Tottenham Hotspur sold their highly-rated forward Chris Waddle to Bernard Tapie's Marseille in 1989 in a deal conducted at this hotel. Marseille initially offered £2 million, and when Tottenham turned down the bid upped it to £3 million. This too was rejected and so negotiations continued here. Terry Venables, who was then Tottenham's manager, believed Marseille would match the world record fee of the time – £6 million – so that rivals would see what a big club Marseille were. However, when the bidding reached £4.25 million Tottenham caved in – and decided to tell Waddle the news.

Eaton Square

Located to the west of Victoria station and built in the 1850s, the immaculately designed Eaton Square has been home in recent years to such celebrities as the actress Joan Collins, the theatre impresario Andrew Lloyd Webber and various Chelsea players and officials, including Gianfranco Zola and José Mourinho.

When Roman Abramovich moved to London in 2003 and bought Chelsea Football Club he decided he would like to live here too, given that Eaton Square is only a few miles from Stamford Bridge. Abramovich picked out a particular house he admired, and his people phoned the owner to ask if he minded Irina Abramovich and three friends viewing the property.

No, the owner didn't mind, but there was just one problem: he wasn't planning to sell. Nevertheless he let the Abramovich party take a look inside, hoping that this would be the end of the matter. The Russians, however, were so impressed with the house, and the owner's art collection in particular, that they made an offer of £40 million. 'I'm sorry, it's not for sale,' was the response.

A few days later Abramovich's people phoned again. 'We would like to increase our offer to £60 million.' Again the owner said no. Within a week they were back on the phone. Now it was an offer the owner surely couldn't refuse: £100 million. He refused. And so Roman and Irina Abramovich had to be content with luxurious but less exclusive Lowndes Square in Knightsbridge.

José Mourinho rented a flat in Eaton Square when he became Chelsea manager in 2004. With his Mediterranean background and better education than the typical English footballer, Mourinho naturally felt no empathy with the oversized Hertfordshire mansion lifestyle as sent up in *Footballers' Wives*. But life wasn't all chic Belgravia elegance for the spoiled one. In May 2007 the then Chelsea manager was shockingly arrested, not for crimes against football management but in a row over his Yorkshire terrier. He resisted officers who wanted to quarantine the dog for fear it had entered the country without the necessary jabs. The problem was soon sorted out and Mourinho received a caution for obstructing police.

Hans Crescent

Thirty luxury apartments at 1 Hans Crescent, an Edwardian block where the actress Mae West once lived, were bought within ninety minutes of going on sale in August 2001. The buyers included the former Wimbledon centre-forward John Fashanu, who paid a tramp to queue overnight for him.

→ **Wimbledon Football Club**, p. 230

Harrods, 87–135 Brompton Road

Mohamed al-Fayed, the owner of this world-famous store, became football news in 1997 when he bought Fulham. Occasionally some unusual football business was conducted here. For instance, in November 2002 al-Fayed hauled in Fulham manager Jean Tigana for the first of several grillings over the worth of his French striker Steve Marlet, who had cost £11.5 million but was not delivering. Al-Fayed suspected foul play, that he had been cheated and that a number of people involved in the transfer, including Tigana, had dishonestly made money out of the deal. The courts later found Tigana innocent of any wrongdoing. The football world realised that the Fulham boss had simply been guilty of the age-old managerial sin of bad judgement. He hadn't foreseen what a dud signing Marlet would be.

It was also at Harrods that representatives of Fulham and their fellow relegation strugglers, Wigan and Sheffield United, met in May 2007 to decide what they wanted to do about fellow relegation contenders West Ham. The Hammers had broken League rules in fielding Carlos Tevez but had not been docked points in punishment and thus had stayed up at the expense of the Sheffield club. Despite much media exposure their campaign to get West Ham relegated fizzled out and Sheffield United dropped down.

✪ When Ossie Ardiles, newly arrived at Tottenham in 1978 from Argentina, asked a policeman how to get to the famous store he was given directions to Harrow, the north-west London suburb ten miles away.

→ Ardiles arrives at Tottenham, p. 116

Harvey Nichols, 109–125 Knightsbridge

West Ham's costly mid-1990s Romanian international Florin Raducioiu was shopping at this ever-fashionable store in 1996 when his mobile phone rang. On the other end was the club's manager, Harry Redknapp. 'Where are you, Florin?' asked the manager. 'In Harvey Nichols, shopping,' replied the midfield star. 'Oh, sorry, to bother you, it's just that kick-off is only a few minutes away and you were supposed to be playing, if you remember.' A few weeks later Raducioiu was sold to Español at a loss to West Ham of £600,000.

→ Harry Redknapp's foreign legion, p. 57

Knightsbridge Crown Court, Hans Crescent

Eddie Ashby, Terry Venables's long-time financial adviser, was convicted on 23 October 1997 at Knightsbridge Crown Court (now being rebuilt as luxury flats) of breaching the bankruptcy laws, and given a four-month jail sentence. Minutes later Venables deftly avoided being tackled by the press about his connection with the disgraced businessman by announcing, 'I knew nothing about his bankruptcy.'

A year later Venables appeared at the court to face nineteen charges of serious misconduct under the 1996 Company Directors' Disqualification Act. A judge accused him of 'deliberately and dishonestly' misleading a jury when giving evidence at Ashby's trial. Venables was banned from being a company director for seven years.

→ Terry Venables at Tottenham, p. 117

Wellington Club, 116a Knightsbridge

A drinking club popular with the best-paid Premiership players, the Wellington was where England captain John Terry, his incorrigible former team-mate Jody Morris and Wimbledon's Des Byrne were caught up in a fight on 4 January 2002 that left a receptionist with a half-inch facial gash. John Terry was taken to Belgravia police station on suspicion of assault, and of being drunk and disorderly. When the case was tried, the court heard that Terry had hit a Wellington bouncer so hard that he had broken a bone in his hand. However, the centre-half's barrister claimed that it was self-defence and that the footballers were the victims of a conspiracy by the nightclub's management aimed at concealing various 'dubious practices' regarding the running of the club. Asked to choose between the word of the footballers and that of a nightclub doorman, the jury understandably sided with the former: the Chelsea pair were cleared of assault, though Byrne was convicted of throwing a bottle at the bouncers.

→ Jermaine Pennant arrest, p. 23

CHELSEA, SW3, SW10

Alexander's (1960s), 138a King's Road

Below Mary Quant's pioneering boutique, the first of many in 1960s London, was Alexander's, a restaurant owned by Quant's husband, Alexander Plunkett-Greene. Plunkett-Greene was something of an eccentric and had once turned up at Quaglino's, the fashionable St James's eaterie, in a suit with no shirt and a row of buttons painted on his chest. A typical Swinging Sixties dandy, he enticed to Alexander's patrons such as Princess Anne, the actor Richard Attenborough (a one-time Chelsea director) and the Chelsea players Peter Osgood and Alan Hudson, who would go there after training on Fridays. 'I didn't speak to Princess Anne,' Osgood told the writer Clive Batty, author of *Kings of the King's Road*. 'She was royalty after all. We'd have loved it if she'd come across and said "Hello", but you can't approach, can you?' To Hudson the secret of the place's success was the chef, Pepe, who, he once claimed, could 'serve up David Webb's underpants and convince you that you were eating rack of lamb with truffle potatoes'.

Chelsea Harbour, Lots Road

A luxury Thames-side gated complex, situated at some distance from the picturesque delights of the area, it has been home in recent years to several Chelsea players as well as Terry Ramsden, the one-time Walsall chairman who is believed to have lost £52 million on the horses – not all in the same race.

Club Dell' Aretusa (1950s–1970s), 107 King's Road

George Best had his own chair by the bar at this fashionable 1960s King's Road nightclub. Dell' Aretusa was also a regular haunt of the Beatles and showbiz personalities such as the actor Richard Harris, who would arm wrestle with the Chelsea striker Tommy Baldwin here. Dave Sexton, the Chelsea manager of the time, often dropped in on a Friday night, not to socialise, but to check whether his players were out clubbing. Only occasionally did he find anyone breaking the pre-match curfew because the owners tipped off the players that Sexton had arrived and delayed him at the entrance while they escaped out the back.

→ **China White, p. 27**

King's Road

One of London's most famous and longest streets, King's Road is synonymous with the 1960s when Chelsea was at the centre of 'Swinging London' and Chelsea Football Club was briefly the most fashionable in the country.

It was an exciting place. As George Graham, the dapper Scot who arrived at the club from Aston Villa in July 1964, later recounted in his autobiography, *The Glory and the Grief*, 'for a red-blooded male, stepping foot in the King's Road was like a passport to paradise. There were so many beautiful, long-limbed girls.' This was echoed by Ron 'Chopper' Harris, Graham's craggy team-mate, whose fierce tackles made even the Shed faithful at Stamford Bridge quake in their boots. Harris put it a slightly different way. King's Road was 'crawling with Richards'. When the journalist interviewing him expressed puzzlement and pushed for further explanation Harris revealed that he was simply using the kind of ingenious cockney rhyming slang that came naturally to him, and that 'Richard' was short for 'Richard the IIIs – birds'. At the end of the decade the Chelsea players, particularly Peter Osgood, Alan Hudson and Charlie Cooke, became known as the 'Kings of the King's Road', which Clive Batty used as the title for his 2004 book on the period.

But it wasn't always so chic here. One cold night in the 1930s Hughie Gallagher, the highly rated Chelsea forward who had played in the Scotland team that beat England 5–1 in 1928, was walking along King's Road in his trademark double-breasted tweed suit when he was approached by a tramp and asked for some money. Hearing the man's Glaswegian accent Gallagher took out a wad of notes and stuffed them into the man's hands. He then took off his Savile Row overcoat and, despite the cold, gave that to him as well. Gallagher himself came to a tragic end, committing suicide in 1957 by lying on a railway line.

→ **Green Street, p. 55**

Lord Palmerston, 648 King's Road

Peter Osgood and Alan Birchenall were among those who drank in this pub near Stamford Bridge after matches in the late 1960s and early 70s, taking advantage of the lock-in which would start when the curtains were drawn at 11 p.m. After Chelsea's Fairs Cup match against DWS Amsterdam in 1968 Osgood and Birchenall dropped in as usual, but when Birchenall went to get the drinks he was buttonholed at the bar by a ferocious-looking man wearing a Crombie overcoat. The man harangued Birchenall about just how badly he and the team had played. The player nodded – anything for a quiet life – but asked the barfly how he could bear to wear such a heavy coat in the clement weather. At that point the man opened the overcoat to show the sawn-off shotgun secreted inside. Birchenall rushed off and dragged Osgood out of the pub with him, mid-pint. A few days later they read of a gangland shooting that had taken place that night on the Fulham Palace Road. When Birchenall later mentioned this to the Lord Palmerston landlord he was told to keep quiet.

✪ One King's Road pub which does survive is the Chelsea Potter at 119 King's Road, where the players also used to gather after matches. On one occasion Osgood and Co. arrived at 8 p.m., despite having just played at Newcastle. This left them plenty of drinking time before rolling home in the early hours of Sunday morning complaining to their wives of the inordinately long coach trip they had just endured.

Markham Arms (pre-1990s), 138 King's Road

A pub heavily patronised by the 1950s Chelsea beat set, the Markham Arms was where the 1960s Chelsea players headed after midweek training to refuel on shepherd's pie and beans. They also often congregated here after Saturday away games, implementing two rules: no women and no outsiders. Drinks were bought after a £10 whip round, and the talk was solely about football – what had gone wrong with the match, how to deal with troublesome opponents and how to fend off the management.

After closing time the players would head off to a nearby club where football would be replaced on the agenda by women. The club's manager, Dave Sexton, disapproved of the gatherings, but as star midfielder Alan Hudson later explained to the journalist Rob Steen: 'Sexton couldn't handle the fact we conducted our team talks without him. If it had been [Stoke manager] Tony Waddington he'd have been drinking there with us.' The pub closed in the 1980s and is now a bank.

Phene Arms, 9 Phene Street

A once elegant pub, currently shut, named after the eccentric local late-nineteenth-century barrister-architect-scientist Dr John Phené, it was also the local of long-time Chelsea gadabout George Best after he retired from playing. Best primed staff to lie to wives, girlfriends and creditors who would then happily maintain he wasn't in the pub when indeed he was. Occasionally Best ventured outside to make trips to the betting shop, the off-licence on the corner or Pucci's pizzeria on the King's Road. As some cynics noted, his lifestyle – pub, bookie's, offie, pizza joint – was little different from the kind of existence he might have led had he never left Belfast, albeit in more luxurious surroundings.

→ Best in court for drink-driving, p. 157

Pucci Pizza, 205 King's Road

A favourite eaterie of George Best, it closed shortly after his death in 2005. In the 1960s the pizzeria was a regular haunt of the fashionable Chelsea set, diners often including the Rolling Stones' Mick Jagger and the actor Jack Nicholson, and King's Road watchers saw its closure as another nail in the coffin of the once ultra-chic street.

→ Gazza's kebab, p. 42

CLAPHAM, SW4

Clapham Common

Clapham Rovers, founded in 1869, played at various times on Clapham Common and Tooting Bec Common. The club competed in the first ever FA Cup in 1872 and are best known for being the first team named after a part of London to reach the final, losing to Old Etonians in 1879 at Kennington Oval. (They cannot really be called the first *London* team to do so as the Cup was won in its opening season by the Wanderers, based at Battersea Park.) Playing for Clapham in that game was James Prinsep who was only seventeen years and 245 days old, and remained the youngest player to feature in the final until 2004 when his record was beaten by Millwall's Curtis Weston. Prinsep was also England's youngest international when he made his debut against Scotland in April 1879 and kept that record until Wayne Rooney was capped in February 2003. The club are now defunct. In 1996 a local Sunday League team called Clapham Rovers began playing but have no connection to the original team.

Clapham High Street

When Clapham resident Mrs Tapsell went shopping on the High Street one morning in November 1945 she bumped into a group of Moscow Dynamo players sauntering along taking a break from football during their pioneering tour. Not only did she recognise them but she proceeded to do a most unClapham-like thing: she addressed them in fluent Russian, to the Soviets' amazement. Mrs Tapsell had worked in Moscow before the war, despite the near total absence of contacts between the Soviet Union and Britain at that time. Surprisingly, the newspapers failed to pick up on this unlikely occurrence so no one knows what the touring party said to the Clapham housewife.

→ Tottenham High Road, p. 111

EARL'S COURT, SW5

Cromwell Hospital, 198 Cromwell Road

George Best was admitted to this private hospital for the first time in March 2000. By then he was a bloated parody of his former self, his liver destroyed by years of alcoholic abuse.

After his liver transplant, Best became particularly susceptible to infections, and in October 2005 he was back at the Cromwell with flu-like symptoms. He developed a kidney infection and complications leading to internal bleeding. Best's condition deteriorated and he died on 25 November.

FULHAM, SW6

Barbarella's, 428 Fulham Road

A favourite for Chelsea players in the 1960s and 70s as it was only a couple of minutes' walk from the ground, Barbarella's was where Alan Birchenall, Charlie Cooke, Peter Osgood and John Boyle enjoyed a lunch in 1969 washed down with fourteen bottles of wine. Cooke paid for the meal by cheque but it was sent back by the bank as the signature was illegible. Soon there was worse news. The Chelsea management had found out about the players' bacchanalian binge and they were all dropped, which allowed a seventeen-year-old Alan Hudson to make his debut. Even that was not enough to prevent Chelsea being thrashed 5–0 by Southampton.

→ Pucci Pizza, p. 201

Bellwood, 444 Fulham Road

Gus Mears, who founded Chelsea Football Club in 1905, lived in a mansion called Bellwood at 444 Fulham Road in the first decade of the twentieth century. In 1910 Mears sold the property, the adjacent No. 446, and the land behind to the music-hall impresario and theatre builder Oswald Stoll, who wanted to build a new venue. When Stoll found himself unable to obtain planning permission for his venture, he donated the land to a war charity, which in 1916 put up a block of flats, the War Seal Mansions.

→ John Charles at Ronan Point, p. 79

Butchers Hook, 477 Fulham Road

The pub which stands opposite the main entrance to the ground is crucial to the history of Chelsea. It was at a meeting here, in what was then the Rising Sun, on 14 March 1905, that the club was conceived as Chelsea by a group of men who became the first board of directors. The *Fulham Chronicle* was amazed by the news and commented that the new football team would be 'no more connected with the neighbouring borough than with Timbuctoo'. They were partly right for Chelsea FC play not in Chelsea but in the shabby Walham Green end of Fulham.

Fittingly, it was in the same pub around a hundred years later that former chairman Brian Mears, who had given way to Ken Bates in 1982, had lunch with Chelsea's new owner, Russian billionaire Roman Abramovich. As Mears later recalled: 'Abramovich was walking around and I introduced myself to him. He was with someone who explained who I was. I can't speak Russian and I don't know how his English is. In truth, I hardly spoke to him.'

→ The Drayton Park pub, p. 104

Chelsea (1905–), Stamford Bridge, Fulham Road

Because of the severe congestion on Tottenham High Road one match day in 2003 Russian billionaire Roman Abramovich gave up his plan to buy Tottenham Hotspur and instead turned his attention to Chelsea. Now, instead of passing his time dabbling in fantasy football, the man *Forbes* magazine claimed was the twenty-first richest person in the world, with a fortune worth over $13 billion, could tinker in real-life football.

Abramovich bought Chelsea that summer, saving them from bankruptcy, which was allegedly only four days away. He then provided the funds for the acquisition of a batch of world-class players. The final piece of the jigsaw would be the appointment of a high-achieving manager. So the popular but laid-back Claudio Ranieri, despite taking the club to second place in the Premiership in the 2003–04 season, was ousted in favour of José Mourinho, who had just won the European Cup with Porto.

Chelsea were now ready to conquer football, and over the following couple of seasons they undoubtedly conquered England, even if they fell short of European domination. All this to a soundtrack of frequent mutterings from opponents and rivals about how they had 'bought' success ... unfairly; how they had too much money and were spoiling it for everyone else – as if no other club had ever used its financial muscle to prise a player away from a smaller rival.

A stadium but no club

There was nothing new in the moans about Chelsea using their bank balance to gain advantage. Exactly the same complaints had been heard a century earlier, in 1905, when the club was formed. Unlike almost every other important League club Chelsea were an Edwardian rather than Victorian creation. They came into existence purely through the desire of two businessmen brothers – Gus and Joe Mears – to find a football club to play at the stadium they already owned: what is now Stamford Bridge.

That original stadium, of which nothing remains, was built in 1877, nearly thirty years before the club was founded, as a home for the London Athletic Club. Being so close to the Lillie Bridge ground, venue for the second FA Cup Final (→ p. 226), it was not an initial success. Just 6,000 turned up for the opening event, and a few years later the developers, the Waddell brothers, were so much in debt they fled the country. The stadium continued to be used for athletics until 1904 when Gus Mears bought the freehold with his brother, Joe, and the athlete Fred Parker, who had performed here. Mears planned to redevelop the site into the finest sporting arena in the country with a capacity of 100,000. Having a football club to play here as well would maximise revenue, and so the owners invited neighbours Fulham to move in. When Fulham said no the brothers considered scrapping the idea altogether and selling the land to the railway company, whose line ran alongside, for a coal yard.

Parker didn't like that idea. He and Gus Mears agreed to meet on the site to discuss the matter. As they walked around, Mears's dog bit Parker's leg. Parker was livid and began wiping away the blood, but when Mears quipped: 'Scotch terrier – bites before he speaks,' Parker's annoyance faded.

Mears was so delighted that he changed his mind about selling the land. The two men decided to form a club to play at the revamped ground. They suggested the names Kensington, Stamford Bridge (the Stamford Brook runs alongside) or even London, but eventually opted for Chelsea, even though the land is in Fulham.

Those behind the new Chelsea Football Club wanted to join the Football League immediately rather than pay their dues in the lower divisions. Other clubs were horrified by the idea of a brand-new club going straight into the League, but after intense canvassing in the bar of Covent Garden's Tavistock Hotel, involving, some said, well-filled brown envelopes, Chelsea scrambled enough votes to join at the start of the 1905–06 season – entering the League without having kicked a ball.

Bankrolled by the Mears brothers, Chelsea FC signed a number of established players including Willie 'Fatty' Foulke, the highly rated 22-stone Sheffield United goalkeeper. Chelsea employed two boys to stand behind Foulke, simply to emphasise his weight. They were the first ball-boys in football. An irrepressible character, Foulke memorably retorted once when insulted about his weight: 'You can call me anything you like but don't call me late for lunch.'

Stamford Bridge stadium was redesigned by the indefatigable Archibald Leitch, responsible for impressive new grounds in Glasgow for Celtic and Rangers. It featured a 5,000-seater grandstand using earth excavated during the construction of the Piccadilly Line for the banking. Within a season Chelsea were attracting ample gates of 18,000 and had been promoted to the First Division of the Football League itself, where they remained for three seasons. Yet, despite the high expectations that came with their unusual genesis, Chelsea's first forty-nine years of existence yielded no trophies. The only high spot was an FA Cup Final appearance in 1915. This took place during the Great War and was held at Old Trafford, to ensure Londoners did not neglect their war duties to attend the match. It became known as the Khaki Cup Final, so great was the number of uniformed soldiers present, and Chelsea lost 3–0 to Sheffield United. It barely warranted a mention in the press.

The Russians are coming

On 13 November 1945 Stamford Bridge was the setting for one of the strangest football matches ever seen in Britain. Chelsea played the touring

Moscow Dynamo team at a time when not only were there no European competitions between clubs but football fans had been starved of sporting action during the six years of the Second World War. The match should have been played at Wembley, but there was a bus strike and spectators would not have been able to reach the national stadium easily. Moscow were distraught. They particularly wanted to play there and requested the authorities to order the strikers back to work. Nevertheless, Stamford Bridge it was.

People came to the game en masse to pay their respects to the Russians for their role in fending off the Nazis in the war. They were also curious to see what foreign footballers looked like and how they played. On the day itself crowds began arriving soon after breakfast, and the gates had to be shut an hour before the afternoon kick-off. The attendance was officially listed at 84,000 but reports claim there were perhaps 100,000 in the ground.

Many climbed over walls and gates to gain entrance. One hefty paratrooper shinned up the stand, fell through the roof, and landed in one of the few empty seats, according to a barely believable legend. Roy Bentley, who went on to star in Chelsea's 1955 League Championship win, managed to get in by crossing the West London Railway and clambering up the back of the stand. Chelsea's owner, Joe Mears, took his son, Brian, who became the club's chairman in the 1970s. They gained entrance legitimately and the youngster was mesmerised by the spectacle. When he asked if it was like this every match, he was told: 'Shut up and get on with your ice cream!'

Before the kick-off the Soviet players, their shirts emblazoned with an ornate letter 'D', came on the field and did something never previously witnessed in England: they handed each of their opponents a bunch of flowers. They also spent fifteen minutes warming-up before kick-off, which English clubs didn't do in those days. The newspapers had dismissed Dynamo as enthusiastic amateurs. 'Do not expect much from this bunch of factory workers,' wrote the *Sunday Express*. 'These pale boys are far too slow for the top drawer,' claimed the *People*. Another journalist watched Dynamo training and announced the players were so slow you could see them thinking.

The reality was different. Dynamo amazed the crowd from the kick-off with their precise passing and athleticism. Yet it was Chelsea who scored first and even took a two-goal lead. The Russians were, however, considerably fitter than the Londoners and gained control in the second half. When they scored their first goal, the Soviet radio commentator, Vadim Sinyavsky, screamed (in Russian): 'He's through! He has scored! Yes, comrades, you can kiss him.' The game ended in a 3–3 draw.

Pensioned off

By the 1950s Chelsea were considered second-rate. They were a music-hall joke watched by the Chelsea Pensioners, superannuated uniformed ex-servicemen who attended home games and were featured on the cover of the match-day programme. Yet there had been no shortage of big-name signings. In 1930 it was to Chelsea that the 'Wembley Wizard' Hughie Gallagher was sold from Newcastle. After the war the much admired centre-forward Tommy Lawton joined for a big fee of £11,500 – to get away from his wife, he claimed. Lawton scored thirty League goals in forty-two games for the club but to little avail as Chelsea finished fifteenth. In 1952 another major striker, Ted Drake, having retired from playing, became manager.

During his playing career, Drake had a reputation as a joker. Once, when he was at Arsenal, the coach was explaining team tactics to the squad using little tumblers of water to represent players. Drake picked up one, downed the contents and before the astonished manager could remonstrate announced: 'The centre-forward's drunk.' But when he took over at Chelsea he became more professional. He removed the pensioner icon from the programme and replaced it with a lion. He made some inspired signings, and installed a tight regime based around selfless team-building and hard work. The simple things were the most effective: the players trained with the ball, unlike at most clubs, and before a match Drake would shake each player by the hand and wish him 'all the best'.

In his first season Chelsea were nearly relegated, but within three years they were champions. No one in football could believe it. It was not even as if they were worthy champions. Their points tally was the lowest ever for a team winning the League. They lost as many as ten of their forty-two games. (Under José Mourinho they lost only two League games in one stretch of sixty matches.) How could a team that lost 6–5 at home to Manchester United in the autumn go on to win the League? many later puzzled.

Chelsea themselves were amazed, but the squad's celebrations were low-key, especially when compared to the modern-day histrionics that are now *de rigueur*. There was no on-pitch presentation of the trophy and no lap of honour. As centre-forward Roy Bentley explained, 'The players just had some nuts in the boardroom with our wives.' Another group went to a nearby café 'for a cup of tea and some chips', and full-back Stan Willemse, a former Marine commando, caught a train back to Brighton to watch his greyhound race.

The winning squad was, however, treated generously by the Chelsea board. They were invited to a tailor's and told they could choose between a suit or an overcoat as a reward for their endeavours. Winger Jim Lewis was an amateur (he was a Thermos flask salesman the rest of the time) and therefore not allowed to accept so blatant a handout. He was instead given an illuminated scroll in a frame, which he hung in his toilet for fifty years.

As champions Chelsea had qualified for the new European Cup to begin that autumn of 1955. The football authorities intervened and urged the club to withdraw so that they could concentrate on domestic football, thereby setting back Chelsea's progress immeasurably. Fifty years on it seems barely believable that Chelsea could have agreed not to participate.

Kings of the King's Road

During the 1960s King's Road, the one-time royal route from Westminster to Fulham Palace that runs through the heart of Chelsea, became one of the hippest streets in the country thanks to its boutiques, nightclubs and colourful crowd of *habitués*. The glamour rubbed off on to the club and made it the most fashionable in the country. It helped that so many of their players – Peter Osgood, George Graham and Charlie Cooke – oozed class and strode the pitch with a swagger, even if, as one Arsenal fan memorably later told a journalist, 'Osgood wouldn't run five yards for the ball, but he'd run fifty for a fight.' Chelsea even had the leading actor Richard Attenborough on the board, while the stands were dotted with other theatricals – Leonard Rossiter, Tom Courtney, Michael Crawford, John Cleese and Marty Feldman. There were also one-off visits by Hollywood stars Steve McQueen and Raquel Welch, whom Jimmy Hill brought into the dressing room. (When US Secretary of State Henry Kissinger paid a visit, the FBI wanted to check out the ground first but were told by the local police inspector that he couldn't allow the Feds to walk around the stadium with guns.)

The Chelsea squad tapped into the showbiz, 'booze and birds' lifestyle – perhaps too much. For instance, just hours before a crucial League match against Burnley eight players broke the curfew and were sent home by no-nonsense manager Tommy Docherty. Nevertheless Chelsea entered their first sustained period of success at this time, winning the new League Cup (in 1965), reaching the FA Cup Final two years later (a defeat to Tottenham in the first all-London final) and consistently finishing high enough in the League to qualify for European football.

Chelsea's newly found hip status wasn't welcomed by everyone. In one memorable incident from the 1970s TV sitcom *The Likely Lads*, Terry Collier tries to enliven a dull dinner party thrown by an insufferable Londoner who has moved north by asking him which team he supports. 'Chelsea,' comes the reply. 'Chelsea,' groans Collier, 'I hate Chelsea. Them and all their showbiz supporters. They represent everything I can't stand about London.'

The wit and wisdom of the Doc

'I talk a lot. On any subject. Which is always football,' Tommy Docherty, manager of Chelsea from 1962 to 1967, once quipped. Docherty endured a tough wartime Gorbals upbringing before developing into an explosive wing-half, but his greatest weapon was his gift of the gab. After retiring from the playing field he became one of the most voluble managers in football while taking charge of Chelsea, Manchester United, Derby and Aston Villa, amongst others.

Docherty could have made a good living as a stand-up comedian. His ideal board of directors, he often said – but not during his interview for the Chelsea job – comprised three men – 'two dead, one dying'. George Best's problem, according to the Doc, was that he was a light sleeper – when it got light he went home to sleep. 'Ron Atkinson couldn't be here,' he once told an audience. 'His hairdresser died – in 1946.' When he found out that a rival was going for the same job as him, he told one of the interviewing directors: 'If you appoint him you won't get a coach, you'll get a hearse,' and added that football was a 'rat race – and the rats are winning'. He was once questioned by journalists about allegations that he was being investigated by police for the rapid purchase and sale of three players at Derby in 1980 and responded in typical fashion: 'I've always said there's a place for the press, but they haven't dug it yet.'

Into the 1970s, with the flamboyant and bullish Docherty replaced as manager by the calm and reflective Dave Sexton, Chelsea's achievements continued. In 1970 they won the FA Cup for the first time. They followed this the next year with their first European trophy – the Cup Winners' Cup – victory achieved in a replayed final against the legendary Real Madrid after a 1–1 draw.

In 1972 Chelsea recorded what is still the highest ever aggregate total for European cup football, beating Luxembourg's Jeunesse Hautcharage in the European Cup Winners' Cup 21–0 over the two legs. The scoreline may have reflected not just the ineptitude of the Grand Duchy's team, but the fact that one of their players wore glasses and another had only one arm. Yet despite this massacre Chelsea went out in the next round against unfancied Atvidaberg of Sweden, and it would be twenty-three years before they returned to Europe.

The playing strength declined measurably as the 70s ended. Sexton bought inconsequential second-raters such as Bill Garner and Chris Garland, discipline declined as key players feuded with the manager, and it was no surprise when Chelsea were relegated in 1975. They struggled, often as a Second Division club, for the next fifteen years.

Bates Hotel

Money was tight for Chelsea in the early 1980s and the club were bailed out by the irascible and unlikeable Ken Bates who bought them for £1 in 1982, inheriting £2 million worth of debts. Things didn't go well for Bates at first and relegation to the Third Division was only just avoided in 1983. But in 1984 Chelsea were promoted back to the top flight thanks to the new spearheaded attack of Kerry Dixon and David Speedie.

With Bates and his quick tongue in charge the club were rarely out of the news. He once told former chairman Brian Mears that a leper would be more welcome at the club than him, while his suggestion that the fences around the pitch should be electrified to stave off the hooligans, the Chelsea Headhunters, who inhabited the notorious Shed part of the ground, was not greeted with universal acclaim. In 2002 the Chelsea Independent Supporters Association, sued Bates for libel after he described the fans as parasites. He settled out of court.

Meanwhile, the Mears family's involvement declined. David Mears sold his stake to property developers, Marler Estates, who announced a plan to bulldoze Stamford Bridge and replace it with luxury flats. By then everyone realised how this once great stadium had declined. In the early 1920s Stamford Bridge had been considered good enough to host the FA Cup Final while Wembley was being built. But the ground failed to live up to its original billing as a super stadium. Although it was used for other sports including the obscure (shinty, a Scottish game similar to hurling) and popular (speedway from 1929 to 1932, greyhound racing from 1937 to 1968), little investment was made to update it until the 1970s, when a new East Stand was built. It cost the then colossal sum of £2 million as a builders' strike and shortages of materials sent the bills spiralling out of control, and it crippled the club financially, coming at a time of economic uncertainty. But many said the stand was too grand, and made the ground look absurdly unbalanced.

Bates launched a successful 'Save the Bridge' campaign to stave off Marler's plans. He enlisted the backing of insurance tycoon Matthew Harding, with whom he rowed constantly, and managed to complete the ambitious rebuilding transformation of the ground into 'Chelsea Village' with hotel, fancy restaurants, plus, crucially, a football ground.

By the mid-1990s Chelsea had secured safety in the top division and were considered a club with the potential to get to the top. Glenn Hoddle's management was praised in some quarters. Although the football did become prettier as Hoddle preached the qualities that made him one of England's most skilful players in the 1970s and '80s, Chelsea finished fourteenth, eleventh and eleventh with the former England midfield maestro at the helm. In the transfer market Hoddle showed himself to be a poor judge of ability. Million pound-plus sums were spent undeservedly on Paul Furlong, Scott Minto and a rapidly declining David Rocastle.

True, there was an FA Cup Final appearance in 1994 but despite drawing 0–0 with Manchester United at half-time, Chelsea folded in the second half, losing 4–0 in the end.

When Hoddle was inexplicably given the England job in 1996, he was replaced by one-time 'world's best footballer' Ruud Gullit. He brought the FA Cup back to the Bridge in 1997 but was sacked midway through the following season and replaced with another major overseas star – the Italian Gianluca Vialli. Astonishingly, Vialli secured both the League Cup and the European Cup Winners' Cup in his first season, 1997–98. Even if this was eclipsed by Arsenal's greater feat of achieving the League and FA Cup Double that season, Chelsea would also now be playing in the European Champions League. Money could be spent on more and more big-name foreign imports to join the likes of French World Cup-winner Frank Leboeuf at centre-half and the mercurial Gianfranco Zola in attack.

Those who arrived, though, were no longer at their best. By the beginning of the twenty-first century Chelsea had become the Premiership's main resting home for superannuated international superstars looking for one last juicy playing pay-packet before handing their boots in. George Weah, one-time World Player of the Year, appeared at the start of the 1999–2000 season, with no discernible benefit to the team, as did the extraordinarily overrated French World Cup-winning captain, Didier Deschamps – 'the water-carrier', Eric Cantona once called him. This was a collection of Panini stickers (almost) come to life, not a football team. Yet one of the few really talented players in the squad, Chris Sutton, was castigated as a £10 million flop from the moment of his arrival at the Bridge in 1999. Some might say the fault was the manager's for failing to get the best out of one of the great strikers of the era.

Chelsea believed they were 'destined' to win the European Champions League in 2000. When they beat Barcelona 3–1 in the home leg of the quarter-final they celebrated as if they had won the trophy, much in the same way that Newcastle fans tend to greet a home point against Arsenal or Manchester United. Pity they lost the second leg 5–1.

The 'Special' One

It was not under Vialli, nor his Italian successor, Claudio Ranieri, he of the endless squad rotation system that led him to become known as the

'Tinkerman', that Chelsea (almost) reached the promised land. In the summer of 2003 Bates unexpectedly sold the club for £60 million to the Russian oil magnate Roman Abramovich. The club went on a £100 million spending spree, signing many of the best players available, such as Damien Duff, Joe Cole and Claude Makelele. Abramovich gave Ranieri one season to net the title. When the manager could do no better than second in the Premiership and a semi-final of the Champions League, Abramovich sacked him.

The invisible man

In August 2000 Chelsea signed yet another well-known overseas player. This time it was Dutch international and European Cup-winner Winston Bogarde. There was no reason to expect that Bogarde wouldn't follow in the footsteps of fellow countrymen such as Ed de Goey and Ruud Gullit, and star at the Bridge. Instead Bogarde blew it big style, and could be regarded as the biggest overseas flop in English football history, the epitome of the overpaid, over-egoed foreign mercenary.

Bogarde arrived from Barcelona on a four-year contract worth £2 million a year with a ringing endorsement from Chelsea manager Gianluca Vialli. Three weeks later Vialli was sacked. The new boss, Claudio Ranieri, was not impressed with Bogarde and relegated him to the reserves. He was not even given a squad number and was forced to train with Chelsea's youth team. Rather than hand back the already inflated wages he now hardly deserved, Bogarde insisted in taking the lot. 'That money is mine,' Bogarde explained – and to hell with the hard-pressed, ever-fleeced fan, he might well have added.

Bogarde explained once that he had endured a tough upbringing and it was only football that saved him from a life of crime. Clearly he was without free will of his own, except when it came to picking up his pay-packet no doubt. 'Everywhere I came I had a disadvantage, because I am black,' he claimed in his autobiography *Deze Neger Buigt Voor Niemand (This Negro Bows for No One)*, but evidently not so big a disadvantage as to miss out on a million pound-plus sinecure.

At least Bogarde turned out to be an honourable man in one respect, honouring his contract to the letter, always turning up for training, despite being picked only eleven times in four years. The Professional Footballers' Association has yet to explain if this anomaly was what they had in mind when they pressed for the ending of the old feudal transfer system and the abolition of the maximum wage in 1961.

The new manager replacing Claudio Ranieri turned out to be one of the most volatile and controversial figures ever seen in British football – the Portuguese José Mourinho. A man of considerable talent who had won the UEFA Cup and the Champions League with Porto, he surely couldn't fail at Chelsea with all the funds for players available to him. Succeed he did – five trophies in three seasons – which included bringing the Championship back to Stamford Bridge in 2005, the club's centenary, for the first time in fifty years. The title was retained the following year, the first time a London side had achieved this since the 1930s. But to many Mourinho's success was only partially worthy of admiration. Surely with the budget available to him Chelsea should have won everything, in particular the Champions League in which such mundane sides as Bayer Leverkusen and Borussia Dortmund have recently prospered.

Mourinho and Chelsea were more grudgingly accepted than respected or admired. It was not so much the endless slosh of money to buy success that annoyed the rest of the football world, especially when millions were wasted on such nonentities as Veron, Kezman, Kalou and Mikel, but Abramovich's relentless silence, and Mourinho's personality quirks. A supersize ego led him to christen himself the 'Special One'. His confrontational temperament saw him accuse officials at Reading of not being quick enough to call an ambulance to treat his injured goalkeeper. His arrogance led him to tap up another team's player (the Ashley Cole affair, p. 141). His surliness manifested itself in contrived and pointless rows with officials at European games that didn't go Chelsea's way. He falsely accused the respected referee Anders Frisk of talking to Barcelona officials at half-time during a Euro match, and then unfairly sending off Didier Drogba. This resulted in Mourinho's being suspended for two games, and led to

Anders Frisk's decision to retire after receiving death threats. Mourinho's players' behaviour was appalling, yet there was barely a murmur in the press about Michael Essien's dangerous tackling, John Obi Mikel's nauseating 'wot me, ref?' attitude and Didier Drogba's gamesmanship. 'Sometimes I dive,' the Ivorian once admitted.

By late summer 2007 even the lengthening sequence of honours – the FA Cup and League Cup in a relatively 'unsuccessful' season – was no longer enough for Chelsea. The relationship between manager and owner had soured irrevocably. Mostly the disagreements were over one player, former European Footballer of the Year Andriy Shevchenko. Mourinho didn't want him at the club but Abramovich, a personal friend of the Ukrainian striker, did. Abramovich bought him, Mourinho barely played him, and rightly so, for when Shevchenko did appear he looked like a park player.

Mourinho left by 'mutual consent' in September 2007. His replacement could not have been more of a contrast. Where Mourinho was dynamic, Avram Grant, whose sole major management job had been to take charge of the Israeli national side, was dour. His antics made fans and journalists reach for the smelling salts. In a team meeting before his first game, away to Manchester United, he announced a line-up with only ten men. The team's formation would be 4–4–1. Even Chelsea are not that good, to take on United in their own stadium with one player fewer from the start. They put out eleven men in the end but lost the game. Chelsea no longer looked invincible.

Nevertheless Grant took Chelsea to the League Cup Final and the European Cup Final in his first season. This was some sort of achievement; to be only the second London side in football history to come that close to the European summit. But detractors argued that with all that money, all those world-class players and all that media hype Chelsea should win everything every season.

Having won nothing Grant was replaced. Now Chelsea would have a truly world-class manager – like Mourinho – not a stand-in. Luiz Felipe Scolari had won the World Cup with Brazil, yet after a few months, with Chelsea riding high in the table and still in Europe, he was being called a failure, on no discernible evidence.

Along came another truly world-class manager, Guus Hiddink, but only as an interim measure. Despite being touted as a saviour by the same journalists who in turn had lauded Scolari and then derided him, Hiddink also failed to secure the title and the European crown, although some of his players did win prizes for temper tantrums as the club went out to Barcelona in the last minute of the May 2009 Champions League semi-final.

Chelsea off the bench

✪ Chelsea' early twentieth-century reputation as a music-hall joke stemmed from a song, 'The Day That Chelsea Won The Cup', mocking their lack of silverware which was occasionally performed at the **Granville Theatre of Varieties** that stood opposite Fulham Broadway station. The Chelsea supporters' all-time favourite ditty, 'Celery', is based on another old music-hall song, 'Ask Old Brown', which goes: 'Ask old Brown for tea/And all the family/If he don't come/We'll tickle his bum/With a lump of celery.' Contemporary versions have introduced lewder words.

✪ Spectators leaving Fulham Broadway station en route to Stamford Bridge nowadays have to pass a Virgin Megastore. The shop was built around the café where in 1932 the Scot Hughie Gallagher once took refuge from a gang of violent Fulham fans. In the mass brawl that ensued Gallagher was arrested and, though he was later acquitted, he was ordered to put 10s in the poor box.

✪ Stamford Bridge was the home venue for the hybrid London team that contested the first Inter-Cities Fairs Cup Final (later the UEFA Cup) in 1958. London drew the first leg 2–2 but lost in Barcelona 6–0. In subsequent years club sides rather than city teams entered the competition.

✪ Matthew Harding, who invested heavily in the club in the 1990s after answering an advert Ken Bates had placed in the *Financial Times*, was an unlikely figure for a football director: as well as money he had personality, a sense of social responsibility and the common touch. He would happily sit with everyday fans in the Imperial Arms on the King's Road before matches and discuss ways of improving the club. His highly appreciated involvement with Chelsea was tragically curtailed in 1996 when the helicopter in which he was travelling back from a match at Bolton crashed, killing everyone on board.

Fulham (1896–2002, 2004–), Craven Cottage, Stevenage Road

Fulham enjoy the most picturesque setting of any League club. On two sides of their ground are charming Victorian and Edwardian brick houses with whitewashed stone bays and creeping foliage. In one corner stands the quaint, anachronistic Craven Cottage pavilion, and behind the West Stand lies a glorious stretch of the River Thames. However, the scenic location belies a long history of second-rate football watched by a notoriously half-hearted crowd and presided over by a succession of unscrupulous businessmen.

One F in Fulham

Fulham were founded in 1879 as Fulham St Andrew's Church Sunday School by the Rev. James Cardwell of St Andrews church in Star Road, West Kensington – not Fulham. Their first ground was a patch of nearby land known as the Mud Pond. They soon moved to the Ranelagh Club a mile south, changing into their kit at the Eight Bells pub. When the Ranelagh Club folded so did the football team who briefly dropped the title 'Fulham' and became St Andrew's. They then played at a variety of locations close by including Lillie Road by Fulham Cross in 1884; Barn Elms, south of the Thames, for the 1888 season, when they were holders of the West London Amateur Cup; Pursers Cross, off Parsons Green Lane, in 1889; Eel Brook Common (1891) and a ground next to Putney's Half Moon pub in 1895.

A year later Fulham moved to land by the long-standing Craven Cottage, a well-known country retreat for upper-class society. During the building, workers came upon a tunnel joining the Fulham and Putney banks of the river. It was filled in with earth excavated during the building of the new Central Line underground railway.

The club's first match at Craven Cottage was a 4–0 win against Minerva in the Middlesex Senior Cup in October 1896. Two years later Fulham turned professional. They had been playing in the Second Division of the London League, watched by crowds of around 2,000, but now joined the Southern League, whose teams played the best football outside the Football League itself. Despite winning the Southern League Second Division in 1901–02 and 1902–03, Fulham missed out on promotion in the Test matches. Losing one of these play-offs 7–2 to Brentford in 1903 was rather a surprise considering that the club had conceded only seven goals the whole season. At last in spring 1903 Fulham were invited to join the Southern League First Division. But this meant more investment would be needed and so the club committee decided that Fulham should become a limited liability company and issue shares.

Archibald Leitch's new stadium – banked terracing on three sides and one full-length stand along Stevenage Road – opened in September 1905 and could house 20,000. It was time for Fulham to be playing at a higher level, and in 1907 they replaced Burton in the Football League. Meanwhile, with Harry Bradshaw as their first full-time manager, Fulham won two Southern League titles (in 1906 and 1907), reached the semi-finals of the FA Cup in 1908, and rebuilt the ground.

Leading the club's new drive towards greater commercial potential was director Henry Norris. In 1905 he rejected an approach from the owners of newly formed Chelsea to move Fulham to Stamford Bridge, but five years later bought Woolwich Arsenal and attempted to merge them with Fulham at Craven Cottage. When the Football League blocked the plan Norris shifted his attention to Arsenal and helped turn them into a powerhouse, something which Fulham have never become.

Craven comic

The years between the two world wars were uneventful for Fulham, but in 1949 they at last managed promotion to the top flight. It didn't last long but they re-established themselves, reached the FA Cup semi-final in 1958 – where they should have beaten a Manchester United depleted by the Munich disaster but lost a replay 5–3 – and won promotion to the First Division again the following year. The 1958–68 period is now seen as Fulham's golden days. Their chairman was also the most famous of the ninety-two in the Football League: the comedian Tommy Trinder. Despite regularly struggling against relegation, the team was awash with big names. There was Ron Greenwood, who guided West Ham to success in the 1960s; Bobby Robson, who did the same at Ipswich from 1973 to 1982; and Jimmy Hill of the peculiar beard and pointed chin, who led the players' fight to abolish the maximum wage in the early 60s. And, of course, the man who benefited most from this, Johnny Haynes, the first footballer to be paid £100 a week.

Haynes, who ranks as Fulham's greatest ever player with fifty-six caps for England, grew up supporting Arsenal but opted to join Fulham as a fifteen-year-old amateur in 1950, believing it would be easier to become established at Craven Cottage than at Highbury. There was also George Cohen, the tough-tackling full-back, who played for England in the 1966 World Cup Final, and Rodney Marsh, he of the silky attacking skills – a timeless, brilliant idol.

Fulham dropped out of the top flight in 1968, and humiliatingly went down again the following season. Director Eric Miller was to blame. He was determined to sell the club's best players to finance building a new stand. He replaced the riverside terracing in 1972 and the new stand was later named after him, but Miller wasn't around to sit in it much though. Following an investigation by the Fraud Squad he committed suicide in 1977 on the Jewish Day of Atonement.

The wit and wisdom of Tommy Trinder

A comedian and actor, Tommy Trinder became a national favourite in the 1950s with his catchphrase 'you lucky people'. He began compèring the ITV show *Sunday Night at the London Palladium* in 1954 and a year later became chairman of Fulham.

⊕ Sitting alongside war hero Field Marshal Bernard Montgomery watching the young Johnny Haynes star for Fulham at Craven Cottage, Trinder drooled: 'He has a great football brain and is an excellent passer of the ball. Mark my words Johnny Haynes will captain England one day.' 'Only eighteen, you say,' responded the leader of Britain's Second World War troops. 'What about his national service?' 'Ah, you see, there's one problem and that's the sad thing about him,' replied Trinder. 'He's a cripple.'

⊕ Trinder did not believe the maximum wage would ever be abolished so he promised Johnny Haynes that he would pay him £100 a week if ever the bar was raised. When the maximum wage was indeed abolished in 1961, Haynes said, 'I think he regretted it, but he had to live with it.'

⊛ When Fulham went down in 1968 chairman Trinder explained: 'The real reason why Fulham have never won the League Championship is that we could never work up enough speed. That's why we've dropped back into the Second Division – to get a longer run at it.'

⊛ In 1977 Trinder walked out on the club after a boardroom row.

Feet of clay

Fulham arrested the decline in the mid-1970s, even if they couldn't get back to the First Division. The veteran England World Cup hero Bobby Moore joined from West Ham in 1974. Playing alongside him was fellow ex-England international Alan Mullery, and they helped take the club to its first FA Cup Final, where they were soundly beaten by West Ham. A year later George Best, self-exiled from Manchester United and top-class football, came to Fulham. He scored the only goal on his debut, a 1–0 win against Bristol Rovers, and played forty-seven times for the club, scoring ten goals, but departed for the US after a row over money.

Briefly in the early 1980s Fulham looked capable of returning to the First Division. The impressive Malcolm Macdonald was manager and promotion from the Third Division was almost followed immediately by success in the Second Division until the club collapsed at the last. It would be some time before they came close to another challenge. The rest of the decade was overshadowed by turmoil surrounding the future of the ground.

When Fulham missed out on promotion to Division One in 1983 by two points the chairman, Ernie Clay, decided to sell off the club's best players. Two years later he borrowed £1.5 million to buy the freehold of Craven Cottage from the Ecclesiastical Commissioners, and a clause stipulating the right of Fulham to play football here was removed. Clay sold his shares to Marler Estates for £9 million in 1986, but little of this money was made available to strengthen the side.

It was then that things took a turn for the worse. In 1987, David Bulstrode, chairman of Marler, bought Loftus Road, home of Queen's Park Rangers. Just as Henry Norris at the beginning of the century had wanted to merge Woolwich Arsenal and Fulham, now Bulstrode wanted to merge QPR with Fulham under a new ungainly hybrid name: Fulham Park Rangers. They would play at Loftus Road, and Craven Cottage would be redeveloped for housing.

There was a mass outcry. Fans around the country, local councillors and the Football League combined to thwart Marler, and the Department of the Environment granted listed status to the main stand and the Cottage itself. While the battle to keep football at Craven Cottage raged, the team continued to decline. Fulham were relegated to the bottom division for the first time in 1994. The days of Haynes, Cohen, Moore and Best were long gone. By 1996 home gates were averaging 4,000, there were fewer than 1,000 season-ticket holders and only seven full-time staff. The training that took place on Epsom Downs included on one occasion circuits of a park bench.

The Manchester United of the south

That year Micky Adams took over as manager, and through his hard work the corner was turned. He steered the club away from the dreaded drop zone to the Conference and took Fulham up the League. In 1996–97 they finished second in the Fourth Division, winning promotion for the first time in fifteen years. Even though the club reclaimed its ground from the Royal Bank of Scotland there were no resources to strengthen the side. But then the unlikeliest of financial saviours emerged in the shape of Harrods owner Mohammed al-Fayed, who bought into the club in 1997. Although away from football al-Fayed has made himself an absurd figure with his claims that the British security forces assassinated his son, Dodi, and Princess Diana, at Fulham he has been popular.

When he took over he vowed that Fulham would become a Premier League team in five years – and he was as good as his word. Somewhat over the top was his announcement that he wanted Fulham to become the Manchester United of the south, an aspiration that always seemed fanciful given that the latter have drawn in more than 50,000 fans from across the British Isles every match for decades.

Al-Fayed began with the surprise sacking of Adams. But his replacement, Kevin Keegan, was a wise choice. He energised the players and the fans, as he had at Newcastle, and Keegan's Fulham soon cleared the third tier. Even after he left to manage England in January 1999, Fulham's ascent continued under the mild-mannered Frenchman Jean Tigana. On the way to promotion in 2001 they amassed 100 points and over 100 goals.

Just five years after Fulham kicked-off at home against Hereford in the League's basement division in August 1996, they travelled to Old Trafford to meet Manchester United in the Premiership. In their first season back in the top flight Fulham finished only thirteenth, but the fans were delirious that they were there at all; that they had a chairman *not* looking to make a profit on the much coveted real estate that Craven Cottage occupies. Al-Fayed invested £30 million in players so that Fulham could cope in the top division, but when he saw £11.5 million of it go up in smoke in the shape of Steve Marlet he thought again.

The ground remains a problem. For a while it was the only one in the Premiership with standing areas. In May 2002 Fulham left for a temporary groundshare at Loftus Road so that Craven Cottage could be redeveloped as an all-seater stadium, but it looked at one stage as if planning permission would not be granted and the future of England's most beautiful football setting again looked in doubt. Fans formed a 'Back to the Cottage' group and with the support of the House of Lords won the campaign to see the ground rebuilt. But then the club admitted they had abandoned the idea as the costs had risen too high. A company called Fulham River Projects was set to turn the site into flats.

Al-Fayed again rallied round. 'Fulham Football Club have not, I repeat, not sold Craven Cottage. The ground still belongs to us and will remain so,' he announced. Supporters were not entirely convinced, for there was a rider: 'we have set up a structure which would make it possible for us to sell Craven Cottage if as a last resort we are forced to do so'. Nevertheless Fulham returned to the Cottage for 2004–05, a move financed by the sale of the occasionally scoring Louis Saha to Manchester United. Plans to move to White City with QPR and play in a 40,000 all-seater stadium appear to be on hold.

In the Premiership Fulham failed to shine under Tigana and his successors. It was not the lack of financial investment by the Harrods owner but his mostly poor choice of managers, though in 2009 Roy Hodgson surprisingly took Fulham into the top half of the Premiership.

Fulham off the bench

⚽ Craven Cottage takes its name from a 1780 property built by Baron Craven in what had been Anne Boleyn's hunting grounds, which stood where the centre of the pitch is today. The cottage became popular in the nineteenth century with society figures, and was used as a hunting lodge by George IV. In the 1840s the author Edward Bulwer-Lytton moved in, and it was here that he wrote *The Last Days of Pompeii*.

Bulwer-Lytton held dinner parties that attracted the leading figures of the day such as Benjamin Disraeli, later to become prime minister. After attending one such event Disraeli wrote to his sister: 'Our host, whatever may be his situation, was more sumptuous and fantastic than ever. Mrs. Bulwer was a blaze of jewels and looked like Juno; only instead of a peacock she had a dog in her lap.' The cottage burnt down in May 1888 and was rebuilt in a quaint black and white style a few yards away in 1905. Though compact, the new structure incorporated a boardroom, offices and dressing room, and is still used.

⚽ Fulham's best Victorian era player, Billy Ives, emigrated to New Zealand in 1898. Around a hundred years later his London League medal found its way back to Craven Cottage.

⚽ At the start of the First World War Fredrick Charrington, the well-known brewer who had renounced his place with the family firm to become a leading temperance campaigner, came on to the pitch at half-time during a match to urge the crowd to sign up to fight. Unfortunately, Charrington had not sought permission for his recruitment drive and, as soon as he started to speak, two officials dragged him off and threw him out of the ground.

⚽ On his first day as an apprentice in 1960 Rodney Marsh was told to sweep the entire ground, clean the kit room, the bars and the press box, and polish the players' boots. Among them were those Johnny Haynes had worn the previous night playing for England in a 4–2 win over Spain. Marsh emptied a box of its matches and with his knife sliced some of the grass off Haynes's boots into the matchbox to keep as a memento. Marsh also had to undergo an initiation ceremony which involved being thrown into an ice-cold bath and then painted with the whitewash used for the pitch markings. It took a wire brush to remove the paint from his private parts.

✪ One day in the early 60s the morning training session was about to start when someone noticed that Eddie Abrahams, the new player from South Africa – a rarity in those days, before the invasion of foreign players – was nowhere to be found. Rodney Marsh was sent to scour the ground for him, and after half an hour found Abrahams in a large oven used to dry the players' kits. Abrahams was so cold, having just arrived in London from Johannesburg, he had climbed in the oven to keep warm.

✪ On Boxing Day 1963 Fulham beat Ipswich, champions eighteen months previously, 10–1 at the Cottage. As he left the ground the Ipswich chairman John Cobbold was asked for a comment about the 'crisis' at the club. 'There is no crisis,' Cobbold responded. 'But the team are fighting relegation and have just lost 10–1,' the reporter reminded him. 'My dear boy,' came back Cobbold, 'a crisis at the club would be for the boardroom to run out of gin.'

✪ Although Fulham right-back George Cohen helped England win the World Cup in 1966 no further Fulham players had appeared for England in a competitive match by the end of 2008.

✪ During the 1975 FA Cup Final Bobby Moore, by then playing for Fulham, was burgled. He discovered the bad news when he and his wife returned home from the team hotel the next day and saw his football memorabilia neatly piled on the front lawn.

Fulham Road

One of the longest streets in London, Fulham Road has always lived in the shadow of the King's Road, its illustrious neighbour to the south. Nevertheless it has antique shops, fancy restaurants, smart bars and chic boutiques, particularly along a section east of Chelsea FC popularly known as 'The Beach', thanks to its relaxed atmosphere, particularly in the summer.

Before the infamous Chelsea *v* Moscow Dynamo match in November 1945 some of the tens of thousands of supporters converging on the ground went to extraordinary lengths on Fulham Road in their desperation to gain admission, even tearing down gates to use as battering-rams against the fences stopping them getting into Stamford Bridge. In one ingenious wheeze more than a hundred fans entered the disused Chelsea and Fulham station on the corner of Wandon Road and Fulham Road, walked along the tracks of the West London Railway, scrambled up the embankment and climbed the back of one of the stands.

→ **Moscow Dynamo on Clapham High Street, p. 202**

Lillie Bridge stadium, Seagrave Road

Lillie Bridge, a Victorian sports stadium and home of the Amateur Athletic Club, staged the second-ever FA Cup Final in which Wanderers beat Oxford University 2–0 in 1873. The venue was chosen according to the rather biased rules of the time: the holders went straight into the final (where they were 'challenged' by another team in what has always been officially 'the FA Challenge Cup') and allowed them to choose the ground. The kick-off was scheduled for 11 a.m. so that punters could watch the Boat Race afterwards, but the game didn't in fact start until 11.30 as a number of players turned up late. The crowd numbered 3,000. Lillie Bridge fell into disuse once Stamford Bridge opened, half a mile to the south, and was closed altogether following crowd trouble in 1887.

→ **FA Cup finals at the Crystal Palace, p. 183**

White Hart, 563 Fulham Road

Hughie Gallagher, the gifted Scottish centre-forward who briefly played for Chelsea before the Second World War, used to head here before Chelsea home matches and down a whisky or a pint before playing. Fellow players wondered whether such a strategy could backfire. One night the opposing team, out for a walk near the ground, saw Gallagher slumped in a doorway drunk. Yet the next afternoon he was running the match and scored.

BATTERSEA, SW11

Battersea Park

The Thames-side park was where on 9 January 1864 the first ever football match played according to Football Association rules took place. One team was chosen by the FA's president, Arthur Pember, and the other by the secretary, Ebenezer Cobb Morley. The Football Association had been founded only a few months previously, and the game had been scheduled for 2 January, but enthusiastic members couldn't wait for the new year to arrive and so a game without formal rules was played at Mortlake on 19 December 1863 between Barnes (one of the founder-members of the FA) and Richmond (not members). It ended in a goalless draw, after which Richmond abandoned football and turned to rugby instead.

The park continued to be a popular venue for some of the first regulated matches. For instance, Harrow Chequers played the Civil Service here on 14 February 1865, and London played Sheffield in the park in the first recorded city *v* city match on 31 March 1866. The encounter was particularly physical. As the reporter for *Bell's Life of London* wrote: "The game was a very hot one, and though Sheffield were overmatched, many of the Londoners were badly knocked about." Afterwards it was agreed that all football matches should be of ninety minutes' duration.

By then the park had become home to the most successful side of the era: the Wanderers. Formed in 1859, they were based near Epping Forest (and nothing to do with Nottingham Forest), and remained in Woodford until 1863 when, as they put it, they 'wandered' over to Battersea Park. The side consisted mostly of ex-public schoolboys and was captained by Charles Alcock, chairman of the FA in its early years. Wanderers were the greatest team of the era, winning the FA Cup five times from 1872 to 1878. They declined once professionalism set in the following decade and disbanded in 1883.

→ **Griffin Park, p. 271**

PUTNEY, SW15

Bank of England Sports Ground, Priory Lane, Roehampton

The national side's training ground for many years was first used in the 1950s under the management of Walter Winterbottom. Training sessions were occasionally enlivened by the incorrigible Sunderland inside-forward Len Shackleton. When Winterbottom one day told his five England forwards to run down the field passing the ball from one to the other and to shoot once they got into the penalty box, Shackleton interrupted him to ask: 'Which side of the goal, boss?'

England trained at Roehampton during the 1966 World Cup. During one session manager Alf Ramsey waxed on at length about football club directors. For once Jimmy Greaves was silent. 'I'm surprised you haven't contributed,' Ramsey added, and turning to the Spurs striker asked, 'Would you like to give us your view on directors?' 'Not really, Alf,' came the reply. 'There's small choice in rotten apples.' The manager smirked. 'Come, come, Jimmy. I'm certain you of all people can think of something more pertinent to say. We are the England football team. We speak English, the language of Shakespeare.' 'That *is* Shakespeare, Alf,' Greaves countered, aware, unlike Ramsey, that the quote came from *The Taming of the Shrew*.

Fulham's remarkable rise from twentieth position in the Third Division in November 1980 to fourth place in the Second Division by May 1983 may have been down to the training sessions held here at which manager Malcolm Macdonald organised games along the lines of North *v* South, Young *v* Old, Midgets *v* Giants. At the end of these coach Roger Thompson would conduct a poll among the players to find out who they thought had played the worst. The loser would have to buy a Mars Bar for each of the team and run across Putney Bridge in a yellow jersey bearing the legend 'Tosser of the Week' while the other players leant out of the windows of a mini-bus jeering and whistling.

→ Chelsea at the Welsh Harp training ground, p. 135

Fulham (1889–94), Half Moon Ground, west of Biggs Row, south of Lower Richmond Road

St Andrew's, an early incarnation of Fulham, moved to the Half Moon Ground near Putney Bridge in 1889 and became simply Fulham FC seven years before moving to their long-term home, Craven Cottage, on the other side of the river. Fulham shared the ground with Wasps Rugby Club and by now were big enough in their own right to charge spectators 3d a head to watch them. Several hundred turned up for matches, and on Easter Mondays Fulham played charity games known as 'top hat and bonnet' matches. They also competed for trophies such as the West London Association Cup and the West London Observer Cup, winning the latter in 1890. Two years later Fulham joined the new West London League, participated in the FA Cup for the first time, and joined the London League.

→ Craven Cottage, p. 218

The Priory, Priory Lane, Roehampton

The rehab clinic of choice for the nation's celebrities, the Priory has in recent times been a temporary home for a number of high-profile footballers. In 1998 Paul Gascoigne signed in following a four-day drinking binge in Dublin after being excluded from the England World Cup squad. Gascoigne soon discharged himself from the Priory, however, claiming the problem was 'in his head not the bottle'. A friend told reporters: 'To Gazza, drink is part of his culture, it's everyday life, like eating and breathing. He's convinced the demons which are destroying him are in his mind – not in a pint glass.'

Mark Bosnich, an occasional goalkeeper who somehow managed to make the Manchester United and Chelsea first teams at the end of the 1990s, was admitted to the Priory in November 2002 for depression. Stan Collymore, an even more occasional footballer, checked in in March 2004 with depression following revelations that he had been engaged in 'dogging' – having sex with strangers.

WIMBLEDON, SW19

Cannizaro's, West Side Common

The Wimbledon team spent the night before the 1988 FA Cup Final at this plush hotel by Wimbledon Common. Given that it would have been inconceivable for the so-called Crazy Gang to prepare for the club's biggest ever game in a sedate and sophisticated manner, the players ignored manager Bobby Gould's insistence that they stay inside the hotel, and slipped away to the Fox and Grapes pub where a century earlier the newly founded Wimbledon football team had changed before and after matches.

There the bar staff found a ninety-year-old lady whose father had played in one of those early teams. 'It was humbling,' admitted Lawrie Sanchez. 'You could see her eyes glisten with the memory.' It was so humbling that more beer was needed to rouse their spirits. Meanwhile, Bobby Gould had found out that many of his players were absent. Realising he could not stop the remaining ones he gave them £50 to go and join their team-mates.

Eventually the players returned to the hotel, but things turned nasty when battering-ram centre-forward John Fashanu was approached in the bar by a *News of the World* reporter armed with some difficult questions about his faithfulness to his girlfriend. After pacing the corridors in pent-up anger, John Fashanu stopped outside his bedroom door and punched it powerfully. Vinnie Jones – yes, Vinnie! – calmed Fashanu down and took him away to have his hand seen to. Fortunately for Wimbledon his injuries weren't serious and he did not have to miss the final.

The adrenaline rush of all these antics evidently worked for Wimbledon as they won the Cup the following day despite being rank outsiders. Afterwards the players returned to Cannizaro's, placed the Cup on the floor and danced ecstatically round it, before leaving for a celebration in a marquee on the Plough Lane pitch.

Wimbledon (1889–1912), Wimbledon Common

Wimbledon, the most successful club to enter the League in modern times, were formed in 1889 by old boys of the Central School in Camp Road and played their earliest matches on Wimbledon Common as Wimbledon Old

Centrals. They wore a blue and white strip, changed in the Fox and Grapes pub, and for their first game on 2 November that year beat Westminster 1–0. After complaints about the players uprooting the grass Wimbledon moved deeper into the Common. They almost folded in 1910 when a different group of locals got together as Wimbledon Borough. The two outfits merged in 1912 as Wimbledon, and began playing at Plough Lane, swamp land that had been a rubbish dump, in the built-up part of the suburb.

Wimbledon (1912–91), Plough Lane

Wimbledon were the ultimate fairy-tale club, rising through the amateur game to become a League side, climbing through the League divisions to the top flight and winning the FA Cup. But then they dropped down the divisions and almost died in the 1990s when they split into two: AFC Wimbledon and MK Dons.

In 1912 Wimbledon moved to Plough Lane. Success came slowly, but eventually the club became a powerhouse in the non-League divisions. They entered the relatively elevated Isthmian League for the first time in the 1930s and won it four times. After the war Wimbledon came under the care of Sidney Black who took over as owner. He pampered the players as if they were superstars, flew them to Switzerland in 1956 for a friendly against a local Fifth Division team, and secured them tickets for the Swiss Cup Final. Back home he covered the west side of the ground and invested in floodlights.

Amateur hour

Wimbledon won the Amateur Cup in 1963, when Eddie Reynolds scored all four goals with his head, and kept winning the Isthmian League. Now they were ready for a step up – to the semi-professional Southern League. The following decade Wimbledon went on a spectacular FA Cup run during which they became the first non-League side since the expansion of the Football League in 1920 to beat a First Division team (Burnley) at their own ground. In the fourth round they held the reigning champions, Leeds, to a draw at Elland Road. Fans queued through the night for replay tickets, but they were all sold within a couple of hours and fights broke out with touts. In the end a waterlogged pitch prevented the replay taking place at Plough Lane and the game was staged at Selhurst Park where a 45,000-plus crowd saw a Johnny Giles deflection send the Yorkshire team through.

Around the same time there was a buzz of excitement as it became known that a consortium including George Best was to take over the club, and that Best himself would become player-manager. The plan fell through, but the club's exploits and three more Southern League championships rewarded them with election to the Football League in place of Workington, at the expense of favourites Altrincham, in 1977.

In August 1982 Wimbledon were in the Fourth Division after going up and down a number of times. Yet by August 1986 they had risen astonishingly to the top division. Wimbledon even managed to top the table briefly that September, finishing the season a credible sixth, which would have been good enough to bring European football to SW19 had not the Liverpool fans gone on the rampage in Brussels and brought about a ban from Europe for English clubs.

However, along the way Wimbledon made few friends. It was not because of their rise but because of the horrendous, brutal, non-football that the club increasingly turned to in the 1980s as they reached the top, disfiguring the decade with a hit, hump and hoof strategy that turned Pele's 'beautiful game' into a barely licensable form of martial arts.

Sides new to the top flight are usually stuffed with unknowns who remain unknown as the team slips back into oblivion. But Wimbledon were different. Practically all their players were instantly memorable and seemed to represent a particular spirit and personality. There was Dennis Wise, the impish rogue with an angelic smile but a penchant for bile. He could actually play a bit. There was John Fashanu, the battering-ram centre-forward with too much to say for himself. He couldn't play so well. There was the overgrown goalkeeper nicknamed Lurch (Dave Beasant), the studious midfielder who began to look like Ronnie Kray (Lawrie Sanchez), and worst of all, the untameable lunatic who squeezed Paul Gascoigne's testicles during a match and went on to become a minor movie hardman (Vinnie Jones).

'This is all Liverpool'

At the end of 1986–87, Wimbledon's first season in the top flight, Dave Bassett, the manager who had taken them there, left for Watford. Bobby Gould more than maintained the momentum, and in Wimbledon's second season they achieved what nobody had previously thought possible – that a team fresh from the non-League could win the FA Cup. In doing so they knocked out Newcastle, the team who act as if the Cup is perpetually theirs as a divine right, at St James's Park. Although the next two rounds to get to the final were only against Watford and Luton, their opponents in the final were the near invincible Liverpool, Champions ten times in the previous sixteen seasons.

On the journey to Wembley the Wimbledon players watched the build-up to the match on TV. When they heard ex-Liverpool defender Alan Hansen ask: 'Can you see any Wimbledon fans? This is all Liverpool', they became fired up. Even more arrogantly along Olympic Way before the match the Scousers sang: 'Underground, overground, wombling free. You'll be so lucky if we only score three.' Yet it was Liverpool who couldn't get one, not even when they were awarded a penalty in the second half with Wimbledon leading 1–0. No one had ever missed an FA Cup Final penalty at Wembley, and John Aldridge had scored twenty-nine goals that season. But Dave Beasant saved and proudly led the team up the steps to the Royal Box to collect the trophy half an hour later.

The Crazy Gang

Childish capers or necessary pranks needed to foster team spirit? All clubs have practical jokers who strike when the players are holed up together in hotels, but Wimbledon of the 1980s and '90s took this to absurd lengths with wild antics that earned them the nickname 'Crazy Gang', a term coined by Tony Stenson of the *Daily Mirror*.

Putting deep heat in underpants and salt in the tea were just two of the many pranks in which team members indulged as part of a rite-of-passage. Players would go back to the dressing room and find their clothes doctored – the trouser legs tied into knots, the toes cut out of their socks, or even their shoes nailed to the floor. John Hartson's gear was regularly burnt and thrown out of the training-ground windows. On one occasion he walked around for several hours with a note pinned to his back displaying the word 'bollocks'. It was not the humour of the situation that rocked observers but the fact that the word was spelt correctly.

Then there was the time in 1994 that three Wimbledon players were selected for the England squad. Dean Holdsworth recalled how 'Warren Barton, John Scales and myself were all called together. We were on top of the world until after handshakes and congratulations we went to drive home, only to find the tyres on all our cars had been let down.'

Nobody was immune. One day 'the lads' took chairman Sam Hammam's car, drove it several miles away to an obscure location and left it there. They then journeyed back to the ground, went into his office, presented him with the keys, and told him his car was within ten square miles of Plough Lane and that he should go and find it.

Many assumed the craziest of the Crazy Gang was Vinnie Jones. After all the midfield tyrant once threatened to rip Kenny Dalglish's ear off and 'spit in the hole'. Jones was sent off thirteen times in his career, earned the record fastest booking from the kick-off (five seconds), and received a suspended six-month ban for presenting a documentary called *Soccer's Hard Men* in which he described how to pull up a felled opponent by the armpit hair, scrape studs down his leg and squeeze a testicle or two – without the ref noticing.

Perhaps crazier, but less dangerous, except to himself, was the little-known winger Steve Parsons. At Dave Beasant's twenty-first birthday party Parsons was found in the attic sitting on the window ledge throwing potted plants in the air and cracking them on his head.

Wombled out

Winning the FA Cup was the end of the dream. In chairman Sam Hamman's opinion the club had gone as far as it could go, especially given that there was no European competition coming Wimbledon's way thanks to the Liverpool-induced ban. He announced that every player was up for sale, and Dave Beasant and Andy Thorn left for Newcastle.

Hamman was even planning a merger with Crystal Palace to create a south London superclub at Selhurst Park. However, unhappy fans discovered he owned land around Plough Lane and probably stood to gain millions if the merger went ahead and he sold the land to developers. They opposed him so vociferously he was forced to drop the scheme. Instead Hamman announced plans to build a new all-seater stadium elsewhere in Wimbledon's home borough of Merton. Plough Lane was supposedly too small and redevelopment to meet the new compulsory seating rules was impossible, given the proximity of two busy roads and the River Wandle. The club and the council looked at fourteen alternative locations in fifteen years but found nothing suitable.

At the end of the 1990–91 season Hamman half got his way about merging with Palace by deciding to ground-share at Selhurst Park while continuing to look for a new site.

The last game at Plough Lane was a 3–0 defeat to, ironically, Crystal Palace, after which the reserve team used Plough Lane until it was demolished in 2001. But was there any real need to leave? Not according to the *Daily Mirror*'s Tony Stenson. 'I looked into it at the time. The club had been given five years by the Football League to get the ground up to scratch. Plough Lane could easily have become a 25,000-capacity stadium.'

At Selhurst Park Wimbledon prospered under Joe Kinnear in the mid-90s, finishing in the top half of the Premier League and reaching the finals of both the League Cup and FA Cup in 1997. They slumped after Kinnear was forced to quit following a heart attack.

In 1997 Hamman sold 80 per cent of the club to two super-rich Norwegians for £25 million. That year Wimbledon outlined plans to move, not to another part of south London, but to Dublin where perhaps they could break up the locals' bizarre disposition to support Liverpool or Manchester United at the expense of Dublin teams. However, the Football Association of Ireland blocked the move and Wimbledon, having been relegated from the Premiership in 2000, left in 2003 for the nightmare world of Milton Keynes. There they became the awkwardly named MK Dons, known to detractors as Franchise FC. South-west Londoners who could not accept the move founded a new and obviously non-League side, AFC Wimbledon, playing way down the League pyramid but trading on the history of the mutilated outfit.

One day a Wimbledon side will play again at Plough Lane in a new stadium, though probably not in the top division, and the fans will wonder why the early guardians of the club allowed a team that had risen so far to fall apart so fatally.

The Womble of Wimbledon Common

Egil Olsen's career as an ice-hockey star and professional poker player, his shabby demeanour, his wellington boots and his treks across Wimbledon Common to get to the training ground, should have made him the ideal Wimbledon manager, even if he did advocate Marxist-Leninist policies. He had turned Norway, a country of no international pedigree, into a feared outfit, but he had done so utilising an ugly style of hoofing the ball up from the back, bypassing midfield, to the head of a giant arms-and-legs striker. Perfect then for Wimbledon.

True to the Crazy Gang's traditions, Olsen was humiliated on his first day in 1999: his clothes were burned, the tyres of his car let down and his boots filled with shaving cream. But the tenure of the former Norway boss in south London was a disaster. Under Olsen Wimbledon dropped down the table to face a relegation battle. He was dismissed in spring 2000 just before Wimbledon went down, probably never to return.

Further south-west

KINGSTON

AFC Wimbledon (2002–), Kingsmeadow Stadium, Kingston Road

AFC Wimbledon were founded in 2002 by Wimbledon fans who objected to the club's move seventy miles north to Milton Keynes as MK Dons. The birth of the first club to be founded by supporters (FC United in Manchester are another) raises an insoluble philosophical conundrum.

Surely the owners of a football club have the legal right to move it where they like and change the name to what they like, regardless of the fans' distress. New fans will soon appear at the new location, and in time the objectors will fade away. After all, can anyone dismiss Arsenal because they left Woolwich for the other side of London?

However, those who opposed Wimbledon's move stressed that the owners were merely the custodians of the club and that football is not a typical business and cannot be judged on purely economic grounds; that a football club has a history and soul attached to its locale. A move to another part of London might be just about tolerable, but uprooting to an entirely different city some distance away was unacceptable.

Fans opposed to the move came up with a name that was legally different enough but evidently loyal to the area in AFC Wimbledon. Of course the new club would not be able to compete at the same (League) level as the Wimbledon that transferred to Milton Keynes; they would have to start much lower down the football pyramid.

To find players AFC held trials on Wimbledon Common and soon signed some good enough to play at the eighth level of the League – the Premier Division of the Combined Counties League – playing their home games at the Kingsmeadow Stadium in Kingston.

Claiming Wimbledon's traditions and honours for themselves, AFC Wimbledon reached an agreement with MK Dons in 2006 over the use of the name 'Wimbledon' and MK Dons sent Wimbledon's honours back to London. But as 1988 FA Cup Final scorer Lawrie Sanchez has pointed out: 'I have a great respect for what AFC Wimbledon have done – and the fans have the same great memories as I do – but AFC Wimbledon have never won the FA Cup. The 1988 Cup Final has been consigned to history – it belongs to neither club. It belongs solely to the players who played in it and the fans who watched it.'

AFC Wimbledon attracted 4,657 spectators, an astonishingly large crowd at this lowly level, for their first match, a friendly against Sutton. The club soon won promotion, and in 2004 established a record – at any level – run of seventy-eight League games without defeat. It remains to be seen whether the new Wimbledon can maintain the momentum and rival their predecessor's astonishing success.

SUTTON

Sutton (1913–14, 1919–), Gander Green Lane

Long one of the best-known non-League sides, Sutton were formed in 1898 at the Robin Hood Hotel near the ground following a merger between Sutton Guild Rovers FC and Sutton AFC. They wanted to play in caps of claret and gold, but when that was found to be too expensive settled for amber and chocolate.

Sutton have mostly played in the best leagues below the Football League – Isthmian League, Athenian League – and reached the Amateur Cup Final twice in the 1960s. In 1970 Sutton were drawn at home in the Cup to League Champions Leeds, and 14,000 packed out Gander Green Lane to watch the semi-professional side lose 6–0. It looked as if any chance of real improvement had faded in 1985 when, even though the club won the Isthmian League, they refused to be promoted to the GM Vauxhall Conference (the fifth tier of football). However, after they retained the championship they accepted promotion. Soon after, in 1989, Sutton achieved the remarkable feat of not just beating a First Division side in the FA Cup (Coventry City) but becoming the non-League team to knock out the highest-placed First Division side in the modern history of the competition – Coventry were then fourth in the League.

In the twenty-first century Sutton have not been as successful as their 1980s predecessors and have struggled to stay at the highest non-League level.

7 West London

BAYSWATER, W2

The Football Association at Lancaster Gate, No. 22 (1929–71), No. 16 (1971–2001)

Despite their no-doubt good intentions, it would be hard to find another English organisation as powerful as the Football Association, football's governing body, that has been so riddled with ineptitude and incompetence. If a decision crucial to the development of football in England has to be made, it is practically certain the FA will make the wrong one. For instance, in 1929 around the time that the FA first moved to Lancaster Gate, an oddly shaped but exclusive street of Georgian villas north of Hyde Park, it withdrew from football's international body, FIFA, in a row over amateurism and payments to players. In their letter of resignation the FA explained that as FIFA had only recently been formed it did not yet have the knowledge 'which only experience can bring'. Consequently England refused to send a team not just to the first World Cup, held in Uruguay in 1930, but to the following two that took place prior to the Second World War – decisions which they rue to this day.

Yet the FA's thinking was typical of, rather than an exception to, the prevalent thinking of the time. Charles Sutcliffe, a leading figure in the Football League, the FA's northern rivals, dismissed the 1934 World Cup as a 'joke', claiming that the British Home International Championships between England, Scotland, Wales and Northern Ireland was 'a far better World Championship than the one to be staged in Rome'.

England Roused

That year Stanley Rous, a former amateur goalkeeper and top referee, became FA secretary. Rous recalled in his autobiography that Lancaster Gate was 'in many ways a quiet backwater when I arrived on 4 August 1934, to start my work. There was no problem parking my Hillman Minx as there was rarely another car in the road.'

Rous stayed as secretary from 1934 to 1962, and later as president of FIFA became the most powerful man in world football. When he began his tenure there were only five members of staff at No. 22, previously the Eden Court Hotel, home of the Association of British Launderers and Cleaners. Disciplinary cases were 'very rare, not more than five or six a year needed personal hearings', mostly because players were in those days allowed to practically assault an opponent short of outright GBH without being penalised.

After the Second World War the FA at last allowed England to enter the World Cup, and so a manager was appointed for the first time – the astute and genial Walter Winterbottom, who took on the job in July 1946. There was almost no media interest, which contrasts sharply with the current climate when the suitability and status of the England manager appears to be football's main story. Outside Lancaster Gate a photographer asked the FA secretary, Sir Frederick Wall, if he could pose for a picture with Winterbottom. 'No. Why should I?' Wall responded and walked away.

It was not Winterbottom, however, but a selection committee who chose the squad and team. The committee consisted of men who knew little about the game and was for many years chaired by a Grimsby fish merchant, Arthur Drewry. He was in charge of picking the England squad and team for the 1950 World Cup in Brazil, a task hampered by the goodwill tour of Canada which the FA, with extraordinary incompetence even by their standards, organised for the same time and the decision to allow Manchester United to withdraw their players from both the squads that were travelling to the USA and Canada.

Absent from the England World Cup squad was the country's best player, Stanley Matthews, who was sent on the Canada trip. There was an outcry and at the last minute a compromise was reached. Matthews would fly down to Brazil for England's second match. But Drewry refused to change a winning team, and Matthews could only stand by while England's expected walkover against the USA turned into an embarrassing 1–0 defeat.

England continued to decline until Alf Ramsey took over from Walter Winterbottom in 1963. The taciturn ex-Tottenham man became England's first sole selector. At Lancaster Gate Ramsey was given a 'stark office, little more spacious than a large cupboard on the third floor', according to his biographer, Max Marquis, but was later promoted to something more roomy on the ground floor. Between internationals Ramsey read his letters, replied to the sensible ones, enjoyed lunch with a club manager or trusted journalist, and headed off in the evening back to Ipswich via the Central Line tube to Liverpool Street. Such unprotected mingling with the public today would probably put some recent incumbents at risk of a lynching.

Ramsey evidently knew what he was doing for he fashioned a team that won the 1966 World Cup. Even if all England's games were held at Wembley, it was some achievement to win five out of six matches. (Thirty years later Terry Venables managed two wins in five games at Wembley when England staged their only other home tournament – Euro '96.) During the 1966 tournament Ramsey was summoned to Lancaster Gate to answer for Nobby Stiles's horrendous tackle on French player Jacky Simon in their group game. Stiles trained with a sense of foreboding, and when Ramsey called him to one side he feared the worst. 'What were your intentions when you tackled Simon?' asked Ramsey. 'I wasn't trying to hurt him,' explained the midfield player. 'I was playing the ball but I got my timing all wrong.' 'Good,' replied the manager. 'You're playing against Argentina.' England won that game, and in the next match, the semi-final against Portugal, Stiles came into his own, subduing the mighty Eusebio, who was reduced to taking corners. At the end of the final his joyous celebrations epitomised the day.

'Don Readies'

Alf Ramsey was sacked after England failed to qualify for the 1974 World Cup and was replaced by Don Revie, the highly successful Leeds manager. A new era dawned at Lancaster Gate. The restrained gentlemanly days of

Ramsey soon faded. In his first match Revie's England beat Czechoslovakia 3–0 in a European Championship qualifier. But it was the Czechs that went through from the group and even went on to win the trophy while England stayed at home for the second tournament running.

Strangely, Revie forsook the winning ways he had adopted at Leeds while in charge of England. Instead of turning out a settled, steady, line-up he capped a bewildering mass of players, many second-rate (Steve Whitworth, Ian Gillard, Peter Taylor) and mostly ignored the many highly skilled English-born players of what truly was a golden generation (Duncan McKenzie, Alan Hudson, Stan Bowles, Rodney Marsh, Charlie George).

Revie made the hard-working but uninspiring Alan Ball captain and then suddenly dropped him altogether. Ball received a typed letter, thanking him for his services, sent by 'Jill Clarke, Team manager'. Ball took Revie's lack of signature on the letter as deliberate; as 'the final twist of the knife', he claimed in his autobiography. Revie kept getting his selections wrong. For a qualifying game against Italy in Rome in November 1976 he packed the team with defensive players to outmuscle Italy. With little quality in midfield England had no answer to the Italians' craft and creativity, and lost 2–0, a result that eventually meant England failed to qualify for the World Cup – again. It can't have helped that he bamboozled the players with *megillah*-like dossiers they couldn't understand, made them relax at their hotels with games such as bingo and carpet golf, and tormented himself with a host of mind-boggling superstitions – hatred of the colour green, loathing of ornamental elephants and fear of peacocks (he had the bird removed from the Leeds United crest).

Ted Croker was FA secretary at this time. He came over as an uncontroversial administrator, not someone who would charge his suits, haircuts and holidays to expenses, and not someone at all likely to supplement his wages by selling tickets to tout king Stan Flashman. It was the England manager, Don Revie, not the bureaucrat Ted Croker, who was the epitome of the venal, money-grabbing football mercenary of the period.

Revie once asked for £200 from journalists wanting to interview Malcolm Macdonald after the Newcastle striker had scored five against Cyprus, and then pocketed the money himself rather than give it to the player. Revie was well-known inside the game for offering bribes to opponents to throw matches. Bob Stokoe and Frank McLintock were just two of the football men who later revealed this. And in the late '60s Revie sent Alan Ball £100 sweeteners to try to entice him to leave Everton for Leeds.

In July 1977, with the England team about to *not* qualify for a third successive tournament, Revie learned that the *Daily Mirror* was going to run an exposé on him. He quit the England job and sold his story to the *Daily Mail*. In the article Revie claimed the pressures were intolerable. 'I sat down with Elsie one night and we agreed that the job was no longer worth the aggravation,' revealed Revie. 'It was bringing too much heartache to those nearest to us. Nearly everyone in the country seems to want me out. So I am giving them what they want. I know people will accuse me of running away and it does sicken me that I cannot finish the job by taking England to the World Cup finals in Argentina next year. But the situation has become impossible.'

The FA were livid for they did not receive his letter of resignation until a few hours after the article appeared. But what could that *Mirror* exposé have been that made the 'situation' 'impossible'? Twenty-four hours later the *Mail* broke the sensational news that Revie had been hired to run football in the United Arab Emirates for four years for a tax-free payout of £340,000.

There were cries of 'traitor'. Sunderland manager Bob Stokoe was furious. 'Revie should have been castrated for the way he left England,' he cried. Football League secretary Alan Hardaker was perhaps more cutting when he quipped: 'Don Revie's decision doesn't surprise me in the slightest. Now I can only hope he can quickly learn to call out bingo numbers in Arabic.' Sir Harold Thompson, FA chairman, attempted to exact revenge. Thompson, an Oxford academic, had never liked Revie, the badly spoken Yorkshire oik. Once at a dinner Thompson turned to the England manager and said, 'When I get to know you better, Revie, I shall call you Don,' to which the England boss responded, 'And when I get to know you better, Thompson, I shall call you Sir Harold.' Now Thompson accused Revie of bringing the game into disrepute. Revie refused to attend the hearing in which he was suspended indefinitely from any involvement in English football but he appealed to the High Court and won, although he had to pay two thirds of his costs, a fitting rejoinder, many said, for the man they called 'Don Readies' because of his penchant for taking ready cash.

With Revie gone, it seemed certain that the England job would go to Nottingham Forest's Brian Clough, the only viable candidate. Clough was invited for an interview and took the chance he had been waiting for to belittle Sir Harold Thompson whom he believed to be a 'stroppy, know-all bugger'. He also berated the FA for having England play in shirts he described as 'horrible, garish red, white and blue – cheap and nasty', which hardly endeared him to Ted Croker, who had struck the deal with the kit company.

At the end of the session Clough met his friend and colleague Peter Taylor outside and told him he had 'pissed' the interview. 'Can't miss', were Clough's words. He did. Ron Greenwood, a mild-mannered, non-controversial fellow who had guided West Ham to a few cups before losing inspiration, was chosen. Clough had received only one vote. He later called the whole interview a 'sham . . . cut and dried for Greenwood'.

Ron Greenwood came over as erudite and capable, but his England teams did little more than muddle through in what was a relatively uneventful period for English football. He quit in 1982 after his England team had exited the World Cup without losing a game but without scoring a goal in the second phase.

'What can I say about Peter Shilton? Peter Shilton is Peter Shilton. He has been Peter Shilton since the year dot'

Bobby Robson, Greenwood's replacement, lasted what now seems an eternity – eight years. His first task was to qualify for the 1984 European Championships in France. He failed by losing at home to Denmark. Robson offered to resign in favour of Brian Clough but the FA rejected the idea and Robson was free to muddle through for nearly seven more years.

At the 1986 World Cup England were struggling, unable to score in their first two games against Portugal and Morocco. Salvation came through two unlikely sources: injury to England's captain Bryan Robson and the sending-off of the sideways passing Ray Wilkins. Now England had to change the midfield. Enter Peter Reid and Steve Hodge, and up front Peter Beardsley, a livewire dazzling striker who replaced the wooden Mark Hateley. England were transformed. Gary Lineker, aided by Beardsley, went into scoring overload and England made it to the quarter-finals. Once there, though, manager Robson blew it by introducing John Barnes too late to thwart the Argentinians.

Euro '88 was a different kind of disaster. England qualified in style but then lost all three games, their worst ever performance at a tournament. Hostility towards Robson grew. After England drew a friendly against Saudi Arabia, one newspaper urged: 'In The Name Of Allah, Go', and another more wittily concluded: 'England Mustafa New Manager'. Once again Robson tried to resign. Once again Bert Millichip stopped him.

The 1990 World Cup would be Robson's last. The FA had told the hapless England boss they would not be renewing his contract and he secured himself a job as coach at PSV Eindhoven. The *Sun* greeted the news with: 'PSV Off Then Bungler Bobby'. England qualified for Italia '90 with something to spare. But once again they embarrassed themselves once the tournament got under way. The match against Ireland was a miserable draw; the Dutch game a more creditable draw. By now England captain Bryan Robson was injured again. The public was devastated for the all-action Roy of the Rovers-style hero. They might have been less so had they realised he hurt himself not by pushing his body to the limit for the sake of his country but by mucking about with Paul Gascoigne in his hotel room after they had been out for some liquid refreshment.

Next, England had to overcome the inconsequential Egyptians, and did so. Just. Like four years previously, with Robson injured, England were transformed. A tough Belgium side and the tournament's inspired dark horses, Cameroon, were dispatched and England were through to their first World Cup semi-final since 1966. It wasn't just the ability to win a key match that had changed, the playing system had been overhauled. Out was the holding midfield player *canard*; in was the sweeper. Out were the sleeves-rolled-up workhorses like Steve McMahon; in were thoroughbreds of deft touch like Trevor Steven. Had Tony Dorigo replaced Stuart Pearce England would most likely have made it to the final. Instead they went out on penalties for the first but not the last time to Germany.

Nearly two decades later the jury are still split over whether Robson did well in the end because he was a talented manager or because if you keep someone in charge for long enough he is bound to have a few magic moments amid the dross eventually, rather like Harry Redknapp at club level.

But it was not Bobby Robson's failures as England manager that characterised the 1980s at the FA. This was a time when football was rent asunder by cataclysmic events that have shaped the modern game. In the Bradford City stadium fire of 11 May fifty-two people burned to death. A few weeks later on 29 May Liverpool fans charged Juventus supporters at the European Cup Final at the Heysel Stadium, Brussels, and thirty-nine fans, mostly Italian, died. This led to English clubs being banned from European club football till the end of the decade. And in April 1989 scores of fans were crushed to death at the FA Cup semi-final between Liverpool and Nottingham Forest at Hillsborough.

At the FA it was the era of the committee. The FA created an extraordinary glut of committees. There was even a committee to appoint committees. When Graham Kelly went to work for the FA in 1988 he found files stuffed with memos from 1970s chairman Sir Harold Thompson to chief executive Ted Croker that started 'Dear Croker', whom he would refer to as 'boy' at formal dinners.

Route one and root vegetables

The beginning of the 1990s looked promising. England had reached the semi-final of the World Cup, even if they had muddled through, English clubs would soon be back in European club football after the Heysel ban, and the press were excited at the appointment of the new England manager, Graham Taylor. No previous England boss had ever used the long ball game in which defenders bypass midfield to get the ball up to a big striker as quickly as possible. Taylor's Watford had played in this style while rising from the Fourth Division to second place in the First behind Liverpool and reaching the FA Cup Final against Everton. His Aston Villa side were more rounded, but just when it looked as if the Midlands team were going to win the League in 1990 Taylor's nerve failed him and they were pipped by Liverpool.

The media gave Taylor a chance. He qualified for his first tournament, the 1992 European Championships (which is more than Robson or McClaren did). Maybe England would hump and hoof it in style all the way to the Euro '92 Final? Taylor's squad, however, was disastrous. Two of the most talented English players of the period, Peter Beardsley and Chris Waddle, were inexplicably overlooked, but room was found for Andy Sinton and Carlton Palmer. Once again England failed to win a game. Taylor shocked the nation by taking off Gary Lineker in the last group game, just when England needed to score, and they never found the net again. The result of that last match was Sweden 2 – England 1, immediately rejigged in the *Sun* as Swedes 2 – Turnips 1 with Taylor's head transmogrified into the losing root vegetable.

Things then deteriorated sharply and England failed to make the 1994 World Cup as Taylor stumbled from self-inflicted disaster to self-inflicted disaster, needlessly changing formations, selecting players who were palpably short of international stature (Lee Sharpe, Gary Pallister), losing the lead when they were cruising, getting only one shot at goal in a 2–0 defeat to average Norway. England needed to beat San Marino, several thousand leagues below them in international capability, in their last match, but a weak Stuart Pearce back pass allowed San Marino to take the lead after only eight seconds – only their second goal in ten matches. England did turn it round to win 7–1 but Holland beat Poland and England were out. Taylor quit in November 1993.

Can we not knock it?
England manager Graham Taylor was filmed for *Cutting Edge*, a 1993 fly-on-the-wall documentary which turned out to be one of the most absurd TV football programmes ever made. The documentary followed Taylor and his assistant, the barely articulate Phil Neal, at the training ground and in the dugout at two World Cup qualifiers.

Poland 1–1 England, May 1993
England centre-half Des Walker knocks a misplaced pass to John Barnes. Taylor is befuddled and coins one of the great football sayings:

Taylor: 'Ooooh, fucking . . . Do I not like that!'

Poland win the ball, break downfield and score.

Taylor: 'What a fucking ball. What a ball, eh, from Des to Barnesy. What a fucking . . . It was our possession.'

Phil Neal: 'I know.'

Taylor: 'It was from our free-kick. We've come square, and the ball . . . Des and Barnesy, eh? Fucking ball, eh? You can talk till you're fucking blue in the face, can't you?'

Neal: 'Yes, boss.'

The game kicks off again.

Taylor: 'Come on. Bigger, bigger.'

Another misplaced pass.

Taylor: 'We've done that fucking ... CAN WE NOT KNOCK IT? They've done everything that we told them not to do. Everything that we told them not to do.'

Holland 2–0 England, October 1993

After Dutchman Ronald Koeman brings down David Platt on the edge of the area ...

Taylor: 'Linesman, linesman, what sort of thing is happening here? You know it, you know it, don't you? Absolutely disgraceful.'

Linesman mutters. Koeman stays on the field.

Taylor: 'Linesman, linesman, that's a disgrace ... Hells' bells!'

Koeman later scores.

Taylor: 'I'll tell you, they don't fucking deserve. Fucking. That is absolutely shocking. We'll have to get Wrighty on shortly.'

Neal, parroting him: 'We'll have to give Wrighty a go.'

Taylor turns his attention once more to the beleaguered linesman: 'You know we've been cheated, don't you?'

Linesman motions him back to his technical area.

Taylor: 'I have a metre. I have a metre. You know. It's all right.'

Linesman is getting fed up. Goes to report Taylor, who pleads for mercy: 'I won't say anything else. Come on, don't. But I'm allowed to stay in the metre.'

Linesman lets him off with a warning. However, the peace is soon broken.

Taylor: 'Even if he doesn't see it as a penalty, he has to go. You know that. I know you know it, so ... And then the fella scores the free-kick.'

Suddenly an outbreak of bonhomie from Taylor: 'You can't say anything. I know you can't say anything. I know that.'

> Again it's shortlived.
>
> Taylor: 'But, you see at the end of the day, I get the sack. Will you say to the fella, the referee has got me the sack? Thank him ever so much for that, won't you?'

Football came home . . . almost

Taylor's replacement was the 'people's favourite', Terry Venables. As a manager Venables had won the Spanish League with Barcelona – hardly a major achievement when the club ranks as one of the greatest in the history of football – and the FA Cup with Tottenham. In 1994, the year he took over as England manager, Venables was entangled in six libel actions, eight trials in the High Court, six official inquiries and four police investigations. Nevertheless FA chief executive Graham Kelly was insistent that he was the perfect choice: 'I led the consensus to appoint the best man and ignore Venables's business dodginess. I hadn't seen any evidence to disqualify him as a coach.'

The players loved Venables, for it was quite clear he let them get away with practically anything short of murder. At the end of a gruelling pre-Euro '96 tour to the Far East he gave them a night off to 'let their hair down'. They went into binge mode at Hong Kong's Jump Club, where Teddy Sheringham was photographed at the end of the long night having two bottles of spirits poured down his neck as he sat in the club's so-called 'dentist's chair'. On the plane taking them home the players showed that they were in no mood to end their one night off by wrecking two television screens and a table top – one player had to be restrained from entering the cockpit!

Here was the chance for the FA to take a principled stand. The governing body that had wrung its hands so many times over hooliganism from the fans in the previous thirty years now had the ideal opportunity to make an example of hooligan players before things really got out of hand; before, for instance, a future in which England internationals would regularly get caught for drink-driving, film themselves having sex, get into 'self-defence' altercations with nightclub bouncers, indulge in binge-drinking and find themselves locked up for a week over New Year to 'protect the public'.

Instead of kicking the troublemakers out of the squad, the FA allowed the matter to remain in-house, and Venables's response was to castigate not the players as yobs and slobs but the press as traitors: 'It's awful but we're getting hardened to it. We just don't understand why it's necessary – there are a few [journalists] who seem like traitors to us. They're turning the public against the players which can turn them against us in the stadium.'

Some cite the 1996 European Championships as a triumph for England as they went out unbeaten to the eventual winners, Germany, on penalties in the semi-final. Maybe a fully sober England team – tequila- and vodka-free, T-shirts unripped, on friendly terms with aeroplane furnishings – might have waltzed through beating everyone in sight. It wasn't a tough tournament, for this was an era of pedestrian 'world-class' players where the best the Germans could do was Jürgen Klinsmann; the Dutch were at their lowest ebb in forty years and had to resort to Jordi Cruyff and Winston Bogarde; for France, Zidane had yet to mature; and Italy were misguidedly convinced Dino Baggio and Alessandro Del Piero were world-beaters.

Another way of looking at England's endeavours was to point out that they won only two games, one of which was against Scotland, and the other, that sensational 4–1 over Holland, was OTT at the wrong time (much like the later 5–1 over Germany in Munich), for a 4–1 defeat would also have seen England go through.

But it could have been worse. When Venables was appointed the two main FA powerbrokers, international committee chairman Peter Swales (a TV salesman who went on to run and ruin Manchester City) and his side-kick Noel White wanted the antique dealer Gerry Francis. Venables had the job for just one tournament. White refused to grant him the new contract he wanted and he quit England.

The Hod squad

Yet another Tottenham man, Glenn Hoddle, became the next England manager. A gifted midfielder, the post-playing Hoddle was crippled by a penchant for conversing in twisted, tortuous solecisms. His management record to date had been one FA Cup Final defeat for Chelsea whom he had taken as high as eleventh place in the League. Yet he was trumpeted by some sections of the media (particularly the *Sunday Times*) as a progressive choice.

Hoddle's teams played sensible football, his selections were consistent and reliable, and England qualified in style for the 1998 World Cup in France. England had a reasonable tournament, not a great one. They were never serious contenders to win it, even though away from home this would always offer England their best chance, given the proximity of the two countries, since problems increase for every team the further they travel.

Hoddle had been brave enough to pick the eighteen-year-old Michael Owen and rightly omitted the incorrigible Paul Gascoigne after yet another senseless binge, but he hampered England's chances by ignoring many of the best players in the country – the Arsenal defensive unit of Dixon, Winterburn, Keown and Bould alongside Seaman and Adams, and the most talented (sober) English player of his generation: Matt le Tissier. Yet in his 22-man squad for France Hoddle found room for that footballing free zone, David Batty, who missed the crucial kick that brought an England exit in the last sixteen (on penalties, as usual) after a dramatic game against one of their regular *bêtes noires* – Argentina.

Hoddle didn't last much longer in the job, but it was religion, not football, that did for him. Known for his born-again beliefs, he installed faith-healer Eileen Drewery as part of the England coaching staff, and matters descended into farce. One day she laid her hands on Ray Parlour's head and asked him if he wanted anything, to which the tousle-haired one replied: 'Short back and sides, please.' Neither the FA nor the fans had any problem with Hoddle's unorthodox acolyte while results were going well, but in autumn 1998 Hoddle made a disappointing start to the Euro 2000 qualifiers. He was sacked in February 1999 after an interview in *The Times* in which he seemed to be saying that he thought disabled people were being punished for sins committed in a previous life. The comments caused an uproar. Sports minister Tony Banks said he 'would be surprised if Hoddle remained in his job', and prime minister Tony Blair, who at that point had not yet got God in a big way, stated that Hoddle's comments were 'very wrong'. Education secretary David Blunkett, a blind man, joked: 'Glenn's logic means that I must have been a fairly disastrous football coach in a previous life.'

Few supported Hoddle, who said that he was not prepared to resign and claimed his words were misinterpreted. He dug his own grave further when he told newscaster Trevor McDonald: 'At this moment in time I did not say them things.' Perhaps to put Hoddle out of his misery, the FA terminated his contract.

It was then that the FA began a catalogue of errors regarding the role of England manager, something not put right until the appointment of Fabio Capello in winter 2007. Not really sure whether they wanted to win an international trophy at all costs or just to rouse the kind of bulldog patriotism mostly dormant since the Second World War, the FA schizophrenically switched from one stance to the other as each successive manager or caretaker seemed to be chosen simply because he was as different as possible from his predecessor.

Kevin Keegan summed up the perceived best qualities of the English character: loyalty, candour, honest enthusiasm. He had been marginally successful at Newcastle but his all-attacking Geordie side fluffed the 1996 championship despite enjoying a twelve-point lead over Manchester United at one stage. Perhaps he might now lose his nerve with England at the wrong time? The FA should also have wondered why Keegan hadn't actually won a cup or two during his tenure at St James's Park, especially given the hoary footballing legend that Newcastle are destined to win the FA Cup every season.

Keegan took over in February 1999 and soon rekindled England's Euro 2000 qualifying campaign. They reached Belgium/Holland, but there the former Hamburg forward's tactical naivety that had looked touching at Newcastle now became annoying. Though England led Romania and Portugal they lost both games and went out at the group stage. England turned their attention to the next World Cup but lost a qualifier at home to Germany in October 2000, following which Keegan resigned in a Wembley toilet.

By then the FA had a new chief executive, Adam Crozier, a livewire Scot fresh from the advertising agency Saatchi and Saatchi. The FA's fuddy-duddy image would soon be gone in a haze of New Labour-friendly spin buzzwords heralded by a move away from musty Lancaster Gate to stylish Soho Square in 2001 (→ p. 31).

Hyde Park Hotel, Bayswater Road, west of St Petersburg Place

Terry Venables, newly appointed chief executive of Spurs, negotiated the sale of Paul Gascoigne to Lazio Roma on 28 June 1991 at this plush hotel. In attendance, besides the various Tottenham officials, was one Gino

Santin, a London restaurant owner who could speak Italian and assumed the duties of agent to Gascoigne.

When they couldn't agree on the fee Lazio would pay Spurs for the player the men continued their arguing on the street outside. But Tottenham were lucky to be offered anything at all. Gascoigne had badly injured himself in the 1991 Cup Final and wasn't going to be able to play for the foreseeable future. Or as Tottenham owner Alan Sugar explained it, 'We're talking about a fuckin' geezer with one leg.' Lazio paid £5.5 million but Gascoigne, because of his injury, missed the entire following season.

→ Wimbledon at Cannizaro's hotel, p. 230.

Lancaster Gate Hotel, 75 Lancaster Gate

On the eve of England's departure for a match in Portugal in May 1964 a number of internationals broke the curfew to go drinking at the hotel's Beachcomber bar, among them Bobby Moore, Jimmy Greaves and Bobby Charlton. When they walked into their rooms much later they found their passports on their pillows. Each spent a restless night, and faced Ramsey apprehensively the next morning. In his clipped tones, he told them that if it had been practical to do so he would have replaced them all. 'I didn't say you couldn't go to the pub, I didn't say you shouldn't go, I just expected you wouldn't go. We are here on serious business and I thought you all understood that. We are going to win the World Cup.'

Paddington station, Praed Street

Geoff Hurst, England's 1966 World Cup hero, first met the victorious England manager, Alf Ramsey, when teaming up with the England Under-23 party at Paddington station in November 1964. 'The first sight of him was a bit of a shock,' Hurst was quoted as saying in *It is Now!*, Roger Hutchinson's book on the 1966 World Cup victory. 'He didn't seem like a football man at all. He was so carefully dressed, so quietly spoken he seemed more like a businessman or bank manager.'

→ Len Shackleton at King's Cross station, p. 87

Royal Lancaster Hotel, Lancaster Terrace

Major press conferences for the England team often take place in the Royal Lancaster. One of a number of Bayswater hotels popular in the football world, the Royal Lancaster also often hosts the Footballer of the Year awards and is where Manchester United players and officials occasionally stay in London.

In summer 1976 Stan Bowles, then one of the game's top performers, was invited to meet officials from leading German club Hamburg at the hotel with a view to moving there from Queen's Park Rangers. Despite the attractions of such a move the hour didn't suit the fussy Rangers man. 'You know what them [sic] Germans are like – 9.30 a.m. on a bloody Sunday morning,' he later moaned. QPR chairman Jim Gregory was meant to be there with Bowles but didn't turn up. When the player phoned Gregory to find out why the QPR owner told him simply, 'I don't like the Germans.' Bowles pulled out of the transfer, which might well have made him, not Kevin Keegan (who later joined the German side from Liverpool), European Footballer of the Year.

The Tottenham team had lunch at the Royal Lancaster before their League game with Chelsea on 1 December 1990. Alas the driver of the coach parked the vehicle illegally and it was clamped and towed away with the team kit inside. When the players and officials emerged from the hotel well fed and looking forward to get to the game the vehicle had gone. Tottenham arrived at the ground late, handed in their team-sheet late, and were fined £20,000 by the Football Association. On the pitch it wasn't much better for the home side. Gascoigne and Lineker scored but Chelsea won 3–2.

It was from the Royal Lancaster on 2 February 1999 that the FA issued a short press statement making it known that 'with regret the FA and Glenn Hoddle have today agreed to terminate Glenn's contract'.

Nearly nine years later Fabio Capello sat in the same hotel for his first press conference as the new England manager. As the *Daily Telegraph* put it, 'Those in the room had seen off every England manager stretching back to Sir Alf Ramsey. And in their presence Capello looked about as concerned as a man taking his poodle for a stroll. Which in a sense he was, what with Brian Barwick [FA chief executive] walking in a couple of paces behind him.'

→ Sale of Alan Ball at the White House Hotel, p. 133

Royal Park Hotel, 3 Westbourne Terrace

It was at the Royal Park Hotel that the notorious meeting took place in 2005 between Ashley Cole, the underpaid Arsenal left-back, and officials from Chelsea, who wanted to sign the player even though he was under contract to their London rivals.

The story that emerged illustrated, possibly better than any other, how low football had sunk morally. Cole had been driving along the North Circular Road in 2004 when his agent Jonathan Barnett phoned to tell him that Arsenal were only willing to pay the left-back £55,000 a *week*, not the £60,000 he wanted. Cole was so incensed he nearly 'swerved off the road' and knew then that he had to leave Arsenal. It was not about the money, he later explained, but the 'respect', a word often bandied about meaninglessly by those raised in hip-hop culture rather than normal society bound by principle and modesty.

On 27 January 2005 Cole and Barnett were chauffer-driven in the agent's Bentley to the hotel. They walked into a meeting room and just happened to find there Pini Zahavi, a close friend of Chelsea owner Roman Abramovich. The three men chatted for about twenty minutes when who should walk into the room? None other than Chelsea manager José Mourinho and chief executive Peter Kenyon. Cole congratulated Chelsea on their new success and the club's officials told him they wished to buy more players, including the 'best left-back in the world', who just happened to be sitting in the room with them. Mourinho asked Cole if he was happy at Arsenal and Cole revealed that he wasn't (but that it was not manager Arsene Wenger's fault). That was the end of the discussion as far as the player was concerned but the fact that the meeting had taken place was splashed in the *News of the World*.

Four days later Arsenal chairman Peter Hill-Wood declared that his club were ready to investigate allegations of secret transfer talks. 'The Premier League rules are very clear on this matter. If the club is presented with evidence that those rules have been contravened I am sure we will take the matter further,' added the chairman. Arsenal manager Arsene Wenger played a clever hand. He announced cryptically that he had no doubts over Cole's commitment to Arsenal, but by the beginning of March he had rounded on Chelsea, accusing them of 'tapping-up' Cole. 'This case is very sad and very unfortunate because you expect your neighbours in the same city with that power not to behave like that.' Wenger also added how 'arrogant' and 'naïve' Chelsea were to set up such a meeting with Cole in a London hotel.

What irked Arsenal fans was that Cole, already playing for a leading club on a grossly inflated wage, was looking for even more money, and that Chelsea had blatantly twisted League rules knowing that any punishment incurred would be meagre and inconsequential. Indeed, Chelsea were found guilty and given a tiny fine. They were also docked three points but the punishment was suspended and therefore rendered meaningless.

Cole to his credit continued to play superbly for Arsenal, helping them to the European Cup Final in 2006. He left at the end of that season and did join Chelsea who, despite a near limitless pot of money at their disposal, initially failed to match Arsenal's European run. Cole later showed a strange grasp of history by claiming the club had treated him 'as a slave', albeit one on more than £50,000 a week. As *The Gooner* fanzine memorably put it, the accusation, especially from a black man, was 'an insult to those who have suffered slavery'.

→ England at the Hendon Hall Hotel, p. 135

HAMMERSMITH, W7

Hammersmith Palais, 242 Shepherd's Bush Road
Terry Venables took up a singing engagement at this well-known dancehall in 1965, crooning in the style of Frank Sinatra under a reflecting globe at a time when the world was moving towards the rock era led by the Beatles and Rolling Stones. Venables evidently had more talent as an entertainer than as a footballer or manager. Before starring at so prestigious a venue, he had already once come second to the Bachelors in a Butlin's talent contest.

→ Terry Venables growing up in Dagenham, p. 82

Hammersmith Town Hall, King Street
At the height of football club merger mania in the 1980s a group of independent-minded Chelsea fans staged a demonstration outside Hammersmith Town Hall against plans to amalgamate the club with

QPR and Fulham into the monstrous hybrid Fulham Park Rangers. The plan was the brainchild of a property magnate, David Bulstrode, and his company, Marler Estates/Cabra, which owned the grounds of all three clubs and regarded the sites as attractive prime real estate for development.

Meanwhile, the corrupt publishing magnate Robert Maxwell outlined plans to merge Reading and Oxford into Thames Valley Royals. Vociferous fan opposition scotched that scheme as well but the topic continues to rear its head on the radio, particularly on Talksport, which regularly raises the notion of merging, say, Sheffield Wednesday and Sheffield United into one 'super' Sheffield club that could compete with the big sides, ignoring the fact that such a creation would not necessarily be a better team and would sooner or later be challenged locally by the next best Sheffield team, leading to calls for a further merger and so on *ad infinitum*.

KENSINGTON, W8

Kensington High Street

As he watched the traffic lights change from yellow to red on Kensington High Street after the tempestuous 1966 World Cup match between England and Argentina, referee Ken Aston had a blinding flash of inspiration that would change the style of refereeing worldwide.

Why nor issue players with a yellow card for a booking and a red for a sending-off? Previously referees in internationals had to overcome major language problems if they wanted to talk to a player. Aston himself had taken charge of the ninety-minute fight between Italy and Chile at the 1962 World Cup, supposedly a Group B match, that finished 2–0 to the Chileans. During the game one player had to be escorted from the field by armed police, and an Italian kicked a Chile player in the head amid incessant shirt-pulling, flesh-pinching and bollock-crunching. With an ingenious stroke of bumptiousness typical of the over-bureaucratic world of the ref, Aston later explained that the cards were simply meant to confirm a caution rather than be a replacement for it.

→ **Antonio Rattin sent off, p. 147**

Royal Garden Hotel, Kensington High Street, between Palace Green and Palace Avenue

It was at the Royal Garden that England celebrated on the night of 30 July 1966 after winning the World Cup. In the street thousands paid tribute to the England players who were on the balcony holding aloft . . . a replica Jules Rimet trophy. The Football Association were paranoid the real cup might be stolen, as it had been a few months before the tournament and had replaced the real thing with a copy.

Inside the hotel the FA had laid on a party for the victorious England squad but it was a male-only affair. The FA refused to allow wives and girlfriends to join the players for the official celebrations, so Mrs Hurst, Mrs Moore et al ate in the Bulldog Chophouse in another part of the hotel, where they were each presented with a gift for their part in the success: a pair of scissors. (Forty years later the team's chances of recapturing the trophy in Germany were ruined by the presence of the wives and girlfriends, misguidedly supported by the manager Sven-Goran Eriksson. But this was 1966. Feminism hadn't yet reached England and 'girl power' didn't exist.)

Before the festivities began Jackie Charlton placed a card in the top pocket of his jacket that read: 'This body is to be returned to Room 508, Royal Garden Hotel', just in case the night ended in such drunken stupor it rendered him incapable of remembering where he was staying. Which is exactly what happened. Charlton woke up on a sofa in Leytonstone at the home of a complete stranger with whom he had drunk away the night. When he left the house after breakfast the first person he saw in the street outside, astonishingly enough, was a neighbour from his home town of Ashington in Northumberland.

In the late 1980s Terry Venables used to come to the Royal Garden with his financial adviser Paul Riviere after training had finished at Tottenham Hotspur to thrash out details of their board game *The Manager*, a bottle of champagne always on the table. And it was here, usually accompanied by mysterious figures from the Arab United Emirates, that he planned his buyout of Tottenham in 1990. When Venables secured control of the club, Irving Scholar, the outgoing chairman, went up to him and shook his hand with a rousing 'Now go and win the European Cup', something which neither Venables nor his successors have come remotely close to achieving.

→ England stay at the Hendon Hall Hotel, p. 135

Scribes West, 63 Kensington High Street

The drinking club so closely associated with Terry Venables opened in the basement of the Barker's store on Kensington High Street in 1990. Margaret Thatcher was the guest of honour and the newspaper mogul Lord Rothermere, whose *Daily Mail* offices were based in the same building, was one of the shareholders. Venables was not involved until 1991 when he and business partner Paul Riviere bought the club in a deal so complicated that even the Department of Trade and Industry found it hard to understand when they looked into it later.

Owning Scribes West satisfied the Tottenham man's need to be the centre of attention, and the parties held here attracted A-List celebs such as Bill Wyman and Adam Faith, as well as footballers Vinnie Jones and Paul Gascoigne, who were no doubt attracted by the fact that the wooden dancefloor had been purloined from White Hart Lane.

It was in Scribes that the Spurs side celebrated mightily after surprisingly beating Arsenal in the 1991 FA Cup semi-final, the night ending on a schmaltzy note with the Tottenham manager singing 'My Way'. However, Venables's tenure at the club, like his stint at Tottenham, was not always so successful. On one occasion a journalist dining here was told by a worried maître d' that he was the only paying customer; everybody else in the room was a 'freeloader'.

→ China White, p. 27

NORTH KENSINGTON, W10

Queen's Park Rangers (1901–02), St Quintin's Avenue

QPR moved to North Kensington at the start of the 1901–02 season after being evicted from their previous ground. The players changed in the Latimer Arms pub and then had to run along the road to get to the ground. The pitch was never in the best condition, especially after being used for a coronation party for Edward VII in 1902, the facilities were poor and residents who objected to having a football club in their midst took the club to court. The landlord gave QPR notice at the end of the season, and once again the west London side were on the move. They returned to a former ground in Kensal Rise (→ p. 139).

NOTTING HILL, W11

St Mary's Place

Alan Mullery, England's midfield mainstay in the late 1960s after the World Cup, spent the first twenty years of his life in a two-up, two-down terraced house with no inside toilet on this now demolished street. The neighbourhood was so close-knit that if a stranger happened along the road people would come out of their houses to gawp. One day in 1945 three men walked down St Mary's Place, an extremely rare occurrence given that all the local males were away at the war. The young Mullery took no notice of the party but then was surprised to see one of the men knock on his door. It turned out to be his father, whom he hadn't seen for three years.

When Mullery was sixteen he was visited by Frank Osborne, Fulham's whisky-drinking, eighty-cigarettes-a-day general manager. Osborne drove up in a flash sports car, the first motorised vehicle ever seen on the street, and talked Mullery into joining the club. After making his mark at Craven Cottage Mullery moved to Tottenham in 1964. Four years later he became the first England player to be sent off in an international (against Yugoslavia in the 1968 European Championships semi-final). Mullery rushed into the changing rooms and hid from Ramsey in the bath. When the England manager found the midfield player he dragged him up by the hair and raged: 'I'm glad somebody decided to give those bastards a taste of their own medicine.'

SHEPHERD'S BUSH, W12

BBC Television Centre, Wood Lane

When Eamonn Andrews leapt out in front of Danny Blanchflower, Tottenham 1961 Double-winning captain, and announced: 'Danny

Blanchflower, captain of Tottenham Hotspur, Northern Ireland international footballer, this is your life,' Blanchflower replied, 'No, it's not' and stormed off. He was the first person to turn down the mealy-mouthed presenter. 'I consider this programme to be an invasion of privacy,' he explained. 'Nobody is going to press gang me into anything.'

Queen's Park Rangers (1917–31, 1933–62, 1963–), Loftus Road

No major football club has played at more grounds than nomadic Queen's Park Rangers, who have flitted between nearly twenty homes in Kensal Rise (→ p. 139), Brondesbury, Wormwood Scrubs, Kilburn, Notting Hill and White City – but only one in Queen's Park – since forming in the 1880s. And few English clubs have endured so pitiful a time for off-the-field incidents in recent years as west London's leading club: one player stabbed to death, the chairman supposedly held at gunpoint in his office, and a mass brawl, well beyond the usual 'handbags', involving the club and a visiting national side.

In 1917 QPR moved to Loftus Road, still one of the most compact major grounds in the country. The site had been used by the disbanded Shepherds Bush FC, and to get the best out of the new ground they imported the stand from their former Park Royal ground. Three years later in 1920 Rangers joined the newly extended Football League Third Division. Promotion to the Second could then be achieved only by winning the Third Division title and that eluded QPR until 1948. They didn't last long at the higher level and there was no sign of any change to their status until Alec Stock took over as manager in 1959. He ushered in an exciting new era for the club.

Taking Stock

It was not just promotion from the Third Division that Stock secured in 1967 but, contrary to all expectations, a major trophy: the League Cup. Never before had a team from that level won a trophy, and only one team has done so since. This was the first season in which the biggest clubs had entered the competition and for the first time the final was to be played at Wembley. QPR's opponents were First Division West Brom, the holders, then a major club. The Midlanders took a two-goal lead into half-time but a fairy-tale second half saw the underdogs snatch a win with one of the goals coming from that most elusive of strikers, Rodney Marsh; he and Stan Bowles were the club's greatest ever players.

The following season QPR achieved the rare feat of a second successive promotion to land in the top flight. It was to be their first season in exalted company and their last for a few years, for the team found it hard to cope at this level, especially when manager Alec Stock was sidelined for three months with asthma. He was sacked, just when he thought he was going to return to save them from the drop, and QPR were relegated.

An absurd interlude that season was Tommy Docherty's arrival as manager to stay for all of twenty-eight days. Docherty found it increasingly difficult to make any contact with the chairman, Jim Gregory, with whom he desperately needed to discuss buying new players to replace QPR's ageing squad. Finally the manager tracked the chairman down to a health farm in Tring.

'Mr Chairman, Tommy Docherty, remember me? Your manager at Queen's Park Rangers.'

'Tommy, what is it?'

'Mr Chairman, I would like to buy Brian Tiler from Rotherham. Super young player. Will do us a great job.'

''ow much?'

'A hundred thousand.'

'I don't agree. Now I'm busy. Get back to the players you've got.'

'Mr Chairman, it isn't going to work between us. I'm leaving.'

QPR club stayed buoyant in the Second Division. Although Rodney Marsh was sold in 1972, his replacement, Stan Bowles, matched Marsh for magic. In 1973 QPR returned to the First Division a much stronger outfit. This time there was no quick drop. With a powerful goalkeeper in Phil Parkes, the wing play of Dave Thomas and the midfield acumen of Gerry Francis, as well as the brilliance of Bowles, QPR under manager Gordon Jago and then Dave Sexton were for the first time a major force.

At the end of the 1975–76 season Rangers were top of the First Division. The Championship would be a fitting achievement for so skilful and exciting a side. The only trouble was that Liverpool, in second place, had one game left to play. Not for the first time the football authorities allowed Liverpool the kind of leeway that wouldn't be extended to lesser teams. Because the northerners were in the UEFA Cup Final they were given a lengthy break before their last game. Despite going behind to relegated Wolves, Liverpool ran out 3–1 winners, clinching the first of several titles that would be theirs over the next decade.

The odds-on world of Stan Bowles

☉ QPR fans voted Stan Bowles, not Rodney Marsh, their greatest ever player in 2004. Though both players were equally talented, Bowles, prodigal and uncontrollable, was more interesting. His first club was Manchester City. A scout turned up at the Bowles household in a grim part of east Manchester in the early 1960s to discuss terms. But when he asked Bowles's mother which denomination the family were, religious affiliations obviously being of more importance to City than playing prowess in those days, Mrs Bowles responded: 'What's a denomination? You'll have to wait till me husband gets home.' Bowles played for City and a host of other lesser clubs – Bury, Crewe, Carlisle – before hitting the big time with ever-improving QPR in 1972.

☉ Stan Bowles's life was governed not by football but by gambling. As an apprentice at Manchester City in the 1960s he was running bets across town for a Manchester gang 'from pub to pub, when it was illegal to do that. I was earning more doing that than I was from football.'

☉ Bowles's gambling continued at QPR and he would have a bet just before kick-off at a William Hill outside the ground. He once arrived late for the shooting of the television show *Superstars* because he had lost his Daimler in a card game. He requisitioned a milk float instead.

☉ When George Best told Bowles about the statue they had made of him in Belfast the QPR man told Best there was one of him outside Ladbrokes. He also admitted he'd spent all his money on women and gambling, quickly adding, 'But at least I didn't waste any of it.'

☉ At an away game against Cup holders Sunderland in 1973 Bowles and a couple of other QPR players bet on whether they could knock the FA Cup itself off the table on which it was being displayed. As Bowles recalled,

> With the ball at my feet I tore off straight across the park. Everyone on the pitch was just staring at me, and then, bang! The FA Cup goes shooting up in the air. The whole ground knew that I'd done it on purpose. Then the Sunderland fans go ape. They want my balls in their sandwiches. I wound up their fans even more by scoring a couple of goals, and in the end there was a pitch invasion. At least I got my tenner, and my picture on *News at Ten*. And all because I was just having a bit of a laugh.

✪ When the squeaky-voiced Liverpool defender Emlyn Hughes told England manager Don Revie in 1974: 'I don't need money to play for England. I'll play for the three lions on the shirt,' Stan Bowles lost his temper. As he later recalled: 'Here was Hughes suggesting none of us should get paid money for playing! You can play for the fucking lions, and I'll have your £200.'

In the Doc

It was the last time QPR ever came close to winning the League. Long Cup runs peppered the following few seasons but the side were in slow decline. When manager Dave Sexton left for Manchester United in 1977 he was replaced with the inferior Frank Sibley. Two years later Rangers were down. In April 1979 came another strange managerial appointment: Tommy Docherty, who returned to Loftus Road despite his earlier run-ins with chairman Jim Gregory. 'I've changed since the last time we knew each other,' Gregory assured the Doc. 'Little wiser, lot older.' A year later Gregory sacked Docherty for not buying a house in London quickly enough. He soon regretted it and rang the beleaguered manager to tell him he had given him the boot on a whim. Would Tommy return to work? He did, for five months. Then Gregory sacked him again, this time for good, in October 1980.

In Docherty's place came Terry Venables. A brief revival ensued, but Venables, better at producing transient Cup glory than sustained League success, could not take the club back to the heights of the Dave Sexton years. He did, however, lead them to their only appearance in the FA Cup Final, in 1982 against Tottenham. They drew, something of an achievement for a Second Division club, but lost the replay.

A year later QPR returned to the First Division, but this time there were no assaults on the title and no players to rank alongside Gerry Francis or Stan Bowles. A creditable fifth place in 1984 was soured by Venables's departure for a bigger club (Barcelona). Don Revie, the bribe-taking, ex-Leeds boss who had walked out on England, was considered, but he fell out with Jim Gregory, prompting the QPR supremo to announce: 'The terms he asked for then were not those he was seeking when I met him. In view of his increased demands, I have unfortunately come to the conclusion that I no longer wish Mr Revie to be the new manager of Queen's Park Rangers.'

The fans were unhappy with the man who did step in, Alan Mullery, and he found it impossible to emulate his predecessor's minor success. Peter Hucker, QPR's high-quality goalkeeper of the time, later voiced his opinion of the former England midfielder.

> Mullery was a pratt; he was useless, he still is and always will be. He didn't know anything about management, he didn't know how to handle players, he didn't know how to handle the club and he was tactically naive so we were beaten before we started. I'll give you an idea about his football knowledge. At the end of a European game [in the 1984–85 season], having conceded four and gone out on the away-goals rule, he chased us down the tunnel shouting 'come back, come back it's extra-time!' He didn't even know the rules of the game.

By then QPR had installed a plastic pitch at Loftus Road. It was an echo of the 'progress' outlined by Terry Venables in his football novel *They Used to Play on Grass*. The venture was not a success and the artificial surface was abandoned in 1988. QPR finished fifth again that year, but by then Jim Gregory had sold the club to the notorious Marler Estates, who tried to merge them with Fulham as Fulham Park Rangers until the outcry proved powerful enough to bury the plan.

With former captain Gerry Francis as boss from 1991 the club looked as if they might emulate their mid-1970s mini-success, but midway through the 1994–95 season Francis was lured away to Tottenham, even though it was more likely he would have done better staying at Loftus Road and building something solid. The sale of star centre-forward Les Ferdinand to Newcastle in July 1995 for a huge fee proved a watershed. The new manager, Ray Wilkins, replaced him with a string of nonentities and QPR dropped out of the Premiership in 1996 for what has become their longest spell outside the top flight.

The wrong stuff

It was then that Chris Wright, a Rangers fan who had built a viable record company in Chrysalis, took over as chairman. QPR fans were excited that a businessman with hip credibility (the label had released records by Jethro Tull and Procol Harum) and a fan to boot now had control of the club. It seemed the old penny-pinching days were over as Wright announced plans to float QPR on the Alternative Investment Market so that anyone could buy shares.

Alas Wright was unable to bring his record business expertise to football. He had megalomanic plans that the fans would rue. For instance, Wright bought Wasps Rugby Club and announced they would now play at Loftus Road. The prospectus for the deal to bring the two teams together was littered with PR gibberish about 'synergies' and 'economies of scale'. The pitch was dug up (again) and remodelled with rugby in mind. Wasps cost the new hybrid sports club a million pounds a year, money which could be better spent, the fans felt, on QPR. And few turned up to see the oval-balled game at Loftus Road.

Meanwhile, the directors rewarded themselves handsomely. One was paid £100,000 in 'success fees' for working on the acquisitions and flotation. Wright himself was paid £8,000 a month. Money was no object and fifteen youth team players went on full-time salaries. By 2001 QPR had sixty-one full-time professional players and a wage bill more than a third higher than the club's income – and it was not as if they were competing with Real Madrid and Manchester United in the Champions League cash cow.

Another doomed decision was the 1996 appointment of ex-Arsenal assistant manager Stewart Houston assisted, ironically, by his former boss at Arsenal, Bruce Rioch. They achieved nothing, and were succeeded by the barely articulate Ray Harford, who immediately wasted £2.5 million on

Mike Sheron and nearly took the club back to the Third Division. Harford was sacked in September 1998. His replacement, to great surprise, was Gerry Francis, but it was a disastrous homecoming. Francis's magic had worn off, and in May 2001, soon after he resigned, QPR were back in the Third Division for the first time in more than thirty years.

Gun club

Chris Wright quit in February 2001 after supporters tried to storm the directors' box during a defeat to Fulham. QPR went into administration and there were proposals to merge the club with Wimbledon. There had been no sign of QPR edging their way out of the second-tier strugglers/ third-tier promotion chasers rut by August 2005 when news emerged of one of the most bizarre incidents in the history of English football.

QPR chairman Gianni Paladini claimed that a band of thugs had burst into his Loftus Road office before a match and held him at gunpoint demanding he give up his £600,000 stake in the club. Allegedly one of the gunmen warned Paladini: 'Sign, sign the paper or we'll kill you. We're not messing about, we've got guns.' Another assailant pushed something into the back of Paladini's head and said: 'Let's kill him now.' They then slapped the chairman a few times and forced him to sign several documents that would limit his involvement with Rangers.

Several men were arrested for the incident, but some absconded to Europe before the trial. In court the defendants claimed they had merely been discussing the lucrative stewarding contract, which was up for renewal. Paladini was cleverly asked by a barrister: 'Did you ever say to manager Ian Holloway that you would kill him?', to which Paladini replied: 'In a funny way, yes, but it didn't mean anything at all.' Two defendants were cleared.

In February 2006 Paladini sent manager Ian Holloway on 'gardening leave' after a series of rows between them. Fans sided with Holloway, outraged that the chairman had brought in several players over the manager's head.

Holloway's replacement, John Gregory, lasted little over a year. His regime would be remembered for two unfortunate incidents off the pitch. In May 2006 youth player Kiyan Prince was stabbed to death outside the London Academy School in Edgware. A seventeen-year-old boy was later convicted of his murder. At the end of the year several QPR youth team players were horsing around at Earls Court tube station when one fell off the shoulders of another. A Vietnamese architecture student who just happened to be standing nearby was jostled and fell to his death in the path of an oncoming train. One of the QPR youth players, Harry Smart, was severely injured.

Tragedy turned to farce in February 2007 when a 'friendly' between QPR and the touring China national side's youth team ended in a thirty-man brawl that resulted in the club's assistant manager's suspension and the intervention of the police. As former head of youth development Joe Gallen remarked that September:

> A combination of the China brawl, the Harry Smart incident and the stabbing of Kiyan meant I was dealing with police every day. There was a stage where police did not leave the building for about three weeks and all I seemed to be doing was giving statements, making sure the players weren't getting into further trouble, and arranging solicitors to represent them.

Later that year two of the country's wealthiest businessmen, motor-racing mogul Bernie Ecclestone and the engineering magnate Lakshmi Mittal, bought into the club. By 2009 fans were wondering why they had bothered as the team stumbled on in the nowhere land of the middle of the second tier.

QPR off the bench

On 9 September 1939 Loftus Road hosted the first football match of the Second World War, in which QPR beat an army team 10–0. Alas there was no crowd, for no one was allowed in, and the army players have remained anonymous as the authorities would not release their names for security reasons.

⊗ The on-field stunts of QPR's 1970s centre-half Terry Mancini had fans rocking on the terraces. In one match the shiny-pated Mancini took to the field in a long-haired wig. Spectators wondered for a few seconds who the oddly hirsute defender was before Terry Venables whipped the wig off Mancini's head to mass cheering. On another occasion Mancini dropped his shorts and wiggled his behind at chairman Jim Gregory who was stalling over the player's move to, of all teams, Arsenal.

✪ It is often said that QPR have the wealthiest and most influential supporters in the land, namely those who have made the short journey to the ground from the nearby BBC television centre. Or as the writer Chris Horrie once put it, 'Their fans do not shout or clap. They rustle their copies of the *New Statesman*.'

✪ Alec Stock, QPR's successful 1960s manager, provided comedian Paul Whitehouse with the inspiration for his supreme caricature, Ron Manager. An over-enthusiastic ageing pundit, Ron Manager is wont to launch into a string of incoherent reminiscences irrelevant to the point he is supposed to be making, such as 'small boys in the park, jumpers for goalposts, you know . . . wasn't it?' In fact all Ron Manager's aphorisms ended with a redundantly rhetorical: 'Wasn't it?' – taken from Alec Stock's favourite turn of phrase.

White City stadium, Wood Lane

The long-gone stadium was built in a rush early in 1908 for the Olympics on land that had been used for the Franco-British Exhibition. When it opened in May 1908 it was called the Great Stadium, and a capacity of 150,000 made it the biggest one in the world. Later the ground and the surroundings became known as White City after the ever-present white stucco.

After the Olympics the developer Imre Kiralfy hired out White City for athletics, cycling, wrestling and occasionally football. In Easter 1912, during the coalminers' strike, QPR played two games here in the Southern League, one of which, against Southampton on Good Friday, attracted, according to the record books, a crowd of 62,000. This was probably a misprint and should have read 26,000.

QPR later returned to use the stadium as their home ground from 1931 to 1933 because the club's owners wanted to boost the team's image by having them play in a major stadium. More than 40,000 turned out here to watch QPR against Leeds in the FA Cup in 1932, but most of the time the crowd was a fraction of that number and the atmosphere negligible. Despite the directors' good intentions, QPR were losing money playing at White City and in 1933 returned to Loftus Road. They occasionally played first team games here in the early 1960s, the reserves remaining at Loftus Road.

The visiting Moscow Dynamo team trained here in November 1945 during their infamous tour. After Paul Irwin of the *Sunday Express* watched the Russians, he penned the famous report denouncing them as 'just a bunch of earnest amateurs, so slow you can almost hear them think', when the reality was that the team could match any in the land.

White City was used as a World Cup venue in 1966 after the owners of Wembley refused to cancel the regular greyhound racing so that Uruguay could play France on the date specified. The stadium was demolished in 1985 and replaced by a BBC television building.

→ White Hart Lane, p. 113

WEST KENSINGTON, W14

Queen's Club, Norfolk Terrace

A famous private sporting club, best known for its prestigious annual tennis tournament, Queen's was where English football's greatest amateur club, Corinthians, was formed in 1882, taking its name from the city of classical antiquity known for its wealth and trade. At that time, six years before the professional Football League began, many of the game's best players were amateurs who played for fun and Corinthians took their pick of the best of them.

They played only friendlies and refused to enter the FA Cup because their rules forbade them 'to compete for any challenge cup or prizes of any description'. Yet had Corinthians entered the Cup at that time they might well have won it, for they could compete with the best. For instance, in 1884 Corinthians beat Blackburn 8–1 shortly after the Lancashire club had won the Cup.

The club's aim was to develop a squad good enough to challenge the then all-powerful Scottish national side, nearly all of whom came from the Glasgow area and could therefore train together regularly whereas the England players, spread around the country, only met occasionally. Corinthians players dominated the England team before the end of the century, and for two matches against Wales in 1894 and 1895 their players formed the entire England side. But as most of the Corinthians players also turned out for other teams, such as the university sides, the FA does not count them as holding the record for supplying the most players to the England team on any one occasion.

In 1900 Corinthians dropped their opposition to cups and entered the Sheriff of London Shield, beating reigning champions Aston Villa. In 1904 they beat Manchester United 11–3, which remains the latter team's worst defeat. By then Corinthians were spending much of their time touring the world to popularise the game. Their arrival in Brazil galvanised the locals, who founded a club of the same name that went on to become one of the most successful in Brazilian history. Corinthians also went to Spain, where Real Madrid were inspired by them and decided to adopt their white shirts. After Corinthians played in Vienna an Austrian player wrote: 'I remember how they walked on to the field, spotless in their white shirts and dark shorts. Their hands in their pockets, sleeves hanging down. Yet there was about them an air of casual grandeur, a haughtiness that was yet not haughty, which seemed intangible. And how they played!'

The team finally entered the FA Cup after the First World War, but with only limited success. They did, however, play in the 1927 Charity Shield instead of champions Newcastle. In 1939 Corinthians merged with another great amateur side, Casuals, to form Corinthian-Casuals, now based in Kingston.

Further west

BRENTFORD

Brentford (1904–), Griffin Park, Braemar Road

Brentford vie with Leyton Orient for the title of London's least successful long-running League club. Members of the Football League since 1920, they have spent only five seasons in the top division and reached no major finals.

The club was founded in 1889 by members of Brentford Rowing Club, who were unable to use the Thames in the winter, and their first game was against Kew. After playing at a number of local venues (see below), Brentford moved to their long-term home, Griffin Park, in 1904, entertaining Plymouth Argyle in the Western League on 1 September.

Success in the Middlesex cups and a run in the Second Division of the Southern League won Brentford election to the Football League when it was extended to include a Third Division after the First World War. There they made progress, and in 1930 set up an unbeatable record, winning all their twenty-one home league matches. Brentford secured promotion to the Second Division in 1933, and within two years were in the top flight, finishing a highly creditable fifth in their first season (1935–36).

The Second World War spoiled Brentford's momentum, and when professional football resumed in 1946 they were relegated, never to return to the top tier. A further humiliating drop, to the Third Division, came in 1954. The Fourth Division was only four seasons old when Brentford fell into it briefly in 1962. When Brentford went down to the Fourth again in 1967 chairman Jack Dunnett suggested the club should merge with Queen's Park Rangers. Needless to say, the fans realised that any merger with a more powerful rival would be the equivalent of disbanding, and they vehemently opposed the idea.

Since then Brentford have yo-yoed between the bottom two divisions, but made a brief appearance in the second tier when they were promoted in 1992. What's more, due to the renaming of the divisions they jumped up numerically from the old Third Division to the new First Division (formerly the Second).

The club rarely hit the headlines, except in 1998 when new chairman Ron Noades, in a display of footballing megalomania, appointed himself manager as well. Detractors were silenced when in Noades's first season the club won promotion and the chairman-manager won Divisional Manager of the Year, but Noades relinquished both roles in 2000, leaving the club with debts of £8 million. Defeats in the promotion play-offs this century were followed by relegation back to the fourth tier in 2007. That year Brentford announced plans to build a new stadium near Kew Bridge.

In 2009 Brentford won the League Two championship and were also named League Community Club of the Year for the second year running.

Brentford's early grounds

- Brentford's first pitch should have been the Recreation Ground between Lateward Road and Albany Road, but when the local council failed to respond to their request they plumped for the Clifden House ground on land behind the Wesleyan chapel, where they played from 1889 to 1891.
- From 1891 to 1894 Brentford were based at Benn's Field on Little Ealing Lane. It was a mile from the centre of the community, and club officials feared attendance numbers would decline given the lack of public transport – a worry that proved to be well founded.
- In 1894 Brentford moved to Shotters Field, Windmill Lane, land owned by a Colonel Clitheroe who lived in nearby Boston Lodge. There was a pond in the north-west corner of the ground and hardy spectators could watch free by climbing nearby trees. Brentford's first game here, on 22 December 1894, was a 3–0 defeat to the 8th Hussars. Soon the landlord, a Mr Beldam, was objecting to the noisy crowds in what was then a rural neighbourhood. Three thousand spectators, their biggest attendance to date, saw Brentford's first FA Cup match, against the Grenadier Guards, after which Beldam increased the rent. Brentford then quit and, when a proposed site in York Road fell through, they were left homeless (temporarily, it turned out). The site is now covered by Gunnersbury Catholic boys' school.
- From 1898 to 1900 Brentford played at the Crossroads (by the intersection of South Ealing Road with Little Ealing Lane and Popes Lane). The pitch was near the new South Ealing tube station but still some distance from the main centre of support in Brentford.
- For four years from 1900 Brentford played at the Boston Park Cricket Ground. At last they had a ground close to where their supporters (and potential supporters) lived and one that had some

facilities, namely two pavilions. Brentford's first game here was against Chesham Generals on 15 September that year. A crowd of 7,000 saw Brentford play Woolwich Arsenal in the FA Cup in 1902. Soon the football club was the dominant partner, but because of the cricket season Brentford could not play home matches here after 31 March and so they moved to a former orchard owned by the Fuller's brewery company – Griffin Park – where they still remain. The Boston Park Cricket Ground was later wiped away by the extension of the Great West Road.

HEATHROW

London Airport

No sooner had Heathrow opened in 1946 than it was being used by the England squad, eager for the novelty of jetting off to away games at places previously inaccessible to those without the time for a lengthy sea journey. These were the early days of intercontinental air travel, and when the England party set off for the 1950 World Cup in Brazil on 29 June their convoluted thirty-one-hour journey took them to Rio de Janeiro via Paris, Lisbon, Dakar (Senegal) and Recife (Brazil).

Footballers weren't allowed to do anything spontaneous in the early days of air travel. For instance, when Jimmy Greaves bought a cup of tea and a slice of cake while waiting in the airport café with the England party for his first overseas trip in 1959 the FA secretary, Sir Stanley Rous, shouted: 'Greaves, put the cake down. You'll be fed on the plane.' (Some thirty-five years later FA officials turned a blind eye when England players caused several thousand pounds' worth of damage to a plane returning from China.)

That same year the Scotland-raised, Scottish-sounding Joe Baker flew down to London to play for England, having been born in Liverpool. Outside Heathrow he jumped in a taxi and told the driver he was going to the Hendon Hall Hotel. 'But that's where the England team stay,' the driver said. 'Aye,' replied Baker in broad Scots, 'I'm playing for them on Wednesday night.' There was a long silence. Fifteen minutes or so later a police car roared up behind them. The taxi driver had called the police on his radio, asking them to check on whether he had a 'dangerous lunatic in the back of the cab'.

Frank Worthington caused the usually mild-mannered Alf Ramsey to explode with fury when he turned up at Heathrow in 1972 to join the England Under-23s wearing high-heeled cowboy boots, red silk shirt, black slacks and a lime velvet jacket. At least Worthington was no longer in his Pele phase during which he would speak in a made-up language that he hoped sounded like Portuguese. He later became a favourite on the after-dinner circuit, and used to start his spiel by revealing that in America he played for Tampa Bay Rowdies. 'Mind you, before I joined they were just called Tampa Bay.'

In 1986 Robert Maxwell, the newspaper baron who owned Oxford United and was planning a takeover of much of football, summoned Harry Harris, the hapless football reporter of the *Daily Mirror*, which Maxwell owned, to discuss the status of the England manager, Bobby Robson. Harris dutifully turned up – presumably it was for an exclusive interview before the World Cup – only to discover that Maxwell, having hired an entire floor of offices, was proposing to devote the first few pages of the paper to his new campaign: 'Robson Must Go'.

For the corpulent corporate conman, the last straw had been Robson's confusion over a substitution in which he took off Glenn Hoddle by mistake. Evidently, the manager had to go and quickly. Even to the ever faithful Harris this looked to be a Maxwell touch too far. Harris agreed to write the article only if his name were omitted. 'Don't worry. I shall phone the editor and make sure that your name is not on it,' boomed Maxwell, who then left. A few minutes later he returned with bad news. 'Sorry, Harry. It's too late. They've gone to press.' Harris knew it wasn't so and phoned the news desk. Maxwell had never asked them to take out Harris's name, and, as the editor explained, such a piece without the strap of the chief soccer writer would have looked absurd.

Arsenal's Paul Merson had a problem negotiating his way into the right toilet before the team flew off from Heathrow for a pre-season tour in the late 1980s. Having left the others to pay a visit, he was confronted by three doors – male, female and disabled – returning to ask team-mate Perry Groves: 'What am I?'

When Arsenal were due to go on a pre-season tour to Singapore in 1990 the club agreed that the players should meet at Heathrow. The captain, Tony Adams, was at a barbecue in Rainham, Essex, playing drunken cricket in the garden. At 3 p.m. Adams realised he only had an hour to make the sixty miles across the capital to reach the airport. He sped off in his Sierra but crashed into a garden wall, which he destroyed. A breathalyser test showed Adams was three times over the limit. Remarkably, the police allowed him to join the squad at the airport and he arrived with pieces of windscreen in his hair. He was eventually jailed for fifty-seven days for the offence.

WEST DRAYTON

Post House Hotel, Sipson Road

In September 2001 four Chelsea players – John Terry, Jody Morris, Eidur Gudjohnsen and Frank Lampard Jnr – insulted and abused American guests in the bar a day after the September 11th attacks on New York's World Trade Center. The quartet had been on a five-hour drinking binge in the hotel, which was packed with American tourists grieving over the terrorist incident. Once sufficiently fuelled up the Chelsea players began stripping off, laughing and vomiting. It was later explained that Lampard, privately educated and well brought-up, despite his annoying Mockney accent, had been led astray by the rough crowd of proletarian Chelsea players he had been mixing with. The club fined them two weeks' wages each.

QPR training ground, Sipson Lane

A friendly between QPR and the touring China team's youth side on 7 February 2007 ended in one of the worst pitch battles ever seen in English football. Fighting began when Chinese player Gao hit an opponent after being provoked. In the brawl that ensued there were punches, kung-fu kicks and what one witness described as 'absolute mayhem'. Chinese Under-21 international Zheng Tao was rendered unconscious for five minutes and taken to hospital with a suspected broken jaw. Referee Dermot Gallagher was forced to abandon the game. QPR later suspended assistant manager Richard Hill and China sent home seven members of the team.

Gao later apologised profusely. 'I failed to control myself in the match,' adding, as if he were submitting to a Maoist policy directive, 'When facing the provocation I failed to obey the three rules of submitting to the referee, respecting opponents, and not striking back, which caused the incident . . . I sincerely apologise to the fans.' Team-mate Lu Zheng was not so apologetic. 'They kicked us,' he told Chinese journalists. 'If someone suddenly beats you, what is your reaction? It's the instinct for protecting ourselves.' Two QPR players, Jimmy Smith and Pat Kanyuka, later received death threats from a London-based triad gang.

Bibliography

Allen, Matt, *Crazy Gang: The Inside Story of Vinnie, Harry, Fash & Wimbledon FC*, Highdown, Newbury, 2005

Ball, Alan, *It's All About a Ball*, W. H. Allen, London, 1978

Bastin, Cliff and Glanville, Brian, *Cliff Bastin Remembers*, The Ettrick Press, London and Edinburgh, 1950

Batty, Clive, *Kings of the King's Road*, VSP, London, 2004

Beasant, Dave, *Tales of the Unexpected: The Dave Beasant Story*, Mainstream, Edinburgh, 1989

Blows, Kirk and Sharratt, Ben, *Claret and Blue Blood*, Mainstream, Edinburgh and London, 2002

Bose, Mihir, *False Messiah: The Life and Times of Terry Venables*, Andre Deutsch, London, 1996

Bower, Tom, *Broken Dreams: Vanity, Greed and the Souring of British Football*, Simon & Schuster, London, 2003

Burn, Gordon, *Best, George and Edwards, Duncan, Football, Fame and Oblivion*, Faber & Faber, London, 2006

Catton, J. A. H., *Wickets and Goals*, Chapman & Hanton, London, 1926

Conn, David, *The Beautiful Game? Searching for the Soul of Football*, Yellow Jersey, London, 2005

Davies, Hunter, *Boots, Balls & Haircuts: An Illustrated History of Football from Then to Now*, Cassell, London, 2003

Downing, David, *Passovotchka, Moscow Dynamo in Britain 1945*, Bloomsbury, London, 1999

Farror, Morley and Lamming, Douglas, *A Century of English International Football 1872–1972*, Robert Hale, London, 1972

Fenton Ted, *At Home with the Hammers*, Nicholas Kaye, London, 1960

Fynn, Alex and Davidson, H., *Dream On: A Year in The Life of a Premier League Club*, Simon & Schuster, London, 1996

George, Charlie, *My Story*, Century, London, 2005

Giller, Norman, *Football And All That: An Irreverent History*, Hodder & Stoughton, London, 2004

Glanvill, Rick, *Chelsea FC: The Official Biography*, Headline, London, 2005

Glanville, Brian, *Football Memories*, Robson Books, London, 2004

—, *Arsenal Stadium History*, Hamlyn, London, 2006

Goodwin, Bob, *An Illustated History of Tottenham Hotspur*, Breedon, Derby, 1995

Grayson, Edward, *Corinthians and Cricketers*, Sportsman's Book Club, London, 1957

Greaves, Jimmy, *Greavsie: The Autobiography*, Time Warner, London, 2003

—, *The Heart of the Game*, Time Warner, London, 2005

Groves, Perry, with McShane, John, *We All Live in a Perry Groves World*, John Blake, London, 2006

Haynes, Graham and Twydell, Dave, *Brentford F.C.: The Complete History 1889–2008*, Yore Publications, Uxbridge, 2008

Horrie, Chris, *Sick as a Parrot: The Inside Story of the Spurs Fiasco*, Virgin, London, 1992

Hudson, Alan, *Working Man's Ballet*, Robson, London, 1997

Hurst, Geoff, with Hart, Michael, *1966 And All That: My Autobiography*, Headline, London, 2001

Hutchinson, Roger, *It is Now!*, Mainstream, Edinburgh and London, 1995

Inglis, Simon, *The Football Grounds of England and Wales*, Willow, London, 1983

—, *Soccer in the Dock: A History of British Football Scandals 1900–65*, Collins, London, 1985

—, *League Football and the Men Who Made It*, Willow, London, 1988

Joy, Bernard, *Forward, Arsenal!*, Phoenix, London, 1952

Knighton, Leslie, *Behind the Scenes in Big Football*, Stanley Paul, London, 1948

Lewis, Richard, *England's Eastenders: From Bobby Moore to David Beckham*, Mainstream, Edinburgh and London, 2002

Macdonald, Malcolm, with Tomas, Jason, *An Autobiography*, Weidenfeld & Nicolson, London, 1983

Macey, Gordon, *Queen's Park Rangers: A Complete Record*, Breedon, Derby, 1993

Mackay, Dave, with Knight, Martin, *The Real Mackay*, Mainstream Publishing, Edinburgh and London, 2004

Marples, Morris, *A History of Football*, Secker & Warburg, London, 1954

Marsh, Rodney, *Priceless: The Autobiography*, Headline, London, 2001

Mears, Brian, *Chelsea, Football Under the Blue Flag*, Mainstream Publishing, Edinburgh and London, 2001

Moore, Tina, *Bobby Moore*, Collins Willow, London, 2005

Mullery, Alan, *The Autobiography*, Headline, London, 2006

Northcutt, John and Shoesmith, Roy, *West Ham United: An Illustrated History*, Breedon Books, Derby, 1997

Rollin, Jack, *Soccer at War 1939–45*, Headline, London, 2005

Roper, Alan, *In the Days of Gog: The Real Arsenal Story*, Wherry, Norwich, 2004

Scholar, Irving, with Bose, Mihir, *Behind Closed Doors: Dreams and Nightmares at Spurs*, Andre Deutsch, London, 1992

Scovell, Brian, *The England Managers: The Impossible Job*, Tempus, Stroud, 2006

Spurling, Jon, *Highbury – The Story of Arsenal in N. 5*, Orion, London, 2007

—, *Rebels for the Cause: The Alternative History of Arsenal Football Club*, Mainstream, Edinburgh and London, 2006

Steen, Rob, *The Mavericks: English Football When Flair Wore Flares*, Mainstream, Edinburgh and London, 1994

Twydell, Dave, *Football League, Grounds for a Change*, Yore Publications, Uxbridge, 1991

Wall, Bob, *Arsenal from the Heart*, Souvenir Press, London, 1969

Walvin, James, *The People's Game: The History of Football Revisited*, Mainstream, Edinburgh and London, 1994

Winner, David, *Those Feet: A Sensual History of English Football*, Bloomsbury, London, 2005

Young, Percy M., *A History of British Football*, Stanley Paul, London, 1968

Index